Humanoid Encounters

THE OTHERS AMONGST US

1900-1929

Albert S. Rosales

Triangulum Publishing.

Copyright © 2016 Albert S. Rosales

ISBN: 978-1541101449
ISBN 10: 1541101448

All rights reserved. No part of this book may be used or reproduced in any manner whatsoever without permission except in the case of brief quotations embodied in critical articles or reviews.

Cover art center and upper center image by David Sankey. Lower right image by Jim Nichols.

Introduction

The beginning of the 20th century seemed to have set up the stage for things to come in the future as far as humanoid encounters are concerned. In many ways it gave us a taste of the complexity of the modern day encounters. There were rumors in dark corners of strange encounters, as humanity involved itself in yet the biggest war so far; slaughtering millions in Europe. Men looked up at the sky for answers and began to see things which were out of the ordinary. These early reports included reports of abductions, bedroom visitations, flying humanoids, everything that we have today, except in those early years, perhaps they were labeled differently as humans were just beginning to realize that there were indeed others amongst us.

These are my favorites, early pre-modern, pre-Arnold encounters that demonstrate that the others have always been with us. Many of the cases are taken directly from era newspapers that were as puzzled as we are today as to the nature of these visitors.

My hope is that this information will be useful for future generations, be it for entertainment or any other purpose, just hopefully useful. Something strange has been happening, perhaps for thousands of years, mostly ignored, covered up, debunked, but it still happens. Every day someone becomes part of the mystery. 'Others' amongst us are reaching out to us, be it from outer space, other dimensions, other realms, etc. Beware, some might not have the best intentions. But I feel this is a necessary process for our species to make that giant leap forward and become the Universal citizens that we were meant to be.

It would be impossible to mention each and every researcher and person that has helped me amass this incredible amount of information. I have been reluctant in writing a book with all the latest compilations. Many of them have used my research which is free for all to see on-line, they know who they are. Without the encouragement and assistance of my publisher and fellow researcher Ash Staunton, I would still be debating this issue, I thank him.

I also received encouragement from many others, to name a few, Alexander Rosales, Andy Davis, Jaime Brian, Wade Ridsdale, Hank

Worbetz, Gerardo Macias, Sue Demeter St. Clair, Gladys Gonzalez, Robert Othmar Vettiger, Ardy Sixkiller Clarke, Daniel Garcia Ramos, Robert Lesniakiewicz, Patrick Moncelet, Alejandro Barragan, Kay Massingill, Franck Boitte, Jean Sider, Freddy Soisson, Donald Cyr, Jonny Enoch, Lon Strickler, Edwin Joyce, Annie Theriault. Way too many to name here, but they also know who they are. I wish all the best in the future that is to come, sooner than later.

Sit back and read through these 'oldies but goodies;' worldwide cases at the crack of the 20th century. The world was evolving, humanity was changing; for the best? Perhaps not yet, perhaps we are not ready to join the Universal family yet, perhaps we never will.

Albert S. Rosales
December 20, 2016

TYPES OF CE (Close Encounter) CLASSIFICATIONS:

- **Type A:** When an entity or humanoid is seen inside or on top of an object or unidentified aircraft.
- **Type B:** When an entity or humanoid is seen entering or exiting a UFO.
- **Type C:** When an entity or humanoid is seen in the immediate vicinity of a UFO.
- **Type D:** When an entity or humanoid is seen in the same area where UFOs or unknown objects have been reported.
- **Type E:** When an entity or humanoid is seen alone, without related UFO activity.
- **Type F:** When there is a 'psychic' contact between entities or humanoids, but an entity or humanoid is not necessarily seen.
- **Type G:** When there is direct contact or interaction between a witness and a humanoid or entity; either involuntary, as a result of a forced abduction, or as a voluntary contact.
- **Type H:** When there is a report of an alleged crash or forced landing of a UFO with recovery of its occupants, or when an anomalous entity is captured or killed either by a witness or military personnel.
- **Type X:** When the situation is so uncanny that it doesn't fit any of the previous classifications. A new classification, there are several such cases in the files already. I would call these cases, 'extremely high strangeness events.'

1900-1909

Location: (Undisclosed location) Queensland, Australia.
Date: 1900.
Time: Afternoon.

Andy Dickson; a part-Aboriginal, was repairing a fence one day in a remote area on the edge of a patch of trees, when he spotted, approaching across the flat countryside from the west, a big gray-colored "flying machine" (as he later described it). Andy was dumbfounded and "glued to the spot." His horse and a mule carrying equipment ran off. The great "machine" had flown to a point high above him and then descended to capture him within a circular hollow.

The momentary darkness in which he had been enveloped within ended as a bright silver light appeared from above. Three figures; all strangely clothed (not described), emerged from a wide, tall door that suddenly opened from one side of the encircling "machine." These humanoids led him in through the door and he found himself inside a circular room. Andy was then set upon by several more of these men; all of who had blue skin. They removed his clothes and he was petrified with fear; unable to resist.

All kinds of strange, incomprehensible machines were around the room. He was strapped to a metal table and the men touched him all over with hand-held objects. Then they all retreated to another room, leaving another man to release him. Andy quickly dressed. The man took him into another room, through a door that the blue-skinned man opened by touching with a finger. There was a wide, tall window and he could see they were above the clouds.

All this time, none of the crew of this "big flying machine" (as Andy would call it when telling his story over the years) had spoken to him but chattered to one-another in some strange language of their own. He then found himself watching as the craft began descending. Before long, as he watched from the window, the craft landed in a scrubby area. A door opened. At this Andy apparently saw a strange red-colored metallic instrument on a table nearby, and he grabbed it as he made his escape, perhaps as some proof of his experience. He had no sooner left the craft then one of the strange men appeared and gave chase. Grabbing Andy, he took the instrument from him and returned to the craft, which rose up above the trees and flew away as a frightened Andy looked on.

HC addendum.
Source: Rex Gilroy in *Blue Mountains UFO Research Club newsletter*, August 2008, as related to him in 2008 by Mrs. Narelle Cable, the witness' great granddaughter. Type: G

* * * * * * *

Location: Ben MacDhui, Scotland.
Date: 1900.
Time: Late afternoon.

Two men were chipping for crystals on the slope of a mountain, when they suddenly became aware of a giant gray-colored ten-foot tall figure walking towards them. The figure was momentarily lost from sight in a dip on the slope, and then the witnesses became extremely terrified and ran away from the area.

HC addendum.
Source: Graham J. McEwan, *'Mystery Animals of Britain and Ireland.'*
Type: E

* * * * * * *

Location: Kuhmo, Lentiira, Finland.
Date: 1900.
Time: Evening.

Four children, had gone into the swamp and wooded area in order to collect cloudberry. The older children were supposed to keep an eye on the younger ones. An adult had also stayed close by, at the foot of a large pine tree keeping a close eye on the children. Suddenly she became aware that the children were nowhere to be seen; terrified, she ran to the village and immediately a search party was organized and a thorough search was conducted for days, however no trace of the children was found.

However weeks after their strange disappearance, the children suddenly appeared again, standing under the large pine tree. After being interrogated by village elders, all the children could remember was that they were approached by some "friendly people" and invited to fly onboard a "device in the air." According to some of the children, they were able to look down and see the Earth below them. The children were in good health and the adults could not explain how they had gone without food or shelter in the woods for several weeks.

HC addendum.
Source:http://www.suomenufotutkijat.fi/ufodb/ufodata.php?u=161&p=1
Comments: Early abduction? Type: G?

* * * * * * *

Location: (Undisclosed location) New South Wales, Australia.
Date: 1900.
Time: Night.

 A girl was taken at night from between her sisters as they slept beside a billabong, by little humanoid creatures with leathery skin. They took her underground and covered her in animal fat. She couldn't see them because her eyes were covered with the fat but she could hear them. She said they just made guttural noises. She was there for a couple of hours, when she started to hear people calling out her name.
 She began clawing at the tree roots she could feel above her and broke through; she could just make out light and stuck her arm up out of the ground. A man calling out for her ran away as he thought the arm was "from something evil." He came back with her family and they had a tug of war to get her out. Once they did, they built a big bonfire above the spot.

HC addendum.
Source:http://www.reddit.com/r/UFOs/comments/324zve/im_wondering_if_anyone_here_has_any_storiesinfo/ Type: G?

* * * * * * *

Location: Newmarket on Fergus, County Clare, Ireland.
Date: 1900.
Time: Night.

 Residents who lived close to Lough Gaish reported hearing the wail of a 'banshee' which lasted for several nights. When the cries ceased and no one died, the locals doubted whether the sounds actually came from a banshee. A little man in green was also spotted in the area. Matching the description of a 'leprechaun,' a witness tried to grab him for his gold, but the little man vanished.

HC addendum.
Source: http://www.paranormaldatabase.com/ireland   Type: E

* * * * * * *

Location: Sandwood, Highland Region, Scotland.
Date: 1900.
Time: Unknown.

A landholder heard his dog growling and noticed a strange creature lying on a ledge by the seashore, only a few feet from them. The being was described as a female, human in size with beautiful features with curly reddish hair, greenish-blue eyes, and arched eyebrows. The creature, which was mermaid-like in appearance, gave the witness a frightened and angry look, causing the witness to run away from the area.

HC addendum.
Source: Janet and Colin Bord, *'Modern Mysteries of Britain.'*   Type: E

* * * * * * *

Location: Szcyrk, Poland.
Date: 1900.
Time: Unknown.

A shepherdess was grazing her cattle in a meadow when she suddenly noticed in a tree, an extraordinary woman who was later interpreted as the Virgin Mary. No other information.

HC addendum.
Source: woe_@vp.pl   Type: E?

* * * * * * *

Location: Near Mays Landing, New Jersey.
Date: 1900.
Time: Night.

10-year old Amanda was living in her family's farm in the heart of "Devil" county. Her story has become one of the classics of the field. "We heard a scream near the barn one night and ran out of our house," she said. "We saw this thing that looked like a kangaroo. It wasn't such a great big animal; it was about the size of a small calf and weighed about 150 pounds. But the noise it made is what scared us. It sounded like a woman screaming in an awful lot of agony." Amanda said that was the only time she ever actually viewed the creature, but her family often heard it and would follow its tracks, which were eight to ten feet apart and led to a large cedar swamp at the rear of the farm.

Her father had seen the thing once before, when he was sixteen years old. "When the horses heard the Devil scream," she observed, "they would carry on so you'd think they were going to tear the barn down. You could hear the Devil scream a long way off when the horses would quiet down. People may say there's nothing to it but I know darned well there is."

HC addendum.
Source: Loren Coleman and Bruce G. Hallenbeck, 'Monsters of New Jersey.' Type: E

* * * * * * * *

Location: Marseilles near Upper Sandusky, Ohio.
Date: March 1, 1900.
Time: Evening.

On Thursday evening the citizens of Marseilles, a small village southwest of Upper Sandusky, were greatly excited by an alleged airship passing over their place. It was first noticed by Henry Robison, who called the attention of a number of reliable business merchants to the strange sight. It seemed to be about 150 feet high, and had onboard several "gentlemen" passengers. Friday it was the sole topic of conversation.

HC addendum.
Source: Jerome Clark in *Magonia Exchange* quoting the *Cleveland Leader*, Ohio, March 3, 1900. Type: A

* * * * * * * *

Location: Manheim, Pennsylvania.
Date: July, 1900.
Time: Daylight.

Mary Ann Litzenberger was picking blackberries in the Buchtown district when, as she said, "to my astonishment as I gazed across the field nearby, I saw the ghost of a stark-naked man rise up from a fence corner and slowly walk across the field, not looking right or left, but having a worried look on his face. I yelled with all my mighty to her sisters, saying in Dutch, *"A nockisher mon! Don't you see him?"* But they insisted they didn't see anything of the kind.

HC addendum.
Source: Charles J Adams III, *'Pennsylvania Dutch Country Ghosts, Legends and Lore.'*   Type: E?
Comments: Apparitional creature?

* * * * * * *

Location: Vienna, Scott County, Indiana.
Date: August 2, 1900.
Time: Afternoon.

    A mysterious apparition that was seen near Vienna, Scott County, a few evenings since, is causing considerable conjecture. While Mrs. Rhoda Amick and William Norfrey and wife were on their way to a pasture, they saw something in the sky about the size of a human hand floating from north to south. As the speck came nearer, it grew larger and assumed the shape of a child in a flowing robe, the head and feet being distinctly visible, though the latter seemed to be grown together or tied. The object finally floated away and the people who saw it are confident it was some token (omen?) they cannot decipher.

HC addendum.
Source: Kay Massingill in Magonia Exchange.   Type: E

* * * * * * *

Location: Sainte Miande, near Toulouse, France.
Date: September, 1900.
Time: Midnight.

    When a freak storm lashed the Gulf of Lyon and the inland villages were battered by winds of ferocious force, a farmer on the outskirts of the village was awakened by an insistent tapping on the window of his downstairs bedroom. At first he dismissed it as the wind rapping a twig on to the glass but finally he got up and went to the door with a lantern. A strange sight met his eyes.
    In the doorway stood a boy, aged about ten, wrapped in a piece of sacking. His hair was long and yellow; quite unlike that of the local boys; and his face almost luminously pale. He appeared to have no clothes apart from the sack and as he stretched out; his arms towards the light, the farmer noticed that there were only three fingers on each of his long slender hands. As he stood there uncertain of what to do, his wife's voice roused him into action. She had come from the bedroom taken one look at the strange tableau and told her husband to bring the child into the house. She roused the fire in the kitchen, placed the shivering boy before

it and covered him with a blanket. He slept the night on a mattress in front of the fire.

In the morning the couple found him some clothes belonging to the oldest son, but it was soon apparent that he didn't know how to put them on. At first the farmer took him for some dumb waif; a simpleton, but it soon became apparent that he could speak, but in a language they had never heard before. Even the most commonplace things appeared to astonish him. He was bewildered by a cup containing warm milk, and had to be shown how to drink from it. A knife and fork were complete mysteries. When a farm cat strolled through the door the boy backed away, apparently in fright.

The farmer and his wife, totally bemused by their uninvited guest, told the story to the village priest, Father Rene Mouville, a retired Lyons University professor who had entered the priesthood at the age of fifty. Once the priest met the boy, he knew there was no obvious solution. The child was quite unlike any human he had seen before. Even the construction of his body seemed, exceptional: his hips were extremely narrow and his rib-cage almost an inverted V-shape, quite the opposite to a normal chest structure. Just looking at those delicate, three fingered hands made the priest feel a strange sense of foreboding.

The next day he took the child back to his house to be cared for by his housekeeper. He soon found that the boy had a fantastic intelligence. Unable to communicate by any form of language, Father Mouville began by drawing simple diagrams of everyday objects, which received no response. Then one day he wrote down a series of numbers in the form of clustered dots. Immediately the boy took the paper and pencil and began writing dots at high speed. When he passed back the paper, Father Mouville found that he had worked out the cube root and square roots of all the groups of numbers.

As the weeks passed the boy's confidence grew. He began to master simple words, and to go out with the priest on his rounds. He began to be accepted in the village as almost ordinary instead of a curiosity. Basic physical phenomena fascinated him. He would sit for hours by moving water or watching birds in flight and the movement of clouds. It was as though he had never seen such things before.

Then after Christmas, 1900, he became ill. At first the symptoms seemed to be those of a heavy cold, and after a few weeks he seemed to have recovered. But by February he was sick again, this time with a high fever and a deathly pallor. A doctor was sent for and confessed himself mystified. The child's heart was the slowest he had ever heard, almost half the speed of a normal human. He should be taken to a hospital, but in his condition such a journey could well have been fatal. So the boy who came from nowhere became weaker and on the second week of March he died and was buried under an ash tree in the graveyard of Sainte Miande.

HC addendum.
Source: John Macklin, *'Casebook of the Unknown.'*   Type: E or H?
Comments: Shades of Kaspar Hauser. Did the boy come from some unknown subterranean kingdom? Or did the storm that night caused some kind of tear between dimensions in which the unfortunate boy fell through?

* * * * * * *

Location: Andreas, Isle of Man, England.
Date: 1901.
Time: Daytime.

   The young pre-teenage son of a local farming family named John, disappeared one day while out in the fields. Villagers searched but found no trace of him, and the family suffered accordingly. Then, out of the blue, four years after his disappearance, John wandered into the farmhouse, looking barely a day older, utterly disbelieving of the amount of time that his parents insisted had passed.
   According to John' story; strange little men had rendered him senseless in the field. He next found himself in their "land." He could not explain where he now was except that the little men could show him the lives of his family. He was able to describe to family members some of the things they had been up to (including a trip to Ramsey corn market); but while he was in captivity, all his attempts to communicate with them failed. He could observe but not directly interact, despite various almost ghost-like attempts to alert his family. John said he lost all sense of time during this sojourn.
   Then he found himself awakening in a strange spot. Finding that the small men were nowhere in sight, he made his way home, gradually regaining his senses, but still groggy when he found the farmhouse. He could never explain what had happened to him.

HC addendum.
Source: Jenny Randles, *IUR* spring 2004.   Type: G

Location: (Undisclosed location) Western Australia.
Date: 1901.
Time: Night.

"An extraordinary meteor was witnessed here a short time ago. A magnificent ball of fire shot across the heavens from the north-west to the north-east, leaving an almost straight trail of light behind it. At the head of this trail of light appeared a ball of fire, which became gradually diffused around the luminous trail or meteor in convolutions resembling the movements of a serpent.

For some moments the display bore a likeness of a pillar of light with a serpent twined around it. Gradually this semblance was transformed into the figure of a man standing upright, with his arms partly spread and his hands clasped. This form grew gradually into an attitude as if the figure were about to spring, the head and shoulders being inclined forwards and the legs slightly drawn up, and in this attitude it remained till the luminosity, gradually becoming paler, was absorbed in the silver light of the breaking day. Altogether the phenomenon lasted from 10 to 15 minutes."

HC addendum.
Source: Kay Massingill, *Magonia Exchange,* quoting *'Travels in Western Australia,'* "A description of the various cities and towns, goldfields, and agricultural districts of that state," by May Vivienne.   Type: X

* * * * * * *

Location: Alton, Illinois
Date: February, 1901.
Time: Various.

The mysterious woman in black is the all absorbing topic of interest in Upper State street circles in Alton. Her comings and goings are watched with the keenest interest from behind closed doors and speculations as to her identity and object in making State Street her stomping ground each evening is rife.

Many persons believe "she" is a man dressed in woman's clothing. The apparition first made its appearance about two weeks ago and for some time excited little attention, but when every night this creature completely clothed in black and walking slowly up and down in the neighborhood of State and Danforth Streets, continued to be seen, speculation as to what was going to happen became much greater. William Armstrong and Charles Cammell, two well-known citizens of the aristocratic neighborhood, notified the police through Mayor Tony

Young and officers were detailed to learn who the woman was and what her mission on State Street was.

Officers James Young and James Fitzgibbons, dressed in civilian clothes, followed her as she walked up and down State Street and Sunday night they asked her what she wanted. The mysterious woman in black without a word walked a few steps further, and then, crossing the North Alton city limits, asked the officers what they wanted. On being told that they wished to know her business, she told them that she was waiting to meet a friend.

Policeman James Young who spoke with the woman furnishes her descriptions as given above. Prof. William Armstrong, of Danforth Street was one of the first to see the woman. Prof. Armstrong who is a well-known musician in St Louis and who is at the head of the Shurtleff College musical department was returning late from a recital when just as he was going into his gate the woman came in sight. She was walking slowly and after she passed the corner of State and Danforth Streets she turned and retraced her steps, going back up State Street toward the North Alton city limits.

The unusual height of the woman and the way in which she walked suggested a man dressed in woman's clothes. Prof. Armstrong spoke of the matter to his family and found that each member at some time had seen the same apparition. For several nights following they watched as she walked slowly up and down State Street, and thinking that it might be someone who was trying to scare the children of the neighborhood, notified Mayor Young, who had the control stationed.

On the evenings when this woman was seen she began her walk about 7:30 o'clock and continued her vigil until near midnight. She has never been seen with anyone and has seemed to try to avoid meeting anyone who might recognize her. Officer Young the only person, who has spoken to her, is positive that the woman in black is a woman and not a man.

HC addendum.
Source: Magonia list quoting *The Hartford Republican* March 1, 1901.
Type: E?

Location: Bournebrook, West Midlands, England.
Date: Summer 1901.
Time: 8:00 p.m.

Frank Warily; ten years old, was taking a shortcut along a path behind his terraced housing estate. Suddenly he came upon a strange object sitting on the grass and thought that it was a workman's hut. There was a small box-shaped ship's funnel on top and a door on the side. The object was a greenish blue metallic color with a sheen, half the size of a modern car.

Suddenly Frank was confronted by two small beings who stepped down out of the doorway. They were four feet high, clean-shaven, and looked human with no odd features. They wore tight-fitting one piece uniforms with a greenish gray Military look and each wore a dark helmet that masked the eyes and ears almost completely. Emerging from the top were two wires almost like horns on a Viking's helmet. The wires rose nine inches.

One humanoid remained in the doorway. The other moved towards Frank with his arms outstretched, suggesting to Frank to get out of his way. Frank got out of the way and as he was doing this the humanoid scuttled back into the machine and the door closed. There was then a brilliant flash like electric arcing that lit up the perimeter of the object as well as a whooshing sound and the box-shaped craft climbed up into the sky in a curved flight. Frank noticed a pulsating red light at the rear as it ascended.

HC addendum.
Source: Derek James and Phil Bennett, Nufon News #50.   Type: B
Comments: One of the earliest reports of "aliens" seen next to landed object. I wonder why the humanoid was warning the witness to stay away or was his gesture miss-interpreted.

Location: Near Foxford, County Mayo, Ireland.
Date: Summer 1901.
Time: Afternoon.

    Two boys walking back from a stream, sighted a small figure run behind a nearby boulder. They both ran over to the boulder to look and saw a little man about four-foot high; he wore a cap and close-fitting collarless black coat and had curly brown whiskers. The boys became frightened and ran from the area.

HC addendum.
Source: Graham J. McEwan, *'Mystery Animals of Britain and Ireland.'*
Type: E

* * * * * * *

Location: Chesterfield, Idaho.
Date: January, 1902.
Time: Daytime.

    An eight-foot tall hair-covered human monster, visited a party of young people as they skated on the Portneuf River in the field of John Gooch. The creature showed fight and flourished a large stick and giving vent to a series of yells, attacked the skaters; but it being slow of movement, they regained their wagons and got away in safety. A party of young men returned armed and got a good view of the monster warming himself by the fire they had left. The beast was at least eight-feet high, covered with long reddish brown hair, the face was hidden by immense bushy whiskers, and no part of the skin was naked except a small spot above the eyes.
    The boys concluded not to bag the game that night. Measurements the following morning showed the tracks to measure long, by seven and one quarter inches broad, with the imprint of only four toes. The stockmen report having seen similar tracks along the range west of the river, but as far as know no one has ever before seen the animal, which was trekking westward. The people feeling unsafe while this beast is at large have sent some twenty men on its trail to effect its capture. Interested parties are referred to John Gooch, who was at the scene from the appearance to the disappearance of the monster.

HC addendum.
Source: Salt Lake City, Utah, *Deseret News*, January 27, 1902.

Location: Rockport, Ohio.
Date: April, 1902.
Time: Various.

A strange being; apparently half man, half beast, is seen in the country around Rockport and Beaver Dam. The creature puts in an appearance at or near farmhouses. For some time the farmers in that vicinity have been troubled by nightly visits, apparently from intruders bent on securing money or other valuables. It was the scheme of the prowler to attempt to open a window or fumble at the door locks, then move on to the rear part of the house, and after giving the gates and such outposts a good shake, disappear as quickly as he came. The family of Frank Conkleman left their home because of these visits, and while they were gone, the strange being was seen.

The creature is described as resembling a man, although possessed of features coarse and rough, and is said to be covered with hair. The inhabitants of that staid old country vicinity are half crazed with excitement, and the female portion will not venture outside the door after nightfall. It is firmly believed that the strange creature is an insane person who has been at large for some time. The being is attired in dress more peculiar to one of the male sex, although scantily clad. A searching party will be organized to capture the fellow, if possible although his fleetness of foot and abilities at fence jumping almost preclude any idea of so doing.

HC addendum.
Source: *The Tucson Citizen*, April 16, 1902.   Type: E

* * * * * * *

Location: Sassoferrato, Italy.
Date: June 1, 1902.
Time: Afternoon.

"A curious case of popular suggestion occurred yesterday afternoon in Sassoferrato that took on extraordinary proportions. A huge number of people, even from distant towns, poured into Sant' Egidio Parish four kilometers from the city, right at the foot of the mountain called Monte Strega in which the figure of the Virgin with a child appeared; above her shone a bright star. Needless to say, numerous miracles have already been told among the people."

HC addendum
Source: Edoardo Russo, in Magonia exchange list quoting the Milan daily *Corriere della Sera*, June 3, 1902.   Type: E or F?

Location: Northampton Township, Ohio.
Date: August, 1902.
Time: Night.

A blazing ball of fire and a strange animal which vanishes into thin air upon being approached, are terrorizing the people of Northampton Township near Johnson post office. *Both are believed to represent the spirit of John Shaneman, and the theory is advanced by the superstitions that his shade has returned to Earth to point out to relatives the hiding place of his fortune.*
Shaneman was a farmer, and although well to do, lived in a very frugal way and was generally supposed to have a box of money hidden about his premises. Only a few months before he died he sold to the Carrara Paiul Company of Barberton, several acres of land as the site for a factory for which he received about $7,000. He was paid with a check which he cashed at an Akron bank. Upon the death of Shaneman, relatives and others searched high and low about his house and farm for the money received from the Carrara Company and other sources, only $150 was found and that was concealed in an old cupboard. Since then, search for the money has been made at different times but without success.
Shaneman died suddenly, toppling over in his barn from an attack of paralysis. The next night afterward the blazing ball of fire was seen at his home. John Breitenstein, a candidate for County Commissioner two years ago, and a reputable citizen in every way, and Peter Shaffer a neighbor and also a worthy man, were sitting up with the dead man at the Shaneman home.
Suddenly they saw a ball of fire floating about the ceiling of the room. With a cry they left the room. Time passed and the incident was nearly forgotten but some time ago the ball of fire was seen again. It hovered over the Shaneman home, now occupied by Henry Breitenstein and wife. Again it was seen by John Mong, two daughters of Peter Shaffer and by Milton Breitenstein. John Breitenstein says the presence of the fire ball recently awakened him at night and he saw it close beside his window. He arose and tried to follow it. It vanished before going from his premises. Simultaneously with the seeing of the fireball the strange animal was seen at a different locality.
It is said to haunt an abandoned mine near the Shaneman place. It has the features like a wolf. On one occasion George Conrad and Eugene Cady of Barberton pursued the animal but when they came near and struck at it, the creature vanished. Many people are visiting the locality to investigate the supposed apparition.

HC addendum.
Source: Magonia exchange list quoting the *Newark Ohio Advocate* 8-11-1902. Type: F?

Location: Spavinaw Hills, Oklahoma.
Date: September, 1902.
Time: Various.

Great excitement prevails among the full-blood Cherokee Indians in the Spavinaw Hills, two miles southeast of this place, on account of a ghost story. At the home of Davy Vann, a full blood who resides near Eucha Indian Territory, two girls were left alone while the older people were gone to a picnic. On Friday evening the girls declare, rocks and sticks began to fall in the yard thick and fast and they became frightened and ran away to a neighbor's a distance of three miles, and found no one at home except three of the younger Indians. No sooner had the affrighted children arrived at this place; that rocks and sticks began to fall on the roof and in the yard. They looked everywhere, but could see no one.

The family returned from the picnic and the house was again attacked with rocks and sticks and this strange occurrence is still going on there, and is the cause of great excitement. When they go out on the east side of the house, they declare, the rocks come from the west and when they go on the west side of the house, they say the rocks come from the east. *The young son of Mr. Vann went out to look and returned very much frightened, saying he saw a man with a head about two feet long.* The people in the neighborhood of Dave Vann are very much worried over the strange occurrences, whatever it is.

HC addendum.
Source: Kay Massingill in Magonia exchange list quoting *The Hartford Courant* (1887-1922) September 25, 1902.   Type: E?
Comments: Is unfortunate that there is no additional comment or description of the "man with the two foot long head."

* * * * * * *

Location: Iola, Kansas.
Date: 1903.
Time: Night

Four workers on the night shift of a zinc mine encountered a bizarre creature around midnight. The man who saw it first gave a yell and fled. The other men ran to the place to see what was wrong. All took one look at the creature and ran away. It was described as having horns, and long hair, great big eyes, and an inhuman look, although standing erect like a man. It apparently ran off.

HC addendum.
Source: CAUS and Phillip L. Rife, *'America's Nightmare Monsters.'*
Type: E

* * * * * * *

Location: Near Lake Wellington, Victoria, Australia.
Date: May 20, 1903.
Time: Afternoon.

On Monday week two lads named Gill and Luke stated that they had seen a balloon in mid-air in the direction of Lake Wellington. The statement was not then regarded seriously, but some credence is now placed in it, as a young man named Robert Dowd, employed by Mr. Breheny, states that he saw the balloon today about one mile in the air over the Sale to Stratford Road.

He drew the attention of a man named Benjamin White to the object. Dowd says he distinctly saw the oval form with ropes attached, and a man in the car, with network all around him. The balloon disappeared in the direction of Lake Wellington. Local people are unable to account for the strange visitor, as it is felt that if any resident of the lakes district had become possessed of a balloon the fact would have come to light before now.

HC addendum.
Source: *The Age*, May 20, 1903, Melbourne, Australia.   Type: A

* * * * * * *

Location: Stratford, near Indianapolis, Indiana.
Date: September 13, 1903.
Time: Late afternoon.

Area residents spotted a 30-foot long cigar-shaped object circling the area. One witness was alerted to the object by the cackling of his chickens. One man studied the object through a pair of binoculars. He and others saw a canopy on the top center of the object and under it were two figures that were moving backwards and forward as if in rhythm.

HC addendum.
Source: Jerome Clark, *'The UFO Encyclopedia Vol. II.'*   Type: A

Location: Irvington, Indianapolis, Indiana.
Date: September 13, 1903.
Time: 18:00

Did Professor Langley's airship visit Indianapolis at an early hour last evening? If not, whence came and whose was the airship which several residents of the eastern part of the city and Irvington claim, to have seen hovering in that vicinity a few minutes before 6 o'clock?

An airship, or some mysterious creature neither of the Earth nor of the seas; there must have been, for not fewer than a dozen people saw it, and many others saw someone else who saw it, and all along East Washington Street, from Tuxedo to the limits of Irvington, excitement prevailed (especially among young boys) for several hours. The heavenly visitor is said to have appeared from the west and after circling about above the residence of Hilton U. Brown for a few seconds, to have darted off to the north; soon to disappear in the growing dusk.

Difficulty was experienced in finding anyone who had himself witnessed the apparition. John W. Elstun, who lives in the northwest part of Irvington, was reported to have seen it, but upon inquiry, it was found that he had received his information from others. "I did not see the airship myself" said Mr. Elstun by telephone to the Journal, "but half a dozen of my neighbors saw it and are positive that it was an airship. They describe it as a cigar-shaped affair, from which a basket or car was suspended.

In the car were two or three people, but at least two, and one of them was apparently steering the thing. The steering apparatus could not be seen, the airship was too high for that, but those who saw it thought they could detect smoke issuing from one end of the affair, which indicated that there was machinery of some kind. "The airship came from the direction of the city, but no one saw it, I guess, until it had almost reached Irvington. Then it suddenly circled around and started off to the north. No, those who saw it say it could not have been an ordinary balloon, nor merely a cigar-shaped balloon. They are positive it was an airship of some kind and that the men in the car had it under control."

Dr. M. H. Williams, 2912 East Washington Street, is said to have seen the airship, but he could not be reached last night to confirm the report. No one in the heart of the city seemed to have seen the affair, which adds to the mystery, as it was supposed to have come from over the city. No one in Indianapolis has been working on an airship, at least not to the knowledge of the public, and, indeed, there has been no report of Indiana inventors who are seeking to accomplish what Santos Dumont has worked at for years and what Prof. Langley claims to have at last perfected; an airship that is really an airship.

One young witness reported that the airship passed over Tuxedo, veering rapidly to the north. He said it was cigar-shaped, with an under car and a propelling wheel at the stern. The cylinder of the ship was painted red, white and blue and in the car were three men and it moved very fast.

HC addendum.
Source: Kay Massingill in magonia exchange, quoting *The Indianapolis Indiana Journal*, September 14, 1903.   Type: A

* * * * * * *

Location: Van Meter, Iowa.
Date: October, 1903.
Time: Various.

This local town containing 1,000 persons is terribly wrought up by what is described as a horrible monster. Every man, woman and child in the town is in a state of terror, and fully half of them fail to close their eyes in slumber except in broad day light. The monster put in an appearance Monday night. U. G. Griffith; an implement dealer, drove into town at 1 a.m. and saw what seemed to be an electric searchlight on Maher and Grigg's store. While he gazed, it sailed across to another building and then disappeared. His story was not believed next day. But the following night Dr. A. C. Olcott, who sleeps in his office on the principal street, was awakened by a bright light shining in his face.

He grabbed a shotgun and ran outside the building, where he saw a monster seemingly half human and half beast with great bat-like wings. A dazzling light that fairly blinded him came from a blunt, horn-like protuberance in the middle of the animal's forehead, and it gave off a stupefying odor that almost overcame him. The doctor discharged his weapon and fled into his office, barring doors and windows, and remained there in abject terror until morning. Peter Dunn; cashier of the only bank in the town, fearing bank robbery, loaded a repeating shotgun with shells filled with buckshot and prepared to guard his funds next night. At 2 a.m. he was blinded by the presence of a light of great intensity. Eventually he recovered his senses sufficiently to distinguish the monster, and fired through the window. The plate glass and sash were torn out and the monster disappeared. Next morning imprints of great three-toed feet were discernible in the soft earth. Plaster casts of them were taken.

That night Dr. O. W. White saw the monster climbing down a telephone pole, using a beak much in the manner of a parrot. As it struck the ground it seemed to travel in leaps, like a kangaroo, using its huge, featherless wings to assist. It gave off no light. He fired at it, and he believes he wounded it. The shot was followed by an overpowering odor. Sidney Gregg, attracted by the shot, saw the monster flying away. But the climax came Friday night. The whole town was aroused by this time. Prof. Martin, principal of the schools, decided that upon the description; it was an 'ante-diluvian' animal.

Shortly after midnight J. L. Platt foreman of the brick plant heard a peculiar sound in an abandoned coal mine, and as the men had reported a similar sound before, a body of volunteers started an investigation. Presently the monster emerged from the shaft, accompanied by a smaller one. A score of shots were fired without effect. The whole town was aroused and vigil was maintained the rest of the night, but without result, until just at dawn, when the two monsters returned and disappeared down the shaft.

HC addendum.
Source: *The Pittsburgh Press* (Pennsylvania) October 23, 1903.   Type: E
Comments: Early subterranean Mothman type creature?

* * * * * * *

Location: Sourland Mountains, New Jersey.
Date: Winter 1903.
Time: Morning.

On a misty morning, a boy reported encountering a bizarre creature. He first saw an animal he thought was a cow, until it turned and looked at him. "Then I saw what appeared to be a man on the front of the animal, only he was grown into the neck of the animal. It had horns, hands, four hoofed feet, a tail and fire-red eyes." The boy fled.

HC addendum.
Source: Phillip L. Rife, *'America's Nightmare Monsters.'*   Type: E

Location: Szuhabaranka, Hungary.
Date: December 24, 1903.
Time: 8:00 p.m.

Ivan Petrovszki had gone to a local well to fetch some water as his wife waited for him at home which was located nearby. Around the same time a local priest had stepped out of the parsonage, when he noticed a huge beam of light that appeared to be illuminating the entire village from an unknown point above. Looking around for the light source, he noticed a swirling luminous sphere or mass hovering above the well where Petrovszki had gone to get the water.

The hovering light suddenly emitted a very bright flash of light and then shot away and disappeared into the starry sky. Petrovskzi's wife ran screaming towards the well, looking for her husband but he was nowhere to be found. The next day the local police investigated the events and reportedly found a dark circle of about 6 meters in diameter which had melted the snow. They could not find any tracks or remains of Ivan Petrovszki.

HC addendum.
Source: Kriston Endre www.ryufor.hu/Kriston.htm   Type: G?
Comments: Perhaps an early 20th century permanent abduction.

* * * * * * *

Location: Near Moscow, Russia.
Date: 1904.
Time: Evening.

After a powerful thunderstorm swept the area, peasants checking for damage discovered a strange corpse under a fallen tree. According to militia reports of the day "the creature was about one and a half meter in height, covered in dark gray clothing; on its head it wore a kind of a helmet with three short horns." Instead of blood, from the corpse oozed a strange thick violet substance or liquid.

When the body was freed from under the tree it was realized that it was apparently made out of metal, only its face was covered with rough brown skin. The mouth and nose were almost absent, whereas the eyes were unnaturally large and protruding. Incredibly the small creature weighed in at 80 kilograms. The bizarre "android" was shipped to a local morgue where it apparently disappeared.

HC addendum.
Source: UFOLOG.RU.   Type: H?

Location: Fiambala, Catamarca, Argentina.
Date: 1904.
Time: Night.

Several children playing in a field followed a bright light to a dried up riverbed near town. As they approached the light they noticed that it was shaped like a small "table" and on top of it there was a small "angel-like" figure. They attempted to follow the light and the "angel" but it was quickly lost from sight.

HC addendum.
Source: Proyecto CATENT, Argentina. Type: A?

* * * * * * *

Location: Muntii Apuseni, Transylvania, Romania.
Date: 1904.
Time: After midnight.

A farmer was working the fields late using a horse drawn cart when he saw a fiery wheel-like object descend towards the ground near him. The fiery wheel approached rapidly, rotating as it got closer. The farmer stood there stunned as the wheel suddenly changed shape into a humanoid figure that looked at the farmer for a long time without speaking.

HC addendum.
Source: Ion Hobana and Julien Weverbergh, *'UFOs from Behind the Iron Curtain.'* Type: E

* * * * * * *

Location: Cairo, Egypt.
Date: April 8,9,10, 1904.
Time: Noon to 1 p.m. (on 3 consecutive days).

Rose Kelly, who had mediumistic ability, married Aleister Crowley and they spent their honeymoon in Cairo where Rose spontaneously made contact with an entity named "Aiwass" (originally spelled Aiwaz). Aiwass said he was a messenger for the Egyptian god Horus. Crowley had a vision of him, seeing Aiwass as a man dressed in old Assyrian or Persian clothing and having what he described as:

"...a body of "fine matter" or astral matter, transparent as a veil of gauze or a cloud of incense-smoke. He seemed to be a tall, dark man in his thirties, well-knit, active and strong, with the face of a savage king, and eyes veiled lest their gaze should destroy what they saw." Aiwass ordered Crowley to take dictation. For three hours between April 8 and 10, 1904, the entity spoke in a voice that emanated directly out of the air, while Crowley wrote in longhand. The result was *"The Book of the Law"* the seminal work of Thelemic philosophy, which contains the axiom, "Do what thou wilt shall be the whole of the law." In other words, do what you must to surrender to total alignment with cosmic law.

HC addendum.
Source: *'The Confessions of Aleister Crowley.'*   Type: F?

* * * * * * *

Location: Crete, Greece.
Date: January, 1904.
Time: Night.

Christophoros Rodussakis was out hunting for birds, when he saw in the light of his torch; a hairy creature. He described it as a "devil," 1.5 meters (approx. 5ft tall), with long horns. The creature attacked him and they began wrestling on the ground. The witness struck the creature's head many times with a rock, but with no avail. Sometime later, two other beings, described by the witness as one being "Saint Anthony" and "a black clad woman" appeared and then the "demon" seemed to lose interest in fighting and vanished, running away and "emitting sparks."

HC addendum.
Source: Nikolaos Politis, *'Traditions.'*   Type: E

Location: Bronx, New York.
Date: June, 1904.
Time: Night.

Acting Capt. Wilson of the Bronx Park Police Station last night asked the Superintendent of the Zoological Gardens to try to take into custody a big brown 'owl' for which the past three weeks has been scaring the policemen who were assigned to Post 16, which is one of the most lonely posts in the gloomy old Bronx.

For many days it was believed that a winged demon had deigned to hover over Post 16, and the policemen who were assigned to duty there came into the old station in the Lorillard Mansion night after night with wonderful tales of what had happened on the hoodoo post. Policeman Patrick J. Hickey said it was the most horrid thing he had ever encountered.

"It's not an owl," said Hickey, "it's a devil with wings. Sure I know an owl when I see one, but no man ever seen an owl with wings six feet wide. And it "whooooo's" like a ghost in a graveyard, too, when it's not growling beneath its breath. Why, men, he's no owl; he's a devil; and I'm going to get transferred."

And when Hickey was transferred, a German policeman was assigned to Post No. 16, which takes in Lorillard Lane. The German policeman had only been on the post an hour one night when he came running into the station house and shouted:

"I seen it! It had a stick on its claw, and it tried to smash my head. When I ducked it ducked, too, and I had to run behind a tree. I think it is supernatural, that's what I think."

Then policeman Walter Kane was assigned to the "hoodoo" post, and he got a transfer in a hurry after the strange creature on wings had knocked his helmet off while patrolling the lane.

Policeman Frank Campbell, who was sent to the Bronx station from a downtown Manhattan precinct, was on duty on Post 16 only two nights when he encountered "something strange" that flew down from the trees and attacked him. He had not heard of the experiences of the other men who had been on Post 16, but when he entered the station a few nights ago with his face scratched and his helmet battered in, he wrote out this report:

"Shortly before midnight encountered a dark, flying object with four legs and two wings, the beast attacked me, if it was a beast, and I fought back. Has the resemblance of a tall, slim man at times, and at other times assumes the form of a mountain dwarf."

Last night (June 21) Julius Wensch, who resides at Bronxdale, ran into the police station and shouted for help. He told Sgt. Appel who was at the desk, that he had been attacked by something wild that "yelled like a tiger." He said the strange thing had carried away a young woman who was in his company, and he asked for police assistance. Policemen Ollet and Baker were sent to rescue the girl, and they found her running through Lorillard Lane screaming. She explained that a wildcat with wings had attacked her and had torn the feathers from her hat.

The policeman went back to the station and reported that it was undoubtedly the big brown owl which had been frightening policemen for the past three weeks. The acting Captain notified the Bronx Park folks and a squad of men were sent out to capture the thing at midnight. (No additional information as to what occurred).

HC addendum.
Source: Kate Massingill in Magonia Exchange List quoting *The New York Times*, June 22, 1904. Type: E

* * * * * * *

Location: Lawrenceburg, Kentucky.
Date: Early May, 1904.
Time: Various.

The people residing along quiet Chaplin River are suffering the intense agony of ghostly horrors. Several weeks ago Peter Catey, a well-known resident, while out late at night, observed a fierce looking 'apparatus' passing through the air above him at a rapid gate. It resembled a shooting meteor or comet but moved back and forth over the same aerial course.

Upon closer observation he could see distinctly a headless man, apparently standing upon what appeared to be a large plank. He told his neighbors of the mystifying sights which he had witnessed and the whole neighborhood stood at watch the following night and promptly at 2 o'clock, the headless man began darting through the atmosphere.

The more scholarly residents of the Chaplin River section, after viewing the headless man with the instruments, have about come to the conclusion that the terrifying object is an amateur genius who has invented a flying machine and that he is making a personal test of it at night in order to prevent the publicity of it before he gets the apparatus thoroughly perfected.

This is a very reasonable conclusion and serves to account for the man appearing headless, for in passing through the air at such great velocity one would be compelled to hold his head towards his breast to prevent the wind from taking his breath.

HC addendum.
Source: Fabio Picasso in Magonia Exchange, quoting The Hartford Republican, Friday May 6, 1904, Vol. XVI. Type: A

Location: Near Preston, Texas.
Date: September, 1904.
Time: Various.

Nearly a year ago the people living along the river front near Preston were set agog by the appearance in the woods of a strange being in human form. When discovered by a party of hunters on his all fours pawing and neighing like a horse, their attention was first attracted by what they took to be the whining of a startled horse in the undergrowth.

When advanced upon, the strange being ran off on his hands and feet but the pursuers gained upon him so rapidly he sprang to his feet and quickly covering the short distance to the river, plunged headlong from a rather high bank into the water and swam to the Indian side. When he reached that bank he stood up, shook himself like a horse just out of a bath, and with what might really be called a horse laugh ran off into the woods. Some months later he was seen under much the same conditions but this time west of Woodville, on the Indian side.

Only a few weeks ago a man crawled across the road in plain view of several people not far from where the horse-man was first seen but disappeared, the pursuit being somewhat tardy. Since Sunday last the people living near Colbert, ten miles east of Preston, Grayson County Texas, have been hunting for a strangely acting man who crawled about like a snake until pursued, when he would jump to his feet and outrun the fastest horses ridden after him. Others who pursued him on foot say they shot at him at close range but the bullets, if they struck their target, seemed to have no effect.

As late as last evening, children claim to have seen the crawling man again near the Varner place, six miles from Colbert. A phone message from Colbert this afternoon confirms previous reports sent out from Durant about the state of excitement and the gathering of several parties for pursuit, but states that public interest has received something of a chill because some of the parties who were present when the close range shots were tired say that although the peculiar being was in the open and very close, that he disappeared with the smoke of the powder.

At the Varner place he crawled into the henhouse. It is stated that out in the field a dead chicken, bitten in the neck, and from which there was the appearance of the blood having been drawn, was found.

Though with somewhat reduced enthusiasm, the people of the Varner neighborhood are preparing for another big roundup this afternoon and tonight.

HC addendum.
Source: *The Dallas Morning News*, September 3, 1905.   Type: E

Location: Everton, Liverpool, England.
Date: September 10, 1904.
Time: Midday.

   A bizarre figure reported to have been Spring-Heeled Jack, appeared on the roof a local church. He was spotted hanging on the steeple of St. Francis Xavier on Salisbury Street. Onlookers claimed he suddenly dropped from the steeple and fell to the ground. Thinking that he had committed suicide, they rushed to the point where he had landed (behind some houses) only to find a helmeted man, clothed in white, standing there waiting. He scuttled towards the crowd, raised his arms, and took to the air over William Henry Street.

HC addendum.
Source: Mufob Vol. 5 #6.   Type: E
http://www.altereddimensions.net/crime/SpringHeeledJack.aspx

                              * * * * * * *

Location: Poulshot, England.
Date: October 30, 1904.
Time: Night.

   Alfred Fielding and another lay preacher were riding back home in a horse and trap after chapel service, when a tremendous storm suddenly came in. Soon they saw a figure of a woman in white coming towards them along the road. The horse stopped dead on his tracks. Both men watched the girl advancing. She came up level with the lights on the trap, and they saw a beautiful, angelic face and auburn hair, she wore a white flowing dress. Then the figure suddenly vanished in plain sight. The two men searched around but could not find any trace of her.

HC addendum.
Source: Ken Rogers, *'The Warminster Triangle.'*   Type: E

Location: Lake Tinsel, near Sitka, Alaska.
Date: October 31, 1904.
Time: Night.

"Enclosed with this letter is a sketch by Mr. Elgnirk Sirk of the queer "thing" found encased in an iceberg on Lake Tinsel. Last night a party of Esquimaux runners highly excited dashed into Sitka and reported that the mysterious creature had come to life, that Mr. Sirk was ill from the strain and that many of his servants had fled. Business in Sitka is temporarily suspended. Many persons are already on the dog-trail to the interior and a party of one hundred and fifty men left here this morning on skis for the Sirk estate.

My Esquimaux informants state that for nearly an hour after its release the creature lay like a mummy. Then, as night fell, the eyelids quivered and 'rem' was seen to issue from them. All the while Mr. Sirk was engaged in massaging the "thing's" wrists and heart. With the coming dusk animation stirred its body. The lips trembled, the fingers shook nervously.

Suddenly as the moon rose, the tongue protruded and articulation was heard. Mr. Sirk fell over in a faint and all his servants, save three, fled. The remaining servants tenderly put their master, who for two days had neglected to take food, upon a dog-sled and bore him with the strange acquisition to this home. Recovering, Mr. Sirk saw again the weird being and found it wholly alive and seated on a chair like any human creature, dispatching with gluttonous haste all the visible eatables on the servant's table; its first food for possibly 4,000 years.

My Esquimaux messengers added that when daylight came the creature acted as one dead, and remained so until nightfall, when it emerged from its coma, and, bearing itself like a high-caste human, uttered strange speech and made overt attempts to convey its thoughts.

My next letter will be written from personal observation, as it is no longer possible to endure conjecture. I leave for the Sirk estate tonight and will advise you of developments."

HC addendum.
Source: Kay Massingill in *magonia_exchange*; quoting *Philadelphia Inquirer* (Philadelphia, PA) Tuesday, November 8, 1904.   Type: X?
Comments: Unfortunately there is no additional information to this intriguing story.

* * * * * * *

Location: Capel Egryn, Wales.
Date: December 22, 1904.
Time: 5:30 p.m.

Three observers saw a large light "about half way from the Earth to the sky, on the south side of Capel Egryn," and in the middle of it; something like a bottle or black person (figure), also some little lights scattering around the large light in many colors."

HC addendum.
Source: Jerome Clark, *'Unexplained!'*   Type: A?

* * * * * * *

Location: (Undisclosed location) Denmark.
Date: Before 1905.
Time: Night.

All the children of the household were ill with scarlet fever and the main witness had been awake for most of eight nights and was completely exhausted by fatigue; but the worst had now passed and she had gone to lie down for a rest, but to no avail. The night-lamp was burning and the moon was shining through the window, so the room was lit up considerably.
Suddenly the door opened and in came a figure that looked exactly like a "Nisse" (elf), just as these are depicted in fairytales; a dwarf with a long beard, gray clothes. He looked down on each of the children with a friendly expression. The main witness is convinced it wasn't a dream as she could see the shadow of the gnome's hat moving on the wall, each time he bent over towards the bed. When he started approaching the main witness' bed, this one fainted.

The next morning she woke up with a feeling that one of the children was probably going to die now. When she told her husband what she had seen, he laughed at her and said that all the children had recovered fine.

HC addendum.
Source: Thomas Brisson Jorgensen in Magonia Exchange quoting *Sandhedssogeren* (The Truth Seeker) 18-19, 1905. Type: E

* * * * * * *

Location: Northern California, near Oregon border.
Date: Circa 1905.
Time: Unknown.

The reporter of this strange tale was working for the Southern Pacific Railroad; building a track on the northern California-Oregon border area in the early nineteen hundreds. During this project he was dispatched to work on a camp in the woods, they had a base camp that the work crew worked from and each week the work crews would split in to two man teams that would work an area, clearing logs and ground and at the end of one week they would go back to the base camp to check in and replenish their supplies and then set out after the weekend for another week in the woods.

During this time, one of the two man teams came back to camp with only one man; they were told that the other man had disappeared. The group at the base camp apparently gave a brief search to no avail.

The next week the crews went out in two man crews and continued the work on the railroad clearing. Some weeks later, as the camp moved north, the group of railroad workers came upon the missing man; he was naked and hysterical/crazed, and apparently died soon after he was found. He told of being abducted by a female 'ape' that kept him in a large open pit. During the time he was in the pit, the man told of being forced to have sexual contact with the ape many times and said that the ape kept him in the hole or pit by licking his hands and feet raw, so he was not able to escape from the pit. Apparently the reporter saw this man's hands and feet and said that they were completely raw.

IIC addendum.
Source: John Lewis, San Francisco, California.
http://www.bigfootencounters.com/n_california1900s.htm   Type: X

Location: Near Pensarn, Wales.
Date: 1905.
Time: Afternoon.

The witness was on her way to visit her sick grandfather and had decided to go a different route in order to visit a friend. As she was about to turn a corner, an "angel-like" creature appeared before her blocking her path and stretching out both his arms. The figure had golden or fair hair and small white wings that seemed to come out from the middle of his back rather than his shoulders. He was of average height and hovered slightly off the ground completely motionless. The being did not speak but the witness got the "message" that he wanted her to return home. Later that night at home she learned that her grandfather had died.

HC addendum.
Source: *Fortean Times* #68. Type: E

* * * * * * *

Location: Barranco de Badajoz, Tenerife, Canary Islands, Spain.
Date: 1905.
Time: Daytime.

A young girl was sent by her parents to gather fruit in the area just before supper. However, the girl never returned and a massive search was conducted all over Tenerife for her. She was never found. However three decades later (in 1958), the young girl reportedly returned; looking exactly the same as the time that she disappeared. To her, only 15-20 minutes had gone by. (!) According to the girl; as she was collecting pears from a pear grove, she noticed a very tall figure dressed in white standing near her. Strangely she felt no fear but instead felt a strange attraction towards the figure. The entity then invited the girl to follow him and she immediately accepted.

The girl accompanied the humanoid into a nearby cave where there was a descending set of steps which the girl followed the white-clad stranger down. At the bottom of the steps there was a garden in which there were other similar white-dressed entities. The girl remembers speaking for a few minutes with the strange group and later was guided back up the steps by the initial entity which then bade farewell to the girl. Incredibly to the girl, it had only been 15-20 minutes but in actuality 30 years had gone by. (!) Apparently the investigators were frustrated by the lack of cooperation by the local authorities about the event; only one local elderly woman came forward and suggested that the "Girl of the Pears" might still be alive.

HC addendum.
Source: http://www.angulo13.com/badajoz_1.htm   Type: G
Comments: Year is approximate. Time and space seemed to have been compressed inside the cave; while outside it remained "normal." Or maybe the girl was momentarily thrust into the future and then returned?

* * * * * * *

Location: Hudson Bay area, Labrador, Canada.
Date: 1905.
Time: Night.

After some local Indians reported finding strange enormous footprints in the snow, a local French trapper living in an isolated area, came home one night to find his daughter; a girl of 17 or 18; in a state of panic. She said she had seen a huge, black, hairy man come out of the woods opposite the hut and beckon to her.

HC addendum.
Source: Fabio Picasso quoting the *Straits Times* Singapore, December 15, 1913, in Magonia exchange list.   Type: E
Comments: The supposed animal called Sasquatch or Bigfoot shows intelligent behavior here. As far as I know bears don't beckon to people.

* * * * * * *

Location: Quirihue, Itata, Chile.
Date: 1905.
Time: Night.

A nervous young local man came to visit the local priest in a very agitated state, reporting a strange encounter he had several nights before; after a party in which he had danced with a pretty young widow named Doña Francisca. After the dance he had gone outside in the darkness in order to relieve a physiological need; he chose a nearby vegetable garden and was feeling pretty good since the young widow appeared to be responsive to his amorous behavior.
Suddenly as he stood there a dark figure approached him which suddenly grabbed him and scratched his face several times. Defending himself, the young man punched and lunged at the strange figure but was strangely unable to strike him as he couldn't locate a solid body within the dark figure. Surprised he stepped back and stared at the strange figure noting that it somehow resembled a man, perhaps resembling the

widow's dead husband? As he stared at the stranger, its face suddenly seemed to elongate and became as long as a human leg.

Terrified by this he ran back into a nearby house and was told by the foreman that he had probably encountered a "Moro" a dark night creature known to be over-protective of pretty young women, hence its aggressive behavior towards the young man, who assured the priest that the "Moro" followed him for the next several nights and scratched him again.

HC addendum.
Source: Cesar Parra, *'Guia Magica de Santiago,'* quoting Manuel Alarcon. Type: E?

* * * * * * *

Location: Brynerug, Merionethshire, Wales.
Date: February 22, 1905.
Time: Night.

A professional man returning home from a revival meeting suddenly saw a gigantic figure with its arms extended over the road; rising over a hedgerow. He uttered an involuntary prayer at which a ball of fire appeared above, from which descended a white beam which pierced the figure, which thereupon vanished. This was independently witnessed by a gentleman farmer of good standing.

HC addendum.
Source: Mufob Vol. 5 #6, Beriah Evans in *Occult Review*, March, 1905.
Type: E

* * * * * * *

Location: Barmouth, Wales.
Date: March, 1905.
Time: Night.

A young local woman was reportedly visited for three consecutive nights in her bedroom by a humanoid figure totally dressed in black. The figure supposedly delivered a message to the girl, which was too "frightening" to reveal.

HC addendum.
Source: Jerome Clark, *'The UFO Encyclopedia Vol. II,'* and *Barmouth Advertiser* of March 30, 1905. Type: E

Location: Perm, Russia.
Date: April, 1905.
Time: Afternoon.

In a dark corridor of the Orthodox Cathedral of Perm, the witness; Anatol J. Schneiderov saw about 10 paces away, emitting no heat, a red aureole within which was "jumping" a black humanoid 3-4 ft. tall. It had two very large owl-like eyes reflecting red light, a short beak-like nose, and a large mouth running from ear to pointed ear, out of which its dog-like tongue protruded. "It looked at me; it jumped and teased me." Thinking it was a "trick" of some kind, the witness rushed at it, but the aureole and being floated away from him, disappearing when it reached the head of the stairs. Only then did the witness feel fear.

HC addendum.
Source: Witness' letter to J. A. Hynek, November 8, 1973.　　Type: E

* * * * * * *

Location: Philadelphia, Pennsylvania.
Date: May, 1905.
Time: Morning.

Julia McGlone was leaving her workplace when a figure leapt down and assaulted her. The shadowy attacker left her with scratches all over her face and neck. McGlone screamed for a policeman who rushed to her aid. The policeman pulled a gun on the attacker, who "blew blue flames" into his face and leapt up a flight of stairs in a single bound, making his escape. This was only one of a series of attacks perpetrated by a tall, thin man in shining metallic clothing.

HC addendum.
Source: Patty Wilson, *'Totally Bizarre Pennsylvania.'*　　Type: E

* * * * * * *

Location: San Antonio, Texas.
Date: May 4, 1905.
Time: 5:00 a.m.

"The Woman in Black was seen Wednesday night and Thursday morning. Notwithstanding the ban placed upon the matter by the Catholic clergy many of the Mexicans employed the sign of the cross as an exorcism against the apparition which set the west side agog Wednesday night. At (illegible) South Concho Street two un-comical devils were painted on the door. No visit by the Woman in Black was reported at this place and the occupants have assumed that this was as effective as the symbol which was recommended by Don Pedro.

Romaldo Reyes, a Mexican peddler living on South Concho Street, says that about 5 o'clock Thursday morning he started out to purchase his stock of vegetables. He was one of the skeptics, who the night before had failed to place the sign of the cross upon his door. As he opened his portal he saw the Woman in Black, waiting for him, he says. As he stepped out of his door she made a grab for him. He called for his daughter and as the latter came promptly the Woman in Black faded away. The Woman in Black has become very real to some of the residents on the west side and the sign of the cross adorns the majority of the residences on that side of the city."

HC addendum.
Source: Jerome Clark, Magonia exchange, quoting *San Antonio Express,* May 5, 1905.   Type: E

* * * * * * *

Location: Lis Ard, Ireland.
Date: Summer 1905.
Time: Evening.

Martin Brennan was working on a field just below the famous fairy fort when he looked up to see the bank lined with a score or more of the "fairy folk," all life sized, the women mostly young and good-looking and with shawls over their heads. The men wore red or brown coats and some were bareheaded, with tousled brown hair, while others wore conical hats set jauntily on their heads. But all of them, both men and women, had penetrating, staring eyes, which even at the distance of sixty or seventy yards seemed to pierce right through him as he worked with his scythe cutting rushes. Altogether, it was a sight, which made him retire hastily to the human companionship of the farm buildings.

HC addendum.
Source: Dermot Mac Manus, *'The Middle Kingdom.'*   Type: E

Location: Voltana, near Mont Perdu, Spain.
Date: June, 1905.
Time: Daytime.

Five times since the first day of June, a woman robed in white, with long clinging draperies has flown over this town in northern Spain. The people of that entire district of the Pyrenees are in a state of religious fervor and excitement, expecting each day to hear the blast of a bugle; or the call of a voice from the sky. The astounding message of the fifth flight of the woman over the town has just been received at Barbasto, together with the statement that scores of persons standing on the mountainside, scores in the streets of the town, and many from their home and their fields knelt where they were and watched the flight.

The woman; or whatever it was; came from the northwest each time; from the direction of giant Mt. Perdu; one of the highest peaks of the Pyrenees; and disappeared to the southwest among the peaks of the Sierra de Guara. There was no sign of any balloon or wings or other appliances; it was as if a woman garbed as an angel but without wings, floated over the town, slowly, unhurriedly, and three of the five times a strong wind blowing either from the south or the southwest.

Investigations by an English mining expert in that region have shown that over 240 persons have seen, or claim to have seen the mystic figure; to them the symbol of some great happening upon Earth, float from north; evidently from some place on the southern summit of Mt. Perdu, come straight south over the village and disappear over the wooded crest of Tertuso; a low peak south of the town in the Sierra de Guara. The figure appeared to be a woman wearing a long flowing white dress.

On Friday June 16, at 1500 herdsmen from the hills north of town came running in terror toward Voltana, announcing that they had seen the woman in the sky to the northwest approaching leisurely and only a few hundred feet above the ground. Almost before the herdsmen and mule drivers, panic stricken, reached the town, the figure appeared above the trees and the hills to the north and floated gracefully southwards turning southeast over the town and disappeared.

The second appearance threw the entire district into a frenzy of excitement. Wild, weird tales were told of the woman and her appearance. Some vowed that she carried a flaming sword in her hands, others that they saw her lips move in prayer, and some vowed that she carried close to her breast the form of an infant. Many of those who swear that they saw additional phenomena are known to have remained with their faces to the ground during the four or five minutes occupied by the passage of the figure over the town. One woman who saw the figure from the window of her cottage vows that she heard the sweetest song of the entire world, while the figure was passing by.

Three days later; on the Sabbath just before the darkness came, the figure passed over the town again. Fifteen persons saw it but among them were two Jesuit missionaries, who made a careful observation of the figure, but, despite this, could add nothing to what already was known.

On Tuesday morning, June 20, shortly after 7:00 a.m. the figure again passed over the town, this time nearly a mile in the air and in the teeth of a high gale that was blowing from the southeast, off the Mediterranean, and this time the figure was seen plainly by at least two Englishmen, Ben Carniff and Ralph Allison, who were on a walking tour of the country. Carniff carried a pair of small field glasses, which he used to watch the movements of the figure. He admits that he was so astounded that he forgot his glasses until the figure had passed over him and was moving southwest but he says that through the glass it had every appearance of a woman's figure, and that he observed her feet, which seemed to be clad in some soft sole-less sandal, protruding from the flowing draperies when they shifted in the wind.

The fourth appearance climaxed the excitement. The frightened people, who declared, made predictions of every kind or most of them did, that the woman had to come to warn the town of some great calamity, which they believe impended.

HC addendum.
Source: Janet and Colin Bord, *'Unexplained Mysteries of the 20th Century,'* Godelieve Van Overmeire, quoting *Indianapolis Sunday Star* November 28, 1905.   Type: E
Comments: Other sources give the location as Voltana, Ravenna, Emilia-Romagna, Italy.

* * * * * * *

Location: Near Athens, Greece.
Date: July 14, 1905.
Time: Early afternoon.

T. T. Timayenis was lounging near the Phaleron; a romantic spot by the sea. As he stood upon the rocks gazing out over the sea, he was lost in thought when he happened to glance to his right and noticed two young men who were seated about 40ft from him; upon the rocks. Both were tall; towering more than a head above the average man. The witness stared at the two strangers, noticing that they were gazing upon the stars through a large square piece of what seemed to be unusually bright glass.

His eyes could hardly withstand its brilliancy and as he looked upon it with astonishment, he saw the planet Mars and its whole array of life unfolded before his eyes as clearly as one sees a performance upon the stage of a theater. He saw the two strangers lifting their fingers and holding conversation with its inhabitants. He saw the people of "Mars" answer in a sort of language. He saw women and girls of surpassing beauty, tall and stately, with forms "which still haunt his dreams." He also saw birds of a beautiful plumage, flitting about and alighting upon the shoulders of maidens. He saw many amazing sights and heard lovely melodies.

After a while the two strangers withdrew their gaze from the planet and in the twinkling of an eye, Mars shone upon the firmament in its accustomed place. The astounded witness walked towards the two strangers; as they saw him they moved about and asked him in excellent Greek if he could spare a light. The witness offered the strangers matches and cigars, which they accepted. In turn they gave him one cigar, which they stated they bought in Cuba the day before. The witness was more astounded as he told them that Cuba was more than 4,000 miles away.

At this point the two men told him that they came from the planet Mars. The two strangers then proceeded in detailing an incredible tale of civilizations on the planet Mars and ancient strife between different groups. Their enemies, which they called "Pelasgians," were eventually defeated and their survivors fled in their airships and landed in the northwestern part of Greece in the land known today as Albania. They were apparently the first settlers of Greece. They then added that the civilization on Earth was (in 1905) 100,000 years behind the Martian civilization. They also then added that there had not been war on Mars for over 200,000 years and incredibly they had also discovered the secret of immortality.

According to the "Martians," in electricity lay the secret of perpetual life. Every morning the Martians were supposedly "fed" electricity as an antidote against death. The two strangers claimed that the philosophers Socrates and Demosthenes were not dead but were currently alive and well in Mars. Soon the sound of a shrill whistle from one of the Martians (Telemachus) the other called himself Phidias, was answered from a boat by two stalwart men, who immediately jumped into the water, which was no less than 60ft deep. They wore about their feet; long protruding skates of bright yellow metal, strapped with stout wire. This equipment enabled the Martians to glide with safety upon the water.

The witness and the two Martians were then brought inside a magnificent floating airship; there they dined and he was informed that the main objective of their current mission on Earth was to meet the inventor "Edison" in relation to a recent invention, which could prove fatal to humanity. He was then brought back to shore and bade farewell to the Martians.

HC addendum.
Source: T. T. Timayenis in *The Indianapolis Star*, November 6, 1910.
Type: G

Comments: This is a beautiful tale, albeit abbreviated and condensed, not sure if it was meant to be fact or fiction.

* * * * * * *

Location: Between Cly and Goldsboro, Pennsylvania.
Date: October, 1905.
Time: Various.

"People residing along the river midway between Cly and Goldsboro are mystified and some are alarmed over the sight of a strange creature that has its abode in the Susquehanna River. Thus far but two men and their wives have seen the "thing." As it was seen in broad daylight more credence is given to the story than would be had it been seen at night, when people are more prone to see "things." This creature, whether fish or animal, is described as being a large as a man. When seen it came up out of the water erect like a man walking and is described as looking like a man without arms. Those persons who have seen it declare that they are not the victims of an optical illusion."

HC addendum.
Source: Jerome Clark in Magonia list, *Harrisburg Pennsylvania Patriot*, October 23, 1905.   Type: E

* * * * * * *

Location: Lake Creek, Wallace County, Kansas.
Date: December, 1905.
Time: Various.

"Near the premise of young Ockelbaugher, on Lake Creek, Wallace County; roams a disembodied spirit. It has been seen by the very eyes of Ockelbaugher himself and his ghostly discovery is confirmed by Herman Deorfer, Louis Mather and Bert Raines. These men speak of the awful presence of this apparition in words that burnt with convincing belief. The 'ghost' is gigantic in proportions, being about four feet wide and twelve feet high. A ball of fire answers for a head and in flowing robes of flames it flirts over the prairies, frightening men, scaring cattle and causing roosters to crow loudly. He is supposed to be the spirit of one of the aborigines, perhaps Roman Nose, the Indian Chief who fell at the battle of the Arickaree.
Adventurous individuals have camped on the trail of this specter and where it passed through wire fences, the wires were burned off wide enough for a team and wagon to drive through. Men who have seen the apparition scoff at ridicule and insist upon the verity of the testimony of

the senses. The incredulous ask, *"What have you been drinking?"* They refuse to reply to such an insidious question. Whether it is "Smoky water" or a bad brand of booze, they decline to state. Judges from Goodland propose to investigate the subject. The report of their investigations of the testers will be reported. The popular feeling is; *"Show me I am from Missouri."*

HC addendum.
Source: Kay Massingill in Magonia exchange, quoting *The Goodland Republic*, Goodland, Kansas, December 22, 1905. Type: E?

* * * * * * *

Location: Mitchell, South Dakota.
Date: 1906.
Time: Unknown.

Herbert V. Demott, 10, saw a "craft" come down near the well. "As I approached it, a door rolled back and I was welcomed inside." The two occupants, who looked like ordinary men, "sat on camp stools;" they conversed with him, but did not divulge their origin. "The outer shell of the craft was filled with helium gas, and when the lever was moved, the magnetism from the Earth was cut off, allowing the craft to rise." The pilots drew water from the horse trough. "To be used in making electricity."

HC addendum.
Source: Phenomena Research Reporter #3. Type: G

* * * * * * *

Location: Woodville, England.
Date: 1906.
Time: Evening.

While walking between Great Narry Pit and Woodville, Mr. G. Fowler and two companions observed two figures on a nearby path. Fowler hailed and approached the figures. As he did so, they rose up and disappeared over some trees, to the terror of the witnesses.

HC addendum.
Source: Mufob Vol. 5 #6. Type: E

Location: La Celle-Sous-Gouzon, Creuse, France.
Date: 1906.
Time: 10:00 p.m.

18-year old Jules B. was walking home on an isolated road when he encountered eleven to thirteen small beings sitting in the road in a circle. The beings seemed to have short wings on their backs and were wearing gray suits; one of the beings was standing up. The beings on the ground appeared to be sitting on top of some type of transparent cloth that had been placed on the ground. As the witness walked by, the beings turned around and stared at him.

As he walked away one of the beings flew past him, horizontally, with both legs joined together very close to the ground and at high speed. He had on his back what appeared to be a pair of short dark wings that did not move. As the being passed close to the witness, he perceived a slight whistle-like sound. During the encounter the witness noticed an eerie silence in the area. Scared, Jules quickly left the area and did not see the curious beings again.

HC addendum.
Source: Denys Breysse, Project Becassine, and Michel Bougard.
Type: E

* * * * * * *

Location: Nahanni Valley, Northwest Territories, Canada.
Date: 1906.
Time: Night.

Two prospectors; Jerry Walker and a second man named Sam, were in an isolated fog-covered valley looking for furs, when one night several hairy creatures or "monkey-men" began surrounding the camp, coming out of the fog. The creatures seemed to be calling to each other with whistles and howls. Surrounded by a howling band of furry creatures, the two prospectors huddled around their campfire until the morning. They packed and later camped alongside a river.

At night the hairy creatures soon returned. As they moved closer to the campfire, Sam lost his cool, pulled out a gun and ran after one of the hairy creatures. He apparently got lost in the fog, and Walker soon heard him screaming. The creatures attacked Sam, killing him and apparently eating him. When the fog lifted, Walker discovered the grizzly remains of his partner; his head was missing and all the flesh on his body was gone.

HC addendum.
Source: Warren Smith, *'Strange Abominable Snowman.'*   Type: E

* * * * * * *

Location: Near Macy, Indiana.
Date: January, 1906.
Time: Unknown.

"A report comes from Macy, north of Peru, Indiana, that several hunters from that place, while in the vicinity of North Mud Lake, discovered a cave in one of the hills near the new bridge which spans the narrows. The cave showed signs of being used and the men explored it. After entering the cave, they advanced for about 200 feet when they came to a huge flat stone which blocked the way. They removed the stone and found a large room which seemed to have been dug out. At the far end of the room was a living 'object' that seemed to be gnawing at something. It growled and gnashed its teeth like a dog. This so frightened the explorers that they made a hasty retreat.

The men are forming a party to return to the cave and make further investigations. They describe the strange being as about five feet high, stoutly built and covered with long hair. They say that whatever it is, it walks on all fours, but when standing has the appearance of a gorilla. The impression prevails that it is a wild man or a lunatic escaped from some asylum. No affidavit was filed with the story."

HC addendum.
Source: *The Salt Lake Telegram*, January 9, 1906.   Type: E?
Comments: Subterranean species?

* * * * * * *

Location: Near Badain Jaran, Nei Mongol Autonomous region, China.
Date: April, 1906.
Time: Unknown.

Soviet scholar Badzar Baradiin reportedly had a brief encounter with an Almas (hairy Wildman) while he was traveling in the Gobi Desert near this location.

HC addendum.
Source: George Eberhart, *'Mysterious Creatures.'*

Location: Carson, Nevada.
Date: June 20, 1906.
Time: Unknown.

What looks like a combination of Chinese 'devil' and a nightmare was brought to Carson yesterday by J. R. Kenny and Ed Wallis who found the uncanny object high up on Mount Davidson. It is mummified and has a head like a human being; a pair of noses, mouth and eyes, but it has no body. It is provide with wings like a bat and apparently when alive could do most anything from swimming in water to sailing in the air like a kite. Professor Smith took a photograph of it and will send a copy to Professor Fransend of the University of Nevada.

The head is about the size of a baseball and has legs like a frog. Six teeth, three of them broken, grace a mouth which perpetually grins. It is an absolutely unique species of some animal that used to walk, swim or fly, according as its fancy chose.

HC addendum.
Source: *The Fort Worth Telegram*, June 21, 1906, Vol. 23 #4. Type: H?

* * * * * * *

Location: Near Bertha, Burt County, Nebraska.
Date: Late June or early July, 1906.
Time: Evening.

A Swedish immigrant; a man named Carlson, only 17 years of age at the time, was on his way alone in his horse buggy to the local renowned barn dance at Bertha. It was sundown as his buggy was approaching from the east, moving towards the sunset when he saw two "young men" ahead of him walking, each with their suit jackets slung over their shoulders. They were on level ground, about a half mile or more from the dance hall at Bertha. The small grain had been harvested on each side of the road, and the weeds freshly mowed in the ditches on either side of the road.

As Carlson approached the two men, it was his intent to offer them a ride the remaining distance to Bertha. His horse, however, became a little skittish as the distance closed. When Carlson was a half dozen yards or so behind them, he let out a greeting to them, preliminary to offering a ride to them. But with the first sound of his greeting, his horse reared and started to rear repeatedly in place. It took a better portion of a minute for Carlson to bring the horse back under control. The horse, carriage and Carlson were essentially in the same spot as when he called out to these two men. The men, however, were inexplicably gone.

As stated the ground was level, the ditches on the side of the road were shallow with no place to hide, the fields on either side contained only the short stubble of golden straw of the harvested fields of oats, there was plenty of light from the just set sun to expose anyone wearing a dark suit, should they have tried to hide within those few seconds of time. While Carlson had not seen their faces, he was familiar with all the young men who were living and/or working within a ten mile radius, or greater.

The two men did not match the description of anyone he knew. Later at the dance hall, he scanned the crowd several times during the evening and did not see them again. When pressed as who he thought these individuals were, he insisted that they could not have been humans and therefore must have been ghosts. The concept of extraterrestrials was not part of the consciousness of that era.

HC addendum.
Source: Direct from witness's son, Bill Carlson. Type: E?
Comments: I can only conjecture as to whom or what these two "men" were; apparently the horse sensed something strange and Carlson knew that what he had experienced was not a normal event. Time travelers? Or what?

* * * * * * *

Location: Val Vedasco, Switzerland.
Date: August 21, 1906.
Time: Daytime.

"Over 5,000 peasants fled from Val Vedasco on the Swiss-Italian frontier during a great storm on Lake Magione today. The superstitious villagers declare they saw an angel in the sky pointing a finger at the valley. They consequently believed the valley was doomed and in great terror fled from their flourishing orchards, gardens and fields which are now deserted."

HC addendum.
Source: Kay Massingill, Magonia exchange, quoting *Albuquerque Journal*, New Mexico, August 25, 1906. Type: E?

Location: Yakutiya Region, Siberia, Russia.
Date: August 27, 1906.
Time: Afternoon.

During June 1906, Ivan Romanov was hunting in the taiga when he decided to spend the night in the woods. While gathering dry branches for a bonfire, he unexpectedly stumbled into a small pit. After rolling down the pit, the hunter discovered the entrance to a tunnel, which led to an enormous hall. The hall was about 8ft in height and its walls were made out of metal. On both sides of the hall he could see unknown apparatuses. A white light from an unknown source illuminated the hall.

After some time he felt weak and a strong headache and immediately decided to leave the strange tunnel. However on the above date he returned to further explore the site. Once inside he discovered a huge silvery disc-shaped object sitting on the ground and standing around it were four figures, a head shorter than him. The strangers wore silvery coveralls. He made a noise and one of the figures turned to him, he saw that it was not quite human with its eyes somehow different from normal men. The other two then turned to the startled hunter as one of the figures yelled at him (in Russian) to stay where he was and not to move.

Terrified, the hunter leveled his rifle at the figure and shot him directly in the chest area. Immediately from the wound escaped what the witness describes as "blue gas." Terrified, the hunter ran out the tunnel, not looking back. He never returned to the site.

HC addendum.
Source: RU. UFO, UFO Forum. Type: C

* * * * * * *

Location: Orinoco, Indiana.
Date: August 28, 1906.
Time: Night.

John Warner, a retired soldier, was sitting on his back porch that night when he heard a noise in his barn made by his horse. He went to see if the horse was sick and on returning to the house he then heard a rushing noise overhead. On looking upward, he declares he saw a cigar-shaped airship, painted green and carrying green lights, which sailed gracefully down into his garden and stopped. There were four men in the ship, he says, and they informed him they were on their way to New York, from Chicago, and asked him which direction to take. He directed them as far as Seymour when they turned on their power and sailed away.

HC addendum.
Source: Magonia Exchange Image Archive, quoting *Rochport Indiana Journal* 8-31-1906. Type: A

* * * * * * *

Location: Vincennes, Indiana.
Date: Early November, 1906.
Time: Night.

"A phenomenon of unusual nature is said to have been seen in the skies in Vincennes recently. The moon was the cause of it all. The phenomenon according to the witnesses occurred on two different nights and for a time frightened those who saw it. Rev. Everett and wife of Washington, Ind., John Potter and wife and child, who live in Oklahoma, were the witnesses to the thing, whatever it might have been.

Rev. Everett is conducting a revival at the Oklahoma Baptist Church and has been in the city for several weeks. One night according to his story while returning home from church to the residence of John Potter where he resides while there, he noticed that the moon seemed to break to pieces and then suddenly went back into its old position and was as bright as ever.

He said nothing of the matter but one night this week, in company with his wife and Mr. and Mrs. Potter and their son, while again returning home from services they noticed that the moon again seemed to break apart and the image of a man was plainly visible. This lasted for two seconds and was seen by all five of the people. The image then disappeared and the moon went back to its old position and shone very brightly. The minister and the others are of the opinion that the warning was a herald of some approaching catastrophe. No one else as far as is known saw the warning."

HC addendum.
Source: Kay Massingill in Magonia exchange, quoting *Bedford Weekly Mail*, November 9, 1906, Bedford, Indiana. Type: A

Location: Upland, Pennsylvania.
Date: Late November, 1906.
Time: Various.

"These are sleepless nights in Upland. A wild creature, which, according to eye-witnesses, is half man, half beast, has literally terrorized the borough. No one ventures out after dark without a club or lantern, and the more determined carry guns. The perturbation of the residents is such that they are ready to shoot first and investigate afterward. This, they say, is the only way to tackle such weird game.

As no one knows whether the thing is human or not, residents speak of the creature as "it." Tales told by those who have been cuffed and chased by "it" are more uncanny than 'The Headless Horseman of Sleepy Hollow," or "The Hound of the Baskervilles." Judging by the descriptions gathered yesterday from a score of persons who saw the creature it has a body like a bear and a head like a man. Its eyes glitter like hot coals; its voice is sepulchral and changes rapidly to thunderous tones, and it can run like the wind.

Aroused by the actions of the creature, which chased their sisters and sweethearts, the football team of the Upland high school and a number of citizens armed with clubs and guns, descended last night upon the woods at Summit Avenue intending to surprise the thing in its lair. The searchers spread out in a circle and then closed in. In the heart of the woods they found a small bonfire and the remains of a meal, but the mysterious creature had disappeared. Among those who have been chased by "it" are Albert Murphy and Horace Kemmerle. Murphy said, "The thing jumped out in front of me as I was walking Summit Street. From the quick glance that I took the thing looked like a polar bear with a man's head.

I did not stop to investigate, but ran home as fast as I could. The thing followed me for a short distance and then suddenly disappeared. Walter Dunkirk said it chased him while he was walking along Concord Avenue. "It looked like a sheep and walked like a man," he said. "It struck me on the neck and I felt as if I had been struck by a thousand needles." Horace Kemmerle, who was chased along Providence Avenue by "it" said that the creature looked like a sheep with a man's head. He didn't stop to make a minute examination. Policeman Harry Beals, who is the entire force of Upland, said yesterday "this thing has been seen on Summit and Providence avenues and those places are on the beats of the Chester police. I have been keeping my eyes open, however, and the first glimpse I get at this thing I'll run it down anyhow."

HC addendum.
Source: Kay Massingill in Magonia exchange, quoting *Duluth News-Tribune*, MN, December 3, 1906.　　　　　　　　　　Type: E

Location: Ladrillar, Caceres, Spain.
Date: February 27, 1907.
Time: Night.

A sinister looking entity "dressed in tight dark clothes with a little body and a disproportionately large head" entered Ladrillar. It did not walk, it floated just above the ground, and two flying spheres that shone with an intensely bright light accompanied it. Everybody who saw or heard the creature as it moved along the dusty village roads stared at it, first astonished and then frightened, running out of its path or into their houses to shut the mysterious menace out.

Serafina Bejarano Rubio reported that the entity appeared on three consecutive days. It flew in; from not very high up, followed by two powerful round lights. It hardly ever made a sound, but sometimes it shouted. When it shouted, it was loud and frightening and resembled something like *"Uuuua, uuuua."* It was dressed entirely in black and at one point it was seeing floating above some trees near the cemetery. One day a group of frightened neighbors watched from the church door as one of the globes of light passed over a group of children.

A five-year old girl among them inexplicably lost consciousness at that moment and fell to the ground. According to documents, the child, Maria Encarnacion Martin, became ill and died a couple of days later, despite efforts to save her. The cause of death was ruled as unknown.

HC addendum.
Source: Iker Jimenez and Chris Aubeck, *'Return to Magonia.'*
Type: E or C?

* * * * * * *

Location: Ladrillar, Caceres, Spain.
Date: February 28, 1907.
Time: Unknown.

A day after the death of young Maria Martin, the black clad "goblin" was again seen in the vicinity. He is described as 1-meter in height. The local priest, Isaac Gutierrez, reportedly saw the entity and he reported to the Bishop of Coria, forwarding a letter which included the signatures of most of the witnesses.

HC addendum.
Source: http://www.looculto.260mb.com/ovnisenespana/ovnisenespana.htm   Type: E

Location: Near Dikeman Springs, near Dickson, Tennessee.
Date: April 20, 1907.
Time: Afternoon.

Walter Stephenson was out training his pair of bloodhounds and had just finished a long chase with his dogs and sat down on a log to rest, when things got weird. He espied upon the eastern horizon a speck, which he took to be a large kite. He paid little attention to the object, and shifted his gaze temporarily to other scenes. Soon his attention was attracted to a whirring noises and looking upward, he saw that the speck which he had a few moments before discovered in the eastern sky had approached almost directly over him, and that the object was in reality a huge balloon, but of a pattern and appearance he had never in his life before seen.

He discovered that the floating mass was rapidly approaching the Earth. All of a sudden, the observer says, strains of music calculated to charm the spheres burst forth from the balloon, which circled around and around and finally landed at Dikeman Springs. A number of strange people emerged from the car, which was closely curtained with a substance that fairly glistened in the sunshine that temporarily burst through the obscuring clouds, and all going to the big, flowing spring, knelt by it in a supplicating attitude and so remained for a minute or more.

Mr. Stephenson says that while this was going on he sat quietly within speaking distance, and when the strange visitors arose to their feet and he supposed their devotional exercises were over, he asked if he might be permitted to inquire who they were, and what their mission? He said that instantly a visor was lifted by one of the company and the benign face of a lady showed from underneath and said in German, *"Haben sie Beten?"* (Did you pray?) And instantly all were aboard, the airship rose, circled about for a minute or more and was gone in a westerly direction. Mr. Stephenson says that the incident left an impression upon him that he can never forget, and while he knows that it was some human invention, it looked and the music sounded more like that 'of angels than of mortals.'

HC addendum.
Source: Theo Paijmans, *'The Tennessee Aeronaut Flap of 1907,'* citing Evening News (Ada Oklahoma) July 1, 1907, and other newspaper sources.   Type: B?

Location: Bold Springs, Tennessee.
Date: April 21, 1907.
Time: 3:30 a.m.

A Mr. W. A. Smith described as a respected farmer living four miles from the town of Bold Springs, told how he left for town that Saturday morning at around 3.30 am. He was just on his way when he heard strains of music. Shrugging it off, thinking that perhaps a wedding must be taking place, he then noticed that the music came from above. He looked up and "was amazed to see a large balloon of unusual size and strange pattern." Suspended from the balloon was a large closed car from within which the music appeared to come. The car was strung with electric lights, and a brilliant searchlight was carried at the front. No machinery or mechanism appeared in view, and the motive power could not even be surmised.

The balloon directed its searchlight to a large spring, heading directly toward it. Finally the balloon descended slowly to the ground, about 30ft (9m) from the edge of the spring. Smith left his horse tied to a tree and went for a closer look. As he came close he noted a peculiar party of queer-looking persons in strange garb kneeling beside the spring, apparently engaged in silent prayer. Smith decided not to make contact, but as the group returned to their aerial craft, one of them pointed to him uttering some words that Smith could not understand.

In closing, the *Nashville American* remarked: "In justice to Mr. Smith it should be stated that his story was told here Saturday afternoon, nearly 16 hours before the *Sunday American* reached town. In Sunday's *American* appeared a story from Dickson, Tenn., in the adjoining county, chronicling the appearance of a similar aircraft, and crediting the strange visitors with speaking German."

HC addendum.
Source: Theo Paijmans, *'The Tennessee Aeronaut Flap of 1907,'* quoting the *Nashville American*. Type: B

* * * * * * *

Location: Near Pleasant Spring, Tennessee.
Date: April 22, 1907.
Time: Evening.

Herman Schubert, who with his family lived at the edge of town, claimed that the mystery aeronauts visited thereabouts as well. Schubert, who was German, regarded the aeronauts as "merely visitors from what he calls 'the old country.' The Schubert's occupied a large farm with a spring, a natural basin 20ft (6m) wide, at the edge of a 40-acre wood lot.

The spring is the headwater of a small stream, which, from its rise on the Schubert farm, is known as Schubert Creek.

Schubert and his 15-year old son Carl were at the spring-house that Sunday evening. Finishing his work, it was now near dark. Carl sat at the edge of the basin. The old man heard his son calling in a half-frightened tone, so he rushed outside. At an elevation of several hundred feet the two saw a large airship or balloon; from their account it is impossible to decide which.

Suspended from the body of the air machine was a large closed car, very similar to the body of a stage coach, except that it was probably 35ft (10m) long, and had an entrance on either side instead of at the end. The airship landed at the edge of the spring and the Schuberts retreated inside the spring-house to witness the scene from there. Twelve to 14 people were seen walking to the spring "their attitude one of reverence, as though standing on sacred ground, or in a sacred presence."

At the spring the group arranged itself along the edge and knelt, apparently in silent prayer, being thus engaged for several minutes. When the strange aeronauts returned to the carriage, the elder Schubert, addressing no one in particular, asked what they were doing and who they were. The party with one exception, continued unheeding on the way to the car. Only one of the party took note of Mr. Schubert's request.

Turning toward the two this one of the travelers said, without raising the head covering, *"Sie haben nicht gebeten; Rede uns nicht an,"* which Mr. Schubert says is the German equivalent for "Thou has not prayed; address us not." Mr. Schubert spoke to them in German, and the spokesman replied, evidently surprised at hearing the tongue; *"Unsere Wohlfahrt ist noch nicht vallented; in guten Zeit wird die welt alles wissen."* This, Mr. Schubert says, is German for, "Our pilgrimage is not yet completed; the world will know all in time." The spokesman then turned and followed his companions into the car, which rose rapidly and took a southerly direction.

HC addendum.
Source: Theo Paijmans, *'The Tennessee Aeronaut Flap of 1907,'* quoting *Nashville American*, Tennessee, 23 April, 1907.   Type: B

Location: Near Nashville, Tennessee.
Date: April 26, 1907.
Time: Morning.

Mail carrier Asa Hickerson had been delivering the mail and was descending a steep hill with a little log building named Peabody School at the bottom, when his attention was drawn to "sounds resembling the chanting of some weird, funeral dirge, proceeding seemingly from the tops of the forest trees through which his route winded." His horse became restless and all his attention was needed to calm the frightened animal. Pausing briefly, Hickerson left his buggy to adjust the harness, when once more the strange sounds were heard, but now much louder; simultaneously there swooped into plain view a gigantic aircraft that gradually and with the ease of a huge bird, settled softly to the ground, some 50 yards (46m) from where Mr. Hickerson struggled with his now almost unmanageable roan mare.

A group of several men exited the long car attached to the craft, and forming in single file, resumed their long chant, and proceeded slowly to the mouth of an abandoned oil well at the side of the road. There the group conducted a strange ritual. Forming a circle around the well, one of them carrying a long staff plunged it three times in the well after having made "sundry passes in the air" with it. The group then withdrew to the opposite side of the road where the staff, dripping with the oil, was stuck in the moist earth and set alight. The band then joined hands and again lifting their voices in song, slowly circled around and around the flaming rod, while a small spiral column of black smoke whirled slowly upwards.

The ceremony finished, the group returned to the airship. Hickerson too wanted to know what was going on. So he asked, "What are you doing here?" The one who had carried the staff replied in sonorous tones *"Betreue deine sunde und bete!"* (Be healthy and pray) extending his right hand as if invoking a benediction. The huge vessel then with the poise and grace of an eagle rose slowly until well above the forest and headed in a northeasterly direction and was soon lost to view.

HC addendum.
Source: Theo Paijmans, *'The Tennessee Aeronaut Flap of 1907,'* quoting *Nashville American*, Tennessee, 28 April, 1907.   Type: B

Location: Hebden Bridge, West Yorkshire, England.
Date: May, 1907.
Time: Night.

A strange story comes from Hebden Bridge near Halifax. In an old cottage on the moorland heights above the town a young married couple who have recently become tenants of the place, have been worried by noises for which they could not account.
There were knockings and creaking, but an investigation failed to explain their origin. After a time they ceased but were renewed a week or more ago with greater violence than before. Lying awake in bed one night, the husband saw a yellowish light appear, apparently from the room below. Wondering if the house were on fire, he was just about to get up when the light grew brighter; and the figure of a man garbed in black seemed to come through the wall.
With fixed gaze the apparition passed across the room, vanishing in the direction of the stairs. There was no sound and the man in bed was too much surprised to challenge the specter. A former occupant of the cottage witnessed a similar apparition and afterwards became familiar with its appearance. This person declares the spirit to be that of an old man who lived alone for many years in the cottage.

HC addendum.
Source: *West Gippsland Gazette* (Warragul Victoria, Australia 1898-1930), Tuesday 14, May 1907.   Type: E

* * * * * * *

Location: Vilppula, Finland.
Date: Summer 1907.
Time: Unknown.

Some boys playing on the lakeshore saw a bright light approach from the lake and land on the shore near them. A door appeared on the object, and some humanoids emerged. The boys panicked and ran to the rectory; only after some hours could they give a coherent story. Adults who visited the site found both landing traces and footprints in the sand.

HC addendum.
Source: Ilkka Serra.   Type: B

Location: Near Crom Castle, County Fermanagh, Northern Ireland.
Date: September, 1907.
Time: Unknown.

Two women rowing across Upper Lough Erne sighted a small humanoid figure walking on the water from the direction of the nearby castle. No other information.

HC addendum.
Source: Ulrich Magin, *Strange Magazine #4*. Type: E

* * * * * * *

Location: Wenatchee, Washington.
Date: September 16, 1907.
Time: Afternoon.

Residents in the lower end of town were amazed late yesterday afternoon by the sudden appearance of a balloon in the sky above the new bridge, at an apparent elevation of 900 or a thousand feet. The strange craft was moving at a high rate of speed, borne swiftly along by a strong wind, and soon disappeared over the crest of Badger Mountain. The sky craft was of the dirigible class, equipped with a long cigar-shaped gas bag, beneath which hung suspended what seemed to be a cabin with propelling mechanism. The flight of the airship was so swift that but a fleeting glimpse of it was afforded the astonished spectators. Some of the more excited in the crowd claim that they distinctly heard strains of music issuing from the cabin of the sky craft.

According to a hunter who viewed the strange craft through field glasses from the crest of Saddle Rock, three persons were visibly upon the deck of the cabin, two men and a woman of rare beauty. A fisherman who happened to be perched on a log just below the bridge when the balloon passed over, insists that a paper was tossed from the fleetly flying craft, but that it unfortunately fell into the water and was carried away. If a man engaged in any other vocation than fishing had told this the statement would carry more weight and those interested in clearing the mystery.

Omak, September 17, 7 a.m. A strange looking airship has just passed over the town, creating a profound sensation. It was headed northwest: thought to be Japanese war balloon. Superstitious Indians in panic-clamoring for whiskey to quiet their nerves. Town in an uproar.

HC addendum.
Source: *The Wenatchee Daily World*, September 17, 1907, Wenatchee Washington. Type: A

Location: Pittem, West Flanders, Belgium.
Date: 1908.
Time: 8:00 a.m.

Mr. R. V. N. observed a complex phenomenon in the sky. Initially an apparition was seen in the form of a rose, but this afterwards changed into the shape of a lamb. Later still as the apparition neared the witness it assumed the form of a beautiful woman sitting on a seat. It then disappeared.

HC addendum.
Source: George Bonabot, UFO Register, and Project Becassine.
Type: E

* * * * * * *

Location: Alma, Colorado.
Date: 1908.
Time: Night.

Alma had a sensation this week in the shape of a ghost, which appeared at night. People coming from the saloons about midnight saw a strange sight, or imagined they did. One night the phantom was seen near the Thomas saloon, another time it was at the bridge on Main Street. The courageous Almaites gave chase, but when they arrived at the spot the apparition had mysteriously disappeared. Some describe it as a beautiful woman, clad in the finest white lingerie. The spot where the beauty disappeared was fragrant with the perfume of roses and violets.
Others again say it looked to them like a huge elephant, with streams of fire issuing from its trunk, and when they arrived at the spot where it had vanished, the smell of sulfur and brimstone permeated the air. The young ladies of Alma are frightened and will not venture forth in the evening without an escort. The gallant young men act with the greatest of pleasure in this capacity. So far, the 'spook' has not been caught, but it this should be the case, would summarily be dealt with.

HC addendum.
Source: http://mysteriousuniverse.org/2013/10/spring-heeled-jack-in-america/ Type: E

Location: County Meath, Killough district, Ireland.
Date: April, 1908.
Time: Various.

"Belief in fairies or "good people" is still prevalent in many country districts in Ireland, and during the past few days the superstition has been strangely revived in North-West Meath owing to mysterious occurrences in the Killough district. It seems that a strange creature has been observed in the neighborhood. Several persons, both adult and children, claim to have seen it, and describe it as a little man of dwarfish proportions, clad in red, with small peaked cap.

It is to be remarked that this is the traditional appearance of a leprechaun, which is believed to vanish when anyone seeing it calls attention to it, but which, if anyone is fortunate enough to capture it, will, as a condition of its release, disclose hidden treasure to its captor, though if latter turns his eyes off the leprechaun, even for a moment, it will vanish with mocking laughter."

HC addendum.
Source: *Poverty Bay Herald* (NZ) Vol. XXXV issue 11299 June 13, 1908.
Type: E

* * * * * * *

Location: Minsk, Belarus, USSR.
Date: Early summer 1908.
Time: Daytime.

In broad daylight many local residents heard a terrible roar and saw a bright fire appear in the sky and then an enormous "man." The figure of the "man" seemed gigantic and his feet touched the ground. After the figure of the giant man vanished, local residents collected from the streets a large quantity of a substance resembling Jell-O. But once collected, the substance would evaporate into thin air. The substance resembled gelatin or meat jelly, when touched it would shake and it was cold to the touch. No other information.

HC addendum.
Source: www.x-libri.ru archival message, Kosmopoisk and Vadim A. Chernobrov. http://ww.chernobrov.narod.ru   Type: E?

* * * * * * *

Location: Evenkiya area, Krasnoyarsk region, East Siberia, Russia.
Date: June, 1908.
Time: Various.

According to data allegedly obtained by a scientific expedition in 1927 to the area of the Tunguska explosion (which occurred on June 30, 1908) just after the catastrophe, an Evenkian resident of a local hamlet reportedly encountered a bizarre creature, which he apparently captured and took to his home.
According to the description, the entity resembled more a "devil" than a human being. It was dwarf-like, a little more than a meter in height, with large green eyes, smooth shiny skin, with some protrusions on its forehead area and with a short tail. The local man kept the creature in his cattle shed. He told the other residents of the village that he had found the creature in a clearing amid a dense pine forest.
The creature was reportedly injured and very weakened. Despite the protests of his neighbors the man cared for the creature, feeding it and even taking it out for walks at night. (!) As a result of this all the local dogs from the village went into a barking frenzy while the creature was outside. Then the creature mysteriously vanished.
The man claimed that the entity had "walked away into the forest." Soon after the man was stricken with an unknown illness, his hair and teeth began to fall out and he lost a lot of weight, he became very thin and eventually died (radiation illness?).

HC addendum.
Source: 'NLO (UFOs) Over Siberia' in 'Tainy XX Veka' (Mysteries of the 20th century) newspaper, Saint Petersburg, Russia #44, December 2005.
Type: E or H?

Location: Gobilli River area, Khavarovsk, Siberia, Russia.
Date: July 11, 1908.
Time: Evening.

The famous Russian traveler V.K. Arsenyev was trekking along the river when he reportedly found a mark on the path that was very similar to a man's footprint. His dog "Alpha" bristled up snarled and then something rushed about nearby, trampling among the bushes. However it didn't go away, but stopped nearby, standing stock-still. Arsenyev stood still for several minutes and then picked up a stone and threw it towards the unknown "animal."

Then something happened that was quite unexpected, he heard the beating of wings and something large and dark emerged from the fog, and flew over the river. A moment later it disappeared into the dense mist. His dog, badly frightened, pressed itself to his feet. After supper he told the "Udehe-men" about the incident. They broke into a vivid story about a man who could fly in the air. Hunters often saw his tracks, tracks that appeared suddenly and vanished suddenly, in such a way that they could only be possible if the "man" alighted on the ground, then took off again into the air.

HC addendum.
Source: John Keel, 'The Mothman Prophecies.'   Type: E
Comments: Early account of winged humanoid.

* * * * * * *

Location: Bristol, Connecticut.
Date: July 25, 1908.
Time: 6:00 p.m.

An object resembling an elongated gasbag under which was suspended a framework equipped with a propeller was seen flying from north to south over the area. Several observers were able to see a figure inside the object. The craft circled over a local lake and then disappeared, descending towards the nearby Wolcott Mountain.

HC addendum.
Source: Jerome Clark, 'The UFO Encyclopedia Vol. II.'   Type: A

Location: Mullica Township, New Jersey.
Date: November 14, 1908.
Time: Night.

Mrs. Caroline D. Pierce who lives with her son on a farm in Mullica Township has just written a long letter, offering her deep thanks to whoever can tell what she saw outside her window flying over her turnip field on the night of November 14.
It was Mrs. Pierce who saw it, not her son. She says in her letter that she is 75 years old, hoping that she is "of sound mind" and believing the same. Being a Christian, she claims every word that she writes is of purest truth. Her son left her alone in the house, going to Egg Harbor. At 8 o'clock she started to retire. She noticed her bedroom lighted though there was no lamp in it. She saw through her window a bright light. This she thought was made by the burning of her neighbor's house. This was not the case. Presently she saws a ball of fire rise out of the distance and float toward her window. It wandered about over her turnip field, coming so close to her window that she cried aloud. The ball of fire finally arose and disappeared.
Mrs. Pierce noticed that the ball of fire was in the shape of a face, round like the moons. The ears were long, and lay close to the face. The eyes were sunken and the nose and mouth were dark in color.

HC addendum.
Source: Kay Massingill in Magonia list quoting *Americus Times-Recorder*, November 26, 1908, page 4, Americus Georgia.   Type: X?

* * * * * * *

Location: Galway, Ireland.
Date: Late December, 1908.
Time: Night.

"The town of Galway, Ireland is much agitated by the story of a strange apparition which is said to have been seen by some young men on two recent nights. On Saturday after dusk, two young fellows who were walking into the town, along the railway line were suddenly confronted by the strange visitor when within half a mile of their destination; they describe it as "resembling a man, but nine feet in height." It approached them quickly, and when almost upon them suddenly vanished. In terror they ran toward the town but a short distance further the ghostly visitor again stood before them, and then mysteriously vanished.
On reaching Galway they related their strange adventure and a number of their companions arranged to rally forth on Sunday evening

and "lay" the ghost. Accordingly, a party of young fellows left the town after dusk armed with shotguns, pistols and revolvers. Blank cartridge only was carried so that if the "ghost" turned out to be something more material, he might suffer no permanent injury. They hid in a bank near the line at the place where the apparition was first seen and waited.

Their vigil was brief, for they had scarcely settled down when in the distance the tall form was seen approaching in the dusk. On reaching the place where they lay the visitor stood and gazed at them whereupon one young fellow, bolder than his companions, jumped to his feet and presented his revolver fully at the apparition, but no shot came from it and his arm felt powerless by his side. His companions becoming alarmed, jumped to his assistance and there was much confusion in the midst of which the ghost vanished.

The party then without delay, made their way back to the town, where it is said that medical aid had to be summoned to the youthful hero of the revolver. By this time the story had been circulated all over the neighborhood, and on Monday night another band, among whom were some students armed with big sticks, cautiously stole to the hiding place, but though they waited and watched for hours, the ghost failed to appear and they had to return near midnight without having had the satisfaction of "laying" it.

Others in the town who state that they too had seen the strange visitor before Saturday, describe him as "of a grayish color, 8 feet high and tapering toward the top." Some of them credit him with jumping from the railway bridge into the Corrill where he disappeared in the waters. That he was not drowned is proved by the fact that he was seen by the youths on Saturday night and by their friends on Sunday."
-Correspondent, *London Standard*.

HC addendum.
Source: Magonia list, quoting *The New York Times*, December 27, 1908.
Type: E

* * * * * * *

Location: Pont-Fetan-Levek, France.
Date: Before 1909.
Time: Evening.

Three young people were returning home after spending the evening in the village of Kerlann when they spotted something white right beside a hedge. One of them approached the object to see what it could be, but as soon as he got close to it, this object rose in the air while growing larger and moved towards the villages of Kerlear and Keriaval. It was described as resembling a "block of three houses."

The young people, though strongly disturbed, resumed their travel and shortly after they separated, they heard a "terrible cry" which seemed to come from the air, but they did not see anything at all. One of the witnesses experienced a period of paralysis after returning home. Nothing else is known of the event.

HC addendum.
Source: http://ufologie.patrickgross.org/indexe.htm   quoting archaeologist Zacharie Le Rouzic .   Type: X

* * * * * * *

Location: Near Lloyds, Maryland.
Date: 1909.
Time: Night.

At the time that there were numerous strange incidents in the area concerning the disappearance of livestock and of livestock being slaughtered just outside their pastures, Albert Evans a local farmer was driving along a dirt road in his horse and buggy when he saw several bloody cows lying dead in his pasture. He then noticed some kind of half man, half beast standing above one of the cows. The creature was about 7-feet tall, but it was so dark that Evans could not make out any facial details and the like.

HC addendum.
Source: Mark Chorvinsky, *Fate* August, 1992.   Type: E

* * * * * * *

Location: Bauxieres-aux-Dames, France.
Date: 1909.
Time: Night.

A local inhabitant of the village; biologist M. Narcisse Cezard, was walking along a wooded path when he spotted an unknown object landing in a field. Several human-like figures or silhouettes were seen moving around the object. No other information.

HC addendum.
Source: Raoul Robe, *Catalogue Regional.*   Type: C

Location: Georgetown, Delaware.
Date: 1909.
Time: Various.

"More than seven feet in height and swathed in a long black cloak, closely wrapped around its face, a new mystery has been exciting some parts of Georgetown, where it has followed women and young girls and jumped out from behind trees at them. The "Devil in black," as it is called, first appeared several nights ago, when a dozen or so persons saw it during the course of the evening. From behind a tree it jumped at Mrs. William Curdy and sent her screaming with freight into a neighbor's house, while a daughter of Joseph Carnel also was chased by the mysterious stranger until she fell almost fainting into Fred Rust's grocery store.

The men of the neighborhood, informed of the affair, led by William Curdy, ran cross fields, jumped fences and through backyards, with the "Devil" but a few yards ahead of them, but, while crossing the big ditch known as the Savannah, the figure completely disappeared and despite search, could not be found. Again it was seen by several young girls and last night it made its appearance and was seen closely by Mrs. Carn Josephs, who heard a noise as she passed her woodshed. She turned to look and distinctly saw the "Devil" walk out of the shed and after her.

Almost fainting with fear she ran screaming into the house, while her husband ran into the yard with his gun and fired at the tall figure, which was plainly distinguished at the woodshed. In a second it was gone with no trace of injury from the gun. Many superstitious declare that bullets cannot hit it, but some of the more determined men declare it is the work of a practical joker and expect to put a load of shot into it at their first opportunity."

HC addendum.
Source: http://mysteriousuniverse.org/2013/10/spring-heeled-jack-in-america/ Type: E

* * * * * * *

Location: Galway, Ireland.
Date: January, 1909.
Time: Various.

A spectral figure, gray in color and about eight feet in height, is said to have haunted the railway line near Galway for the past few nights. The apparition, which is described as "tapering towards the top," walks from the railway viaduct (says the "Daily Mail") across the Corrib River to a point along the bank of the stream and then disappears.

A number of people have visited the place towards midnight; when the apparition is due to appear. One man declares that he saw it jump from the top of the viaduct into the Corrib where it vanished. It was not "drowned" however, for on the succeeding night it was seen again by a number of students from Queen's College, Galway.

One of the students volunteered to go over and talk to it, but when it appeared he changed his mind. It is further stated that on Sunday evening a party of six men, armed with shot guns, revolvers, and sticks, sallied forth to "lay the ghost." They had been in ambush for a short time only when the specter loomed before them. One of the men raised a revolver, but before he could fire he fell into a swoon. The expedition was abandoned and the man was taken into Galway, where he was medically attended.

These strange reports have created excitement in the district, and search parties are out nightly for the purpose of unraveling the mystery.

HC addendum.
Source: *The Colac Herald* (Victoria, Australia 1875-1918), Friday January 18, 1909. Type: E

* * * * * * *

Location: Beaver Pond, New Jersey.
Date: Middle of January, 1909.
Time: Afternoon.

Several telephone company employees were working in an isolated area when one of the workers walked into the woods. He soon came sprinting back out of the woods and climbed up a telegraph pole. The rest of the men came running when they heard him yelling for help. He had climbed to the very top of the pole and thrown himself onto the lines. A strange creature was climbing the pole after him.

One of the men pulled out a gun and shot at the creature. One shot apparently damaged a wing and it fell to the ground uttering hideous screams. But, before anyone could collect his wits the thing was up and off with long strides. It had a short hop, dragged one wing, and then disappeared into the pine thicket.

HC addendum.
Source: Jerry A. Young, *'Mysterious Monsters.'*   Type: E

* * * * * * *

Location: Woodbury, New Jersey.
Date: January 16-17, 1909.
Time: Night.

A man was leaving a hotel when he "heard a hissing" and saw something white flying across the street. "I saw two spots of phosphorus; the eyes of the beast. There was a white cloud, like escaping steam from an engine. It moved as fast as an auto."

HC addendum.
Source: Loren Coleman and Bruce Hallenbeck, *'Monsters of New Jersey.'*   Type: E

* * * * * * *

Location: Bristol, New Jersey.
Date: January 17, 1909.
Time: 2:00 a.m.

The local postmaster, E. W. Minster, was awakened by strange noises. Being a light sleeper he was used to waking up in the middle of the night. As he tried to go back to sleep, he heard an eerie, almost supernatural sound from the direction of the river. He looked out of his window toward the Delaware River. He saw what looked like a huge crane, except that its body glowed like a firefly's, flying over the river.
The creature had a head with curled horns like a ram's. It also had a long, thick neck and long, thin wings and short legs. He saw four legs. The front legs were shorter than the back ones. It then uttered a mournful and awful sound, like a combination of a squawk and a whistle, and flew away.

HC addendum.
Source: Jerry A. Young, *'Mysterious Monsters.'*   Type: E

Location: Burlington, New Jersey.
Date: January 18, 1909.
Time: Night.

A police officer spotted a flying "jabberwock" with glowing eyes. Soon after, residents of neighboring towns were finding mysterious tracks in the snow, apparently related to the creature.

HC addendum.
Source: Jerome Clark, *'Unexplained!'*   Type: E

* * * * * * *

Location: Gloucester City, New Jersey.
Date: January 19, 1909.
Time: 2:00 a.m.

Mr. and Mrs. Nelson Evans spotted a strange creature on the roof of their shed. They watched it for about ten minutes. It was about 3-feet and a half tall, with a head like a collie dog and a face like a horse. It had a long neck, wings about two feet long, its back legs were like those of a crane and it had horse's hooves. It walked on its back legs and held up two short legs with paws on them. The husband attempted to scare the creature by yelling at it, but it turned around, barked, barked at him, and then flew away.

HC addendum.
Source: Jerry A. Young, *'Mysterious Monsters.'*   Type: E

* * * * * * *

Location: Burlington, New Jersey.
Date: January 19, 1909.
Time: 6:00 a.m.

Mrs. Michael Ryan saw a strange creature prowling through an alley. She described it as having long bird-like legs, a horse's head, and short wings; reputed to have been the "Jersey Devil."

HC addendum.
Source: Jerome Clark, *'Unexplained!'*   Type: E

Location: Morristown, New Jersey.
Date: January 19, 1909.
Time: Night.

John Smith saw the creature (Jersey Devil) and chased it until it disappeared into a pit nearby. George Snyder also saw the creature, and the two described it as follows; "It was three feet high with long black hair over its entire body, arms and hands like a monkey, face like a dog, split hooves and a tail a foot long."

HC addendum.
Source: Loren Coleman and Bruce Hallenbeck, 'Monsters of New Jersey.' Type: E

* * * * * * *

Location: Springside, New Jersey.
Date: January 19, 1909.
Time: Night.

A trolley car operator saw a strange shape cross the tracks and then disappear into the shadows. He said, "It looked like a winged kangaroo with a long neck."

HC addendum.
Source: Loren Coleman and Bruce Hallenbeck, 'Monsters of New Jersey.' Type: E

* * * * * * *

Location: Camden, New Jersey.
Date: January 21, 1909.
Time: 1:00 a.m.

A strange noise was heard at 1 a.m. at the Black Hawk Social Club. One of the members heard the noise at the back window and turned to find the beast staring in through the glass. The club members were immediately gripped with panic. The man attempted to scare the creature, which flew off screaming.

HC addendum.
Source: Loren Coleman and Bruce Hallenbeck, 'Monsters of New Jersey.' Type: E

Location: Gloucester City, Pennsylvania.
Date: January 21, 1909.
Time: 2:00 a.m.

Nelson Evans heard something on the roof of the shed in his backyard. On investigating, he encountered a bizarre creature described as about 3ft and a half tall, with a head like a collie dog and a face like a horse. It had a long neck and wings about 2ft long, and its back legs were like those of a crane, and it had horse's hoofs. It walked on its back legs and held up two short front legs with paws on them. When it saw the witness it turned around and then flew away.

HC addendum.
Source: Jerome Clark, *'Unexplained!'* Type: E

* * * * * * *

Location: Haddon Heights, New Jersey.
Date: January 21, 1909.
Time: 2:00 a.m.-3:00 a.m.

The eyewitness; William Cromley, who worked as a doorkeeper at the Trent Theater in Trenton was on his way home from his job, when he became another eyewitness to see the Jersey Devil from his horse drawn buggy; his horse was very startled to see the creature standing in the middle of the street, and panicked out of fear.
Cromley jumped out of the buggy to see what he described as "a sight that froze the blood in his veins" and caused his hair to stand upright. He described it as a beast with fur and feathers, about the size of an average dog, with the face of a German shepherd with large glowing eyes. He didn't see its feet, but said that it tucked its feet underneath, then the creature hissed at him as it spread its wings and flew off.

HC addendum.
Source: James McCloy and Ray Miller, *'The Jersey Devil,'* 1976.
Type: E

Location: Salem, New Jersey.
Date: January 21, 1907.
Time: Evening.

A local police officer spotted a "devil bird" with one foot like a horse's the other like a mule's. It had a horn on its head and an ostrich's tail, and it was eleven feet long.

HC addendum.
Source: Jerome Clark, *'Unexplained!'* Type: E

* * * * * * *

Location: Haddon Heights, New Jersey.
Date: January 21, 1909.
Time: Night.

A trolley passenger sighted the creature through a window at 2 a.m. The passengers all stared in horror as they watched the Jersey Devil flying near them. When the trolley car stopped, the creature circled above, screaming hissing noises before flying away. The conductor of the trolley, Lewis Boeger, gave this report:
"In general appearance it resembled a kangaroo; it has a long neck and from what glimpse I got of its head its features are hideous. It has wings of a fairly good size and of course in the darkness looked black. Its legs are long and somewhat slender and were held in just such a position as a swan's when it is flying. We all tried to get a look at its feet to see what shape they were but the darkness was too great. It looked to be about four feet high."

HC addendum.
Source: Loren Coleman and Bruce Hallenbeck, *'Monsters of New Jersey.'* Type: E

Location: West Collingswood, New Jersey.
Date: January 21, 1909.
Time: Night.

The town's fire department supposedly confronted the monster (Jersey Devil) and sprayed it with fire hoses as it swooped menacingly overhead.

HC addendum.
Source: Loren Coleman and Bruce Hallenbeck, 'Monsters of New Jersey.' Type: E

* * * * * * *

Location: Burlington, New Jersey.
Date: January 21, 1909.
Time: 6:00 a.m.

A woman heard a noise in the alley near her house and upon investigation she found a creature with bird-like features and a horse's head. The creature appeared as if it were about to leap. The woman immediately shut the window and collapsed in fear. She said; "For some minutes I was so frightened I was unable to scream. My husband and son had already gone to work, and I was finally able to wake my youngest son, who was asleep upstairs." Although no one saw the creature in the alley again, there were small hoof-prints covering the ground. Rumor had it that the mayor of Burlington ordered the police to shoot the creature on sight.

HC addendum.
Source: Loren Coleman and Bruce Hallenbeck, 'Monsters of New Jersey.' Type: E

* * * * * * *

Location: Leiperville, Pennsylvania.
Date: January 21, 1909.
Time: Early morning.

A man walking along a highway spotted the creature early in the morning, and claimed that it ran faster than the cars were driving. He described it as having "skin like an alligator, stood on its hind feet, and was about six feet tall."

HC addendum.
Source: Loren Coleman and Bruce Hallenbeck, *'Monsters of New Jersey.'* Type: E

* * * * * * *

Location: Philadelphia, Pennsylvania.
Date: January 21, 1909.
Time: 4:00 p.m.

Mrs. Davis A. White encountered a creature in her backyard described as having alligator skin and breathing fire from its mouth. Her screams alerted her husband, who dashed outside and chased it to Seventh Street, where shortly thereafter a trolley car nearly hit it.

HC addendum.
Source: Jerome Clark, *'Unexplained!'* Type: E

* * * * * * *

Location: Near Clayton, New Jersey.
Date: January 21, 1909.
Time: Afternoon.

A man walking along the tracks of the electric railway spotted a creature he thought was the "Jersey Devil," just ahead. The creature sniffed the tracks, and then its tail touched the rail. Immediately, the sparks began to fly. After the smoke had dust cleared, 20 feet of track had melted and the creature was gone. The same or similar creature was later seen on the same date just over the border in Pennsylvania. A woman claimed she saw him in her yard. It spit flames from his mouth and left.

HC addendum.
Source: Jerry A. Young, *'Mysterious Monsters.'* Type: E

* * * * * * *

Location: Mount Holly, New Jersey.
Date: January 21, 1909.
Time: Night.

William Cronk saw the creature flying across his yard, saying it looked like a crane. Job Shinn said it had "a horse-like head, long hind legs with claws, and big wings." He said it walked like a man and left tracks everywhere.

HC addendum.
Source: Loren Coleman and Bruce Hallenbeck, *'Monsters of New Jersey.'*   Type: E

* * * * * * *

Location: Camden, New Jersey.
Date: January 22, 1909.
Time: 7:00 p.m.

    Mary Sorbinski became the first human to witness a Jersey Devil attack on another living creature. She heard a commotion in her backyard around 7 pm, and upon remembering that her dog had been out there, immediately went to see the cause of the noise. She was stricken with shock and terror as she saw her dog in the "vice-like grip" of a "horrible monster." Mrs. Sorbinski then began to smack at the creature with a broomstick, and it dropped her dog and began screaming its awful high-pitched cries.
    The creature flew right at Mrs. Sorbinski, but at the last second changed direction and flew away. After it had gone, Mrs. Sorbinski carried her injured dog into the house to find that a chunk of its flesh had been ripped out. She became overwhelmed with fear and panic. Within an hour the house was filled with neighbors, police officers, and others who were curious as to the night's incident. While the crowd gathered, the Jersey Devil made its presence known once more at the Sorbinski residence by emitting its awful screeches. The police officers on scene attempted to fire at the creature, but to no avail. It eventually flew away. This entire incident caused a statewide outbreak of panic and fear.

HC addendum.
Source: Jerome Clark, *'Unexplained!'*   Type: E

* * * * * * *

Location: Salem, New Jersey.
Date: January 22, 1909.
Time: Night.

    Jacob Henderson saw a beast with "wings and a tail" walking through an area of town. Henderson's bulldog growled and drove the beast into the woods.

HC addendum.
Source: Loren Coleman and Bruce Hallenbeck, *'Monsters of New Jersey.'*   Type: E

Location: Salem County, Pennsylvania.
Date: February 24, 1909.
Time: Unknown.

   Local farmer Leslie Garrison reported seeing a six-foot long bird-like creature as it sailed over his property. It reportedly had feet like those of a man. No other information.

HC addendum.
Source: Jerome Clark, *'Unexplained!'*   Type: E

* * * * * * *

Location: Los Tanos, New Mexico.
Date: April 4, 1909.
Time: Early morning.

   Vicente Labadie of Los Tanos, who is well known to all in the neighborhood (though of Navajo nationality) as an honest man who has no need to lie, was at our office on Wednesday this week and told us the following story:
   He says that on April 4th while grazing his sheep on the plain he suddenly felt the ground shake; almost making him fall over and he felt a sort of daze come over him, so he had to grab a hold of something in order not to fall, and at the same time he heard a voice of unknown origin that said, *"Hey, look up,"* which he obeyed and he saw in the sky near where the sun sets, a dark round cloud full of stars that emitted a thunderous noise like that of hailstorm that came towards his location. Afraid, and not knowing what to think, he stood staring at the phenomenon until it passed overhead, traveling towards where the sun rises (east). As the strange cloud passed in front of him he heard another voice that said (this portion is unintelligible on the newspaper scan) but possibly said for him to leave the area.

HC addendum.
Source: Chris Aubeck, Magonia exchange.   Type: F?
Quoting *Bandera Americana* newspaper (Albuquerque NM) May 13, 1909.

Location: Firenze, Italy.
Date: April 24, 1909.
Time: Daytime.

Several witnesses saw a white balloon-like object passing high over the area, two white-dressed figures could be seen onboard the craft. No other information.

HC addendum.
Source: Paolo Fiorino, *UFO Universe,* Oct/Nov 1991.　　　　Type: A

* * * * * * *

Location: Lambert's Point, near Norfolk, Virginia.
Date: April 30, 1909.
Time: 21:30

An airship or propelled balloon passed over Lambert's Point near Norfolk, last night and left consternation in its wake, particularly among the 'negroes.' There was one passenger in the aerial car, but those in the crowd could not tell whether it was a man or woman. The airship was at an elevation of about 150 feet and was apparently in perfect control.

It was about 9:30 o'clock when a strange noise was heard above the roofs of many houses at Lambert's Point, and investigation disclosed the presence of the airship sailing away like some huge bird. The noise made by the propellers on the ship could be heard for some distance, and it was by this means that the presence of the strange traveler of the air was first discovered. The ship made several circles above the houses at the point and then shot away in the direction of Hampton Roads. The noise made by the propellers on the airship caused many negroes to flee from their homes, thinking there was some supernatural visitation.

HC addendum.
Source: Kay Massingill in magonia exchange, quoting *The Washington Herald* (Washington, District of Columbia) Sunday, May 2, 1909.
Comments: Not meaning to be offensive I have transcribed the wording from the original article as it was written at the time.　　　　Type: A

Location: Hampton Roads, Norfolk, Virginia.
Date: May 3, 1909.
Time: Unknown.

"The spectacle of a mysterious airship, occupied by a man and a woman, passing over Sewell's point, was witnessed by more than fifty persons in that vicinity. Those who saw the strange aircraft stated that it resembled an automobile without wheels."

HC addendum.
Source: Chuck Flood in Magonia exchange list citing *Edwardsville Illinois Intelligencer* May 3, 1909.　　　　　　　　　　　　Type: A

* * * * * * *

Location: Chicago, Illinois.
Date: May 9, 1909.
Time: Evening.

Two immense balloons, following closely each other and traveling rapidly toward the south, passed over Chicago early this evening. Both balloons carried lights. One of them has at least two men in the basket. The other was too far away to make out, even with the aid of glasses whether or not there was anyone onboard.
Where the balloons came from and who were the daring aeronauts, speeding through the air nearly a mile high, is a mystery. The lookout at the United Sates life-saving station at the mouth of the Chicago River was the first one to descry the strange-looking objects in the heavens. The lookout called Capt. Charles Carland of the life-saving crew. The latter brought his field glasses to bear on the balloons. With the aid of these glasses he was able to distinguish the forms of at least two men in one of them.

HC addendum.
Source: Kay Massingill in Magonia exchange, quoting *Los Angeles Times* (1886-1922) May 10, 1909.　　　　　　　　　　　　Type: A

Location: Kelmarsh, Northamptonshire, England.
Date: May 13, 1909.
Time: Night.

Three men in a moving car heard what appeared to be a motor engine. Looking up they saw an oblong-shaped airship about 100 feet long. It had lights on the back and on the front. They were able to clearly see the torpedo shape of the object and what appeared to be men on a platform below.

HC addendum.
Source: Jerome Clark, *'UFO Encyclopedia Vol. II.'* Type: A

* * * * * * *

Location: Lowestoft, Suffolk, England.
Date: May 16, 1909.
Time: 1.30 a.m.

A Mrs. Wigg was awakened by a noise similar to that of a motor-car. Looking through the window directly opposite her bed, she saw a dark object pass fairly quickly, heading southwest. It was not very high, and was bottle-shaped, in a horizontal position, and of considerable length; she saw what appeared to be a man steering at the front of the machine. Several other people saw vivid flashes of light or heard engine sounds at that time.

HC addendum.
Source: Carl Grove *FSR* Vol. 17 #1 quoting *East Anglian Daily Times* May 18-19. Type: A

* * * * * * *

Location: London, England.
Date: May 18, 1909.
Time: Night.

Two reported coming upon a strange craft in a city park. They were walking along a fair way when they heard a soft buzzing sound behind them. Then suddenly they saw creeping along the surface of the grass a dimly lit shape resembling a collection of big cigar boxes with the ends cut out. It must have been 200 to 250 feet long. They saw two men on the "airship." The first man, who was near the fore part, seemed to be in a sort of steel wire cage, and had a row of handles in front of him.

The moment they saw the witnesses this first man, who was clean-shaven and looked like a "Yankee" tuned a searchlight on the witnesses blinding them with the glare, the second man, who stood in the middle of the airship looked like a German, and was smoking a calabash pipe. They were on the ground very close to the witnesses and one of the witnesses went up to them. The German like occupant spoke first, "I am sorry, have you tobacco?" The witness gave the stranger tobacco and he was given a pipe in return.

The "German" had a cap and a beard, and a map in front of him. It was fastened on a board, and there were red discs on it, as though they had been stuck in the map with pins. The man at the searchlight was tall with a blue serge suit. The other man wore a fur-lined overcoat and a soft hat. Parts of the airship appeared to be made of some light colored metal-aluminum. There seemed to be some steel rods, which stuck out and kept the airship upright and the propellers off the ground. The airship left without either of the men saying goodbye. It disappeared in 10 seconds, and was gone before the witnesses could see where it had gone.

HC addendum.
Source: Phillip L. Rife, *'It Didn't Start with Roswell.'*   Type: B

* * * * * * *

Location: Caerphilly Mountains, Wales.
Date: May 18, 1909.
Time: 11:00 p.m.

Mr. C. Lethbridge, a dockworker was walking home over the mountain when, at the summit, he came across a tube-shaped contraption on the grass, and two men working on something nearby, they wore "big, heavy fur coats, and fur caps fitted tightly over their heads." Mr. Lethbridge went on, "I was rather frightened, but I continued to go on until I was within 20 yards of them.

The noise of my little spring cart seemed to attract them, and when they saw men, they jumped up and jabbered furiously in a strange lingo." Mr. Lethbridge became even more alarmed when the long object rose from the ground and he was amazed when he saw the two "men" jump into a little carriage suspended from it. Tube, carriage, and "men" rose slowly into the air in a zigzag fashion.

When it was clear of the telegraph wires, two great lights shone out and the object sailed away towards Cardiff. The astonished witness said later he could clearly see two wheels at the bottom of the carriage, and a whirling fan at the tail. The next day trampled grass, torn newspapers, and a quantity of a substance like papier-mâché was found on the scene.

HC addendum.
Source: Charles Bowen, *'The Humanoids.'* Type: B

* * * * * * *

Location: Maindee Wales.
Date: May 19, 1909.
Time: 8:00 a.m.

About 8:00 a.m., W Breighton's little girl pointed out a "big fowl" which would "flap" at times. It came from the Bristol Channel, standing still on occasion, and moving away about 8:30 a.m. Two others saw the object, one, using a telescope, said that the craft was 12 to 15 yards long and was carrying three men.

HC addendum.
Source: Carl Grove, *FSR* Vol. 17 #1. Type: A

* * * * * * *

Location: Maesteg, Wales.
Date: May 22, 1909.
Time: 10:30 p.m.

Lights were seen over Commercial Street, Maesteg. One man, with a telescope, reported an aerial craft, with occupants. No other information.

HC addendum.
Source: Carl Grove, *FSR* Vol. 17 #1. Type: A

* * * * * * *

Location: Near Cudworth, Saskatchewan, Canada.
Date: Summer 1909.
Time: Unknown.

Around the same time that a wandering light kept appearing in the hills; on a Sunday, three children aged six and less saw a beautiful but sad lady carrying a chain and dragging a gold cross across the grass on top of the hill. One of the young children ran up to the exceptionally beautiful woman and tried to pick up the dragging cross, but she, the chain, and the cross disappeared. Nobody else saw the woman except the little boy and the two girls. Within two weeks the boy caught sick and died, while the girls grew up, married and moved away.

HC addendum.
Source: Unidentified in Saskatchewan. Type: E?

* * * * * * *

Location: Olumtsy, near Irkutsk, Siberia, Russia.
Date: Summer 1909.
Time: Night.

Hearing noises a local farmer, Ivan Zharkov, went to his barn and heard a sound resembling the "squealing of a pig." At the same time an unknown creature grabbed and scratched his leg; in the dim light he could not clearly see his assailant. He grabbed a shovel and chased the mysterious being, and it was then that he saw it and described it as a black hairy creature about 5ft tall, like a human, but very thin; it ran quickly away and disappeared from sight.

HC addendum.
Source: http://www.esoreiter.ru/index Type: E

* * * * * * *

Location: Coast of Belgium.
Date: June 7, 1909.
Time: Daytime.

Passengers on the steamer Potsdam, which arrived today from Rotterdam and Boulogne, witnessed a unique maneuver by a balloon over the open ocean off the Belgian Coast.
The balloon appeared to be descending so rapidly that preparations were made to lower a boat and rescue the occupants. The balloon swept down toward the steamer, approaching so close as to almost foul the foremast rigging. As it was about to graze the mast a sand bag was thrown out and the balloon rose slightly and, gradually moving toward the Belgian Coast, was lost to sight. There were two men in the car that made no intelligible response to efforts made to communicate with them.

HC addendum.
Source: Chuck Flood in Magonia exchange quoting *Los Angeles Times* June 8, 1909. Type: A?

Location: Phoenix, Arizona.
Date: July 5, 1909.
Time: Early morning.

"To be awakened from a sound sleep, to see a silent, weird, floating body directly over one's head, dipping, circling and bobbing here and there. Is not an event that will be forgotten very soon. That was what happened night before last to Mr. Turnbull, the picture man, who sleeps on the tin roof of his home during these hot July nights. Mr. Turnbull attended the celebration and coming home very tired, withdrew for the night to his cot on the roof.

How long he had been asleep he could not tell, but during the black, still hours of the morning, when the ghosts walk, he was awakened by a strange hum and subdued clicking of machinery. For several moments Mr. Turnbull could not locate the noise and was commencing to think that perhaps someone was ransacking the house, until the point of an anchor caught the corner of the bed clothes and jerked them off the bed up into the blackness of the night. And yet he could not locate the queer noise exactly, though by this time he knew that it must be directly over his head.

At this moment the moon peeped from out the clouds and Mr. Westburg could see a huge black, oblong object away up, perhaps a mile in the night an object that circled around and around, then shot ahead for some distance, then circled and returned. By this time Mr. Turnbull had collected his senses so that he could call, and waving a pillow in circular swoops, called to the black oval bag overhead what was wanted.

No reply reached him, but the occupants of the airship dropped a miniature parachute, decorated with a hundred lights that before burning out told him the object overhead was the imperial airship from Hong Kong that is taking a world trip and intends to circumnavigate the Earth before the exposition at Japan next year. So precisely did the Mongolians of the upper world figure the downward course of the parachute that after circling for a diameter of over a mile, the weird object dropped in the very middle of the tin porch on which Mr. Turnbull slept.

Though from time to time reports have been received regarding this imperial airship, no one has paid particularly attention to them, but since the event of last night Mr. Turnbull has left no wire unturned to gather information regarding it, and there is no doubt that before tomorrow evening, the greatest advancement in aerial navigation will have been recorded.

Why the airship has not dropped any word before reaching Phoenix is not understood, but the ways of the Chinese are not to be reasoned with and besides they probably are not thoroughly versed as to the cartography of the western coast. When asked as to what he considered the rate the airship was traveling last night, Turnbull said he thought about 150 miles an hour. Why it will take this airy monster a year to go around the globe is another item that cannot be explained, but more than likely they will make side trips somewhere. The messenge that was dropped can be seen in the studio of Mr. Turnbull."

HC addendum.
Source: Kay Massingill in Magonia exchange, quoting *Arizona Republican,* Phoenix, Arizona, July 7, 1909. Type: X

* * * * * * *

Location: Kelso, New Zealand.
Date: July 24, 1909.
Time: Noon.

"Several school children beheld in the air a strange machine, which they described as shaped like a boat with what seemed like a figure of a man seated in it. It approached from the direction of the Blue Mountains, circled high over the school, and then disappeared in the direction whence it came. It was also observed by Mr. James Russell of Kelso."

HC addendum.
Source: *The Daily Times* Jul 6, 26, 1909. Type: A

* * * * * * *

Location: Gore, New Zealand.
Date: July 30, 1909.
Time: 5:00 a.m.

An airship came down near a dredge working on a river some miles north of Gore. About 5:00 a.m. two lights broke through the mist and then the forms of two figures sitting in the air machine could be seen. The dredge winch operator, Mr. F Green, said the ship was narrow and boat-shaped. The object came quite close to the dredge, circling round for several minutes.
At times it moved very fast, at other times it would poise itself and dip like a bird, then rise again. The object shot up into the mist, leaving a yellow glare on the haze; it reappeared in the direction of Otakarama, and then disappeared. Two of the dredge operators saw the object.

HC addendum.
Source: Tony Brunt, *Xenolog* #100/101. Type: A

Location: Port Molyneux, New Zealand.
Date: Late July, 1909.
Time: Unknown.

An anonymous man reported encountering an airship that came down at Port Molyneux. Some Japanese-looking occupants had alighted that conversed with him. No other information.

HC addendum.
Source: Tony Brunt, *Xenolog* 100/101.　　　　　　　　　　Type: B

* * * * * * *

Location: Sounds, New Zealand.
Date: August, 1909.
Time: Unknown.

"A Sounds man out fishing observed an aerial object moving at low altitude. When it was over his launch, the occupants threw out debris, which "fizzled" as it hit the water." No other information.

HC addendum.
Source: Mufob Vol. 5 #6.　　　　　　　　　　　　　　　Type: A

* * * * * * *

Location: Montclair, New Jersey.
Date: August, 1909.
Time: Various.

The nightly appearance of a strange air-sailing craft has mystified and agitated the residents of suburban towns in Northern New Jersey. What is described as an airship; sometimes containing one person and at other times two, has been observed at night making rapid flights high in the air. Attention has been attracted to it by the loud exhaust from its motor. Residents of Montclair are the latest to report having seen it. This airship, which is of the aeroplane model, is believed to belong to an experimenter who has his headquarters in some isolated section and who is preserving secrecy.

HC addendum.
Source: Jerome Clark, Magonia exchange quoting *Morning Oregonian* (Portland Oregon) August 25, 1909.　　　　　　　　　　Type: A

Location: Oamaru, near Sumpter's Hill, New Zealand.
Date: August 2, 1909.
Time: 3:00 a.m.

    A large boat-shaped object with three lights was observed clearly illuminated by the moon, two figures were visible inside. The object flew "at a fast rate."

HC addendum.
Source: Richard H. Hall, *'From Airship to Arnold.'*   Type: A

* * * * * * *

Location: Near Waipawa, New Zealand.
Date: August 3, 1909.
Time: Night.

    A Waipawa man was riding when his horse became restive; he discovered that a large torpedo shaped structure was passing overhead. The airship was painted gray; three persons were visible in it, one of who shouted out to him in an unknown language. The ship rose to a great height, showing lights at prow and stern, and after circling around, disappeared behind a hill. The same night, another resident in the area saw a ship like structure, whence proceeded a humming sound, high in the air.

HC addendum.
Source: Anthony Brunt, *Xenolog* #100/101.   Type: A

* * * * * * *

Location: Mart, Texas.
Date: August 7, 1909.
Time: Early morning.

    Early this morning while splitting wood, City Judge Davis saw an airship slowly passing over the city in a southwesterly direction. He describes it as being about 45 feet long and 15 feet in width, and containing two or three passengers. It is thought to be Mattry's ship from Chicago, en route to Marlin.

HC addendum.
Source: Kay Massingill in Magonia Exchange, quoting *Dallas Morning News* (Texas), August 8, 1909.   Type: A

Location: Cwmdare, Wales.
Date: August 11, 1909.
Time: 7:00 a.m.

"Three persons in Cwmdare declare that they saw an airship last Monday morning. Mr. Evan John Evans, milk vendor, one of three persons referred to, was milking his cows in Gamblyn field at 7'oclock that morning, when he perceived an object descend on the Merthyr Mountain and rise again very quickly. It was cigar-like in shape, similar to the one seen on Caerphilly Mountain. He also saw a person inside, dressed in black. The airship went in the direction of Merthyr. Mr. Evan's son and daughter, who were with him, also testify to seeing it."

HC addendum.
Source: Kay Massingill in Magonia Exchange, quoting *Aberdare Leader* 14, August, 1909, Aberdare, Wales. Type: A

* * * * * * *

Location: Victoria Park, near Perth, Western Australia.
Date: August 15, 1909.
Time: Night.

"The mysterious airship craze has spread to this state. A report was received yesterday from Pingelly that an airship had been passing over the town at night and showing red and green lights, the mysterious visitor eventually passing away in a westerly direction.
Strangely enough, a report of a somewhat similar nature was received from Victoria Park, a suburb of Perth, two or three persons declaring they saw the airship displaying powerful lights early yesterday morning. One man stated it was close to the ground when he saw it, and he distinguished the aeronaut pulling a lever, causing the airship to rise rapidly and pass out of sight at last. A newspaper man went to Victoria Park, and found a number of people, some armed with telescopes gazing at the stars and declaring that varying colored lights were visible, and that it could be distinctly seen turning its course.
It is extraordinary that two fairly circumstantial reports should have originated independently of each other at two places hundreds of miles apart. At Pingelly the phenomenon of colored lights moving quickly across the sky was seen by about a dozen persons and a telegram was dispatched to the Perth Observatory asking whether the spectacle was due to the passage of any astronomical body."

HC addendum.
Source: Zeehan and *Dundas Herald*, August 16, 1909. Type: A

Location: Claremont, Western Australia.
Date: August 17, 1909.
Time: Evening.

"Persons in various parts of the state continue to observe objects in the sky, which they convert into the appearance on an airship. Quite recently a lady in Claremont declared that not only was a veritable airship seen there by her husband and herself, but that its proximity to her house was such that her spouse called out to the occupants to be careful of the chimney, to which reminder he received a reply in some language to him unknown."

HC addendum.
Source: *Kalgoorlie Miner* (WA 1895-1950) Thursday 19, August, 1909.
Type: A?

* * * * * * *

Location: Fishers Island, Connecticut.
Date: August 18, 1909.
Time: 2:30 a.m.

Four men at the island's lifesaving station sighted an airship 60 feet long and 20 feet wide. Moving at a "terrific clip" against the wind, it came from the northeast, its engines whirring, a dazzling white light at its head illuminating the dark, cloud covered sky. "In the center of the object could be seen two dark figures, but the observers could not tell whether they were men; the frames and wings could be seen but the watchers could not clearly make out the huddled figures in the center." Visible for three minutes, the object disappeared in the west.

HC addendum.
Source: Jerome Clark; *'The UFO Book: Encyclopedia of the Extraterrestrial.'* Type: A?

Location: Singapore.
Date: September 10, 1909.
Time: Evening.

To the Editor,

Sir, I shall be greatly indebted to you or any one of the spiritualistic readers of your valuable journal, who will, through its medium, throw some light on the otherwise dark and mysterious object that confronted me last evening, after dusk, while I was enjoying the salubrious breeze all alone in the Government House Domain, with a cigarette in my mouth.

I stood puffing in a meditative mood on a beautiful spot, not very far from the place where I noticed a few rare birds are caged and suddenly, unperceived, I saw face to face a tall figure, dressed in spotless white, with a beautiful and charming face, full of happy smiles, stretching her hand, for the figure was none other than that of a lady of bronze color, and asking for a missive which she said, she had dropped somewhere near the spot where I stood and which, she thought, I might have picked up and secreted in my pocket.

My eyes could not have deceived me. I saw the figure as plainly as anything; my ears could not have deceived me. Her silvery words, I heard distinctly. It was not an apparition. In all conscience I saw a woman before me. I am not cadaverous. I did not forget myself. Bashful of the presence of an unknown lady in that lonely spot, I addressed her in this wise: *"Madam, Pray tell me what missive you want; I saw none and I am sorry you are deprived of it."*

The lady was visibly affected and seemed to have lost all that was precious to her. She asked me to accompany her some distance promising to explain to me what the loss of the missive meant to her. I gladly did so and as we were not very far from the spot we met, to my horror the strange figure vanished into thin air. Imagine sir my feelings. My life had almost gone out of me. I could scarcely move an inch. I thought I was transported into an unrealistic world. I indulged in strange musings and fell down unconscious. I did not know what transpired afterwards.

At 5 o'clock this morning I found myself as usual, on my bed. How and by what means I happened to be in my usual place, I cannot say. All what I have mentioned in this letter is not the figment of my imagination; of this I can assure and reassure you and your readers. Apart from this transformation, either for good or bad wrought in me. I should like somebody to explain the mystery that is behind the appearance and disappearance of the weird figure in the Government House Domain.

HC addendum.
Source: *The Singapore Free Press* and *Mercantile Advertiser*, Singapore Malaysia, September 11, 1909.   Type: E?

* * * * * * *

Location: Scott Township, Ohio.
Date: October 26, 1909.
Time: Daytime.

"M.G. Day, of Scott Township, a farmer, died suddenly today of paralysis. He was stricken when in his barnyard shouting a reply to a mysterious balloon party that had descended low to ask about the location."

HC addendum.
Source: *The Cincinnati Enquirer*, date 27 Oct, 1909.   Type: X

* * * * * * *

Location: Near Algiers, Algeria.
Date: December, 1909.
Time: Night.

Aleister Crowley and his assistant, Victor Neuberg, went into the desert outside Algiers to conduct rituals for the purpose of accessing the high-level aethyrs in the nineteenth call of Enochian magic. Crowley had a number of breakthroughs in consciousness as a result, including the instruction that he would have to confront 'Choronzon' (an evil demon or entity) and cross the Abyss.

In an evocation, a magician stays within the protection of a magical circle and evokes an entity into a separate magical triangle. Crowley intended to break that rule and sit within the triangle, go into trance, and offer his own body for possession; a dangerous magical act.

According to Crowley's account, Neuberg, standing within the protected magical circle, got the brunt of the entity's force. First Choronzon manifested in the form of a seductive female prostitute, and then turned into an old man, and then into a snake. Choronzon told Neuberg he spat upon the name of the Most High. He was Master of the Triangle who had no fear of the pentagram. He said he would give Neuberg words that seemed like great secrets of magic but would be worthless, as a joke.

Choronzon breached the protection of the magical circle around Neuberg and the two wrestled physically. Although some observers have opined that Neuberg wrestled with a demon-entranced Crowley,

Neuberg insisted he fought the entity itself. It had froth covered fangs and attempted to tear out his throat. After a considerable struggle, Neuberg forced Choronzon back into the triangle, and repaired his magical circle.

The two hurled insults and threats at each other, and Choronzon vanished. Crowley and Neuberg felt they had bested the demon and Crowley considered himself to have achieved great magical status as a result. Some critics of Crowley's work believe that Choronzon left a permanent mental and psychic scar upon him.

HC addendum.
Source: Rosemary Ellen Guiley and Phillip J. Imbrogno, *The Vengeful Djinn.*   Type: F

* * * * * * *

Location: Marlboro, Massachusetts.
Date: December 16, 1909.
Time: Evening.

One of the most positive proofs of the existence of the airship comes from ex-councilman B. W. Johnson who says he saw the airship in the south western part of the city, and that it came so low that he could hear a man talking from the craft. The same night another witness name Beauregard reported seeing the airship land on the southern side of Lake Williams.

HC addendum.
Source: Phillip L. Rife, *'It Didn't Start with Roswell.'*   Type: F

* * * * * * *

Location: Quinsigamond, Massachusetts.
Date: December 21, 1909.
Time: Night.

At the time a mysterious aerial object was being reported over New England, Ernest Anderson was walking in the woods near Malvern Road, when he encountered a figure about 6.5ft tall. "I could see its white gown and shining through it, the thin bones of a human skeleton." Emmanuel Johnson had seen the apparition a few days earlier.

HC addendum.
Source: Mufob Vol. 5 #6.   Type: D?

Location: Worcester, Massachusetts.
Date: December 22, 1909.
Time: 7:30 p.m.

An unknown aircraft with a bright searchlight, which had been seen repeatedly in New England, circled Worcester 4 times. "At one point it slowed to a standstill for several minutes. The dark, obscure mass of some sort of airship could be dimly seen. Some observers claimed they could identify broad, projecting wings; others saw figures seated in the center of the machine. No one heard the noise of an engine."

HC addendum.
Source: Lucius Farish. Type: A

* * * * * * *

Location: Boston, Massachusetts.
Date: December 23, 1909.
Time: 7:00 p.m.

On the evening of 12/23, the mysterious aircraft visited Boston, as thousands traced its flight across Massachusetts, it meandered its way to the big city by way of Marlboro, Framingham, and Natick. Here residents said it came within 100ft of the ground. Some claimed there were two men in the aircraft, one standing forward near the headlight, and the second man in the stern. It continued on over Needham and Newton, and arrived at the city shortly after 1900, where it hovered 25 minutes.

HC addendum.
Source: Lucius Farish. Type: A

* * * * * * *

Location: Fernhurst, West Sussex, England.
Date: December 24, 1909.
Time: Night.

On the night of Christmas Eve, Gladys and Gwen Ruffle woke in the night, looked out the window and witnessed an incredible sight. In the sky were two golden doves, which were flying very close to each other, and, as their wings touched; the figure of an angel appeared, surrounded by an aura of radiance. It was quite breathtaking. Dumfounded they just sat in complete awe. The angel vanished and the doves gradually faded into the sky.

HC addendum.
Source: Paul Whitehead, *FSR* Vol. 39 #4. Type: F

1910-1919

Location: Konowaruk, Guyana.
Date: 1910.
Time: Unknown.

The local resident magistrate was prospecting for gold just above the junction of the Potato River when he came upon several short reddish-brown fur-covered creatures that retreated slowly into the jungle without once taking their eyes off him.

HC addendum.
Source: Loren Coleman, *'Curious Encounters.'* Type: E

* * * * * * *

Location: St. Merryn, Cornwall, England.
Date: 1910.
Time: Unknown.

Two witnesses saw a red object resembling a ship among the clouds; the object contained a large number of little dwarf-like creatures that were chattering, laughing, and pointing down at the witnesses.

HC addendum.
Source: Janet and Colin Bord, *'Modern Mysteries of Britain.'* Type: A

Location: Mirror Lake, Sauk County, Wisconsin.
Date: 1910.
Time: Unknown.

A 10-year old girl saw a creature in the woods that looked somewhat like a man but was covered with fur. It peacefully trailed her home, leaving tracks twice as large as her father's.

HC addendum.
Source: http://www.w-files.com/files/ Type: E

* * * * * * *

Location: Near Estella, Navarra, Spain.
Date: 1910.
Time: Night.

Hunter and cow-herder Ricardo Jimenez was returning home on his horse late at night when he was confronted by a short child-like figure standing on the side of the road. The strange creature appeared to be making loud moaning sounds. Concerned, he dismounted from his horse and attempted to grab the figure but was shocked upon noticing that the being had horrible, distorted features and long extremities.

He appeared to have been wearing a white tunic. Jimenez ran back to his horse and left the area but not before the strange creature attempted to grab the horse's reins with long skinny hands. Others in the area had reported encountering the same or similar creature.

HC addendum.
Source: Iker Jimenez, *'El Paraiso Maldito'* (Cursed Paradise) Type: E
Comments: This type of encounter seems to be a worldwide phenomenon and has become almost intertwined with the urban legend motif.

* * * * * * *

Location: West of Karumba, Gulf of Carpentaria, Queensland, Australia.
Date: 1910
Time: Night.

Tom Trent, part Aboriginal, was living with his tribe somewhere in the Gulf of Carpentaria, near the coast on the Flinders River which lies west of Karumba. One night as he lay sleeping in a humpy and the others in his group were seated around a big campfire. Tom woke up to the sounds of screams and yells as a whirring, silvery craft suddenly descended over the people, engulfing the campsite. By his account the glow was immense. As Tom lay crouched in fear, the large saucer-shaped craft remained stationary and all went deadly silent. Then as Tom slinked off into the brush for a better hiding place, the craft began emitting the whirring sound again, then rose up and "shot off" skywards, taking Tom's people with it, leaving a dust-colored smoldering fireplace. Local police took no notice of his story when he tried to report the incident.

Two years after the incident, Tom was again in the region and met a man and woman; members of his tribe and who had been "taken up" that night. They told him how everyone had been abducted by several yellowish-skinned beings of what we today describe as 'typical' extraterrestrials, with thin bodies, long necks, and heads with large round eyes, small nostrils, small mouths and ear holes. They were all clothed in skintight garments.

The information is sketchy but it appears that the tribespeople, about twenty in all, with children both boys and girls, were flown to another world within a few hours. Here were large buildings, perhaps a city. They were, said the couple, apparently the subjects of various researches carried out by more of the strange beings over a period of time, in the course of which most of the people died. The two survivors claimed that they were later flown back to where they had been abducted. These details were passed on by Tom to other family members not present that night, but due to lost information it can only be said that the survivors had been returned to Earth two years later.

HC addendum.
Source: The Blue Mountains UFO Research Club newsletter Jan, 2012.
Type: G

* * * * * * *

Location: Quiquel, Chiloe Archipelago, Chile.
Date: 1910.
Time: Night.

At the time when the native "Chilotes" would trade their agricultural goods using small boats between the ports of Ancud and Puerto Montt, it was reported that a new boat belonging to Alejandro Navarro, equipped with white sails left the above port on its maiden voyage. There were several merchants accompanying their goods onboard the vessel which was piloted by a man by the last name of Guao, better known as "El Piuche."

The ocean was calm as the small vessel quickly reached the entrance to the Chacao Canal. However once there the wind suddenly stopped mysteriously and a cold fog began to envelope the area. Navarro's vessel was accompanied by another small vessel that had been traveling side by side, however the fog became so thick that the occupants of the other vessel could no longer see Navarro's boat. They could hear voices and what sounded like people walking on deck, but could not see the vessel.

The next day was one of unusual splendor, the wind seemed to have been become stagnant in the canals. Very early in the morning the inhabitants of Tenaun, Linlin, and San Juan noticed that the boat piloted by Guao appeared to be adrift among the waves. It remained there most of the morning without signaling or approaching the shore. It was not normal that a boat that had just left port the day before would have already returned.

Several locals approached the boat and boarded it; wondering how the boat had suddenly appeared offshore that morning. Of its ten known passengers and crew, there was only the cargo and goods. The boat appeared undamaged, everything seemed to be in order. Onboard were, sheep, pigs, flour, and other goods, seemingly untouched. Immediately worried family members of the missing crew and passengers launched an investigation, contacting the owners of the boat and later the authorities. Apparently the other boat that had accompanied the unlucky vessel had arrived to port without any incident and were not aware that there had been any problems with Navarro's boat.

Years later a very strange man appeared along the coast. According to the locals the stranger was "educated in appearance," who spoke very little, but who was recognized by the locals as being the pilot Guao or "El Piuche" of that ill-fated vessel years ago. It is even said that a half-brother of Guao ran into him in a cantina at Punta de Chonos. He was wearing strange clothing that "that made noise as he walked," he spoke in a strange foreign accent and once his half-brother recognized him, he confirmed that it was indeed him but soon after; he disappeared from the area, this time for good.

HC addendum.
Source: Antonio Cardenas Tabies, *'Triangulo Pacifico Sur.'*   Type: X
Comments: Translation by Albert S. Rosales.

Location: Invercargill, New Zealand.
Date: January, 1910.
Time: 11:00 p.m.

Several witnesses; among them the vicar, the mayor and a police officer; saw a cigar-shaped object hovering at 30 yards altitude. A man appeared at a lateral door and was heard shouting some words in an unknown language. The opening closed, and the object accelerated and was lost to sight.

HC addendum.
Source: Stuart, *'UFO Warning.'* Type: A

* * * * * * *

Location: Paragould, Arkansas.
Date: January 15, 1910.
Time: Evening.

A large, white airship carrying three or possibly four passengers is declared by many to have passed over Paragould early last night. It carried a powerful headlight and was brilliantly lighted. The machine, apparently a dirigible balloon from the description, was under perfect control, and seemed to be flying a distance of 1000ft above the Earth. It passed over the southern part of the city, heading south.

HC addendum.
Source: Humcat quoting newspaper source. Type: A

* * * * * * *

Location: Near Yangchow, China.
Date: Late March, 1910.
Time: Daytime?

"An unusual case of Chinese 'superstition' occurred near here the other day. In a village eighteen 'li' from Yangchow, a Buddhist priest passing along the streets attracted many of the people by his incantations. The next day, he had it circulated all over the town that he had seen an object riding on a dark cloud. At first it looked like a monkey and then it appeared as a hairy man.

Many of the villagers went out with him to see the being, but failing to show his friends the new messenger; he informed them that it was going to descend on a mount west of Yangchow. So they returned to their homes in great excitement believing this message from the priest. I understand in this way the priest induces the people to give money to build his new temple."

HC addendum.
Source: Fabio Picasso in Magonia Exchange quoting the *North China Herald*, Shanghai April 1, 1910. Type: A?

* * * * * * *

Location: Toti Island, Windward Islands, French Polynesia.
Date: April 20, 1910.
Time: Unknown.

A report of an airship having been seen in the Windward Group (says an exchange) was laughed at as impossible; but it's now reported that it was seen by Europeans and natives to alight on the island of Toti. It is said that it came from a cruiser which was observed in the distance. Toti was visited, and distinct boot prints, cigarette stumps and a "German newspaper" were discovered.

HC addendum.
Source: K. Massingill in Magonia Exchange, quoting the *Sydney Stock and Station Journal* (NSW: 1896-1924) April 22, 1910. Type: B?

* * * * * * *

Location: Belvidere, Illinois.
Date: April 30, 1910.
Time: Evening.

People living in the west edge of town report that a short time before sunset on Sunday evening there appeared in the sky in the direction of Rockford, a cigar-shaped object which appeared to be a dirigible balloon. Objects near each end looked like people.
The body of the object appeared oblong, cigar-shaped at one end, but aside from that being somewhat egg-shaped. It appeared to be moving rather rapidly to the north and in a few minutes was obscured by clouds. They are at a loss to know what the object was.

HC addendum.
Source: Kay Massingill in Magonia Exchange, quoting *Daily Register Gazette* (Rockford, IL) May 2, 1910. Type: A

Location: Vidotville, Maryland.
Date: Summer 1910.
Time: Morning.

Lawrence J. Crone saw a blimp-like ship hovering lower than a tree 200ft away, with an oscillating motion. It was about twice the length of a railroad car, and had windows of different colors of glass. Through the clear glass he could see entities watching him.

They had heads and necks "like pigeons," with pointed heads, no nose or ears, and "two spots for eyes." Their faces were flat, with no chin, and covered with a soft looking gray gown, like fur. He called the ship to the attention of two young men, who screamed and ran away. His mother came out and also saw the UFO, which moved away slowly.

HC addendum.
Source: NICAP. Type: A

* * * * * * *

Location: Barberino di Mugello, Florence, Italy.
Date: Late July 1910.
Time: Evening.

One evening after dinner, several local peasants had gathered in the courtyard to talk before bedtime. Suddenly, out of the clear sky appeared a low flying black creature "resembling a giant bat the size of a man with wings." The head of the monster was pressed into its shoulders and it was surrounded in a shimmering luminous halo. The flying figure flew quickly and disappeared behind some trees. The terrified peasants agreed "that it had been the devil himself."

HC addendum.
Source: Maurizio Monzali, *'Il Giornale del Misteri,'* april 2010. Type: E

Location: Near Listowel, County Kerry, Ireland.
Date: Middle of December, 1910.
Time: About midnight.

    Two men encountered strange lights near Listowel. They noticed a light about a mile ahead of them. At first they thought it was simply a light in a house, but on drawing closer, they could see that it was moving up and down, to and fro; diminishing to a spark, then expanding into a yellow luminous flame. Before arriving to Listowel they were able to distinguish two lights.
    Suddenly both of these expanded into yellow sheets of light about six feet high by four feet across. In the midst of each light they saw "a radiant being having human form." Only the general shape of the figures could be seen. The lights came together so that the beings could be seen side by side within the brilliant illumination. A house intervened between the travelers (who were still moving on) and the lights, and they saw no more of them.

HC addendum.
Source: Paul Deveraux, *'Earth Lights.'*   Type: E?

* * * * * * *

Location: Charleston, South Carolina.
Date: December 7, 1910.
Time: 2:30 p.m.

    "Are things supernatural happening in these modern times? They are, according to the statements of several prominent Charlestonians, who state most positively that this vicinity yesterday received a visitation from the clouds. A mysterious airship; one of the dirigibles, such as that in which Zeppelin achieved immortality; appeared out of the heavens before the rapt gaze of the multitude, floated peacefully over the harbor, over Mount Pleasant, when; swish; there was a dip, a blaze, a visible, but inaudible explosion, the fall of a body from the craft, and then the swift descent of the ship towards terra firma. It disappeared behind a clump of trees, and nothing more has ever been heard of it. Whether it was a real airship or a toy it remains a mystery.
    While the statement of one man in a matter of this kind, as in the event of the appearance of a ghost, might be attributed to the influence of that which is dispensed from the realms of the jungle, wherein sightless tigers roam, the stores of many citizens of Charleston whose sobriety is unquestioned, correspond in every particular, and they are unanimous in saying that the heavenly visitant was an airship; evidently having come here a month in advance of the cay's aviation meet, which

is not scheduled until the first of the New Year. To give the story verbatim, as it was repeated a myriad of times to various members of *The News and Courier* staff. About 2:30 yesterday afternoon, while the pretty misses from Memminger and other city schools were wending their several ways homeward, the mysterious craft sailed into view from no particular place, seemingly appearing from the atmospheric space immediately above a bare expanse of water.

The framework was suspended to a long gas bag, as in the class of air craft known as balloons, and on this framework was perched a figure. Whether it was one of the inhabitants of this mundane sphere, or whether it was a Martian aviator who had passed from the zone of Martian gravity, is not known, but sufficient to say that all agree that a pilot guided the ship as it journeyed towards the hills and dales of the Mount Pleasant side of the harbor.

"Perhaps," suggested one gazer. "Mount Pleasant is having an aviation meet and we have not heard of it." But this theory was discredited, for no special reason except that it was improbable, although not impossible. But to take up the thread of the narrative where it was broken for a momentary comment, the ship sailed majestically over the Mount Pleasant shore and seemingly over the roofs of the houses in the city.

As it was seen by no resident of that place in so far as can be ascertained, local scientists are of the opinion that the navigator has conquered the fourth dimension and was thereby enabled to make himself invisible to the residents of that beautiful little town. The airship sailed out, out, out over the woods until it passed near a house; the location of which is not known. It was then that it was plainly seen to swerve. It swayed, exploded, a flamed; the navigator fell plummet-like to the earth, followed closely by the erstwhile ship.

Mr. Jack Lehman, of No. 32 Savage Street, said most positively that the ship was a large dirigible, not a toy, and he gave a vivid description of the accident which brought its flight to an abrupt termination. Others of those who vouch for the statement of the appearance of the ship are Mr. W. J. D. Heinz, a well-known merchant of the city and his brother Mr. C. H. L. Heinz; several wholesale merchants along East Bay Street and two young misses of the Memminger School, who declare that as they are yet in their teens, their eyesight is perfect and they saw the whole thing.

None of the residents of Mount Pleasant have heard anything of the incident, the crew of the "Sapho" plying between Mount Pleasant and Charleston know nothing of the mysterious visitor and none of the local tugs or boats report any knowledge of the airship. Still the statement has been emphatically made, reiterated, and; who can disprove it? Perhaps an unknown light in the world of aviation has been experimenting near Charleston. Who can say?"

HC addendum.
Source: Kay Massingill in Magonia Exchange, quoting *Charleston News and Courier* (Charleston SC) Thursday, December 8, 1910.   Type: H?
Comments: However nothing is mentioned in reference to any recovery operation.

* * * * * * *

Location: Isle of Man, England.
Date: 1911.
Time: Unknown.

A witness saw a large crowd of "little beings" all dressed in red and all resembling soldiers drilling by marching back and forth on a field. No other information.

HC addendum.
Source: Janet and Colin Bord, *'Modern Mysteries of Britain.'*   Type: E

* * * * * * *

Location: Gumeracha, South Australia.
Date: 1911.
Time: Morning.

A young lad had been working on his father's farm, milking cows. While carrying two buckets of milk, he felt a pain in his head and placing the buckets down, he observed, in front of him some distance away, a disc-shaped object. It was about 10 feet across and was silver and glowing like the moon. He watched it for about 15 seconds, and then it rose into the air and disappeared at a very fast rate into the horizon.

HC addendum.
Source: UFOPIA "*Panorama*" magazine Vol. 3, #5, July-August 1964.
Type: X

Location: Chanute, Kansas.
Date: March 9, 1911.
Time: 2:00 a.m.

Chanute. March 10. Balloons have formed the habit of night prowling, according to the story told by the occupant of a flat on West Main Street. Being aroused at 2 o'clock yesterday morning, he chanced to glance out of the window and saw a large balloon floating away toward the north and west. It was flying low and by the light which it carried, he could distinguish the forms of its occupants. He thinks there were three of them.

HC addendum.
Source: Kay Massingill in Magonia Exchange, quoting *Lawrence Daily Journal-World* (Lawrence, Kansas) Friday, March 10, 1911.   Type: A

* * * * * * *

Location: Bindy Andy, near St George, Queensland, Australia.
Date: May 5, 1911.
Time: 5:30 p.m.

"We have received the following letter from Mr. A. W. Nixon, which will doubtless occasion surprise to readers. Mr. Nixon is in charge of a sawmilling plant at Bandy Andy, distant about 18 miles from St. George on the Mungindi Road and we think his statement can be give full credence:
Dear Sir,-On the evening of the 5th inst. About 5:30 o'clock, while I was returning from work from the top end of Bandy Andy swamp, I suddenly became aware of a strange object in the sky. You will, I feel quite sure, be better able to imagine my surprise than I am able to describe it when I tell you that clearly outlined in the heavens I unmistakably saw an object bearing for its burden two men. One man was to all appearances busy handling some machinery, which gave him a slightly stooping and then assuming a more erect position.
With each motion of the man the object in the air was affected at one time as if it would come down on a long slanting line and then just as quickly it would begin to rise again, the rise apparently being more steep than the proceeding downward movement. The object appeared to me to be about four of five hundred yards high in the air, and was not distant more than half to three quarters of a mile from where I stood had it fallen straight down to the ground. I have no object in writing you that foregoing other than others might be able to support the information I give here. I do not wish any one to think my statement an idle fabrication

and if an affidavit will serve any useful end I am quite prepared to take responsibility of making such.

One or two further small items may be mentioned as of interest to your readers. The object appeared to come from N.S.W. about from the direction of Welltown, and was traveling about north-west as near as I could judge, and should have passed close to St. George. I watched it until it disappeared into the horizon, which I should say would be fully five miles away, the clear light of the declining sun making it easy to discern till the last.

The man who worked the machinery was clad in dark clothing, but the other man was not so noticeable, whilst around the strange object there appeared to be a curious sort of quiver, giving the impression of a bad flicker in a light and of a very rapid motion something too quick for the eye to catch. I hope others will be able to write you in support of this statement, because I am fully aware that there are those who will laugh and perhaps deride this information. If so, I can't help it. But I tell you, Mr. Editor, that our first aerial visitor has come and gone. Let us hope the mission is as harmless as it was mysterious. Yours, etc."
-A.W. Young, Jnr.

HC addendum.
Source: *Zeehan and Dundas Herald* (Tasmania (Australia) 1890-1922), Wednesday 17, May 1911, also *Balonne Beacon* (St. George Queensland. 1909-1954) Sunday 13, May 1911. Type: A

* * * * * * *

Location: Chesterfield, Derbyshire, England.
Date: Summer 1911.
Time: Daytime.

While on a farm near Chesterfield, 6 year old Mary B. saw a long, black, cigar-shaped object hovering 1.5m or so from the ground. It was carrying 2 lights and a cabin in which she could see a man.

HC addendum.
Source: David Clarke citing anonymous letter from witness. Type: A

Location: Palisades Park, New Jersey.
Date: Early September, 1911.
Time: Night.

Frank Goodale, who flies his own airship nightly over Palisades Park, may go down into history as the discoverer of the 'air serpent.' He came down a few nights ago with his hair on end and scared speechless.

When he recovered he said that at a height of two thousand feet he was attacked by a long green thing that had two great wings and seemed to come out of a cloud. He was saved by the search light that was trained on him, for the creature seemed to fear the light and retreated at once to 'his' lair, wherever that was.

HC addendum.
Source: Kay Massingill in Magonia Exchange, citing *East Oregonian*, (Pendleton Oregon), September 7, 1911. Type: X

* * * * * * *

Location: Uspenskoye, Bogoroditskoye district, Tula region, Russia.
Date: 1912.
Time: Unknown.

A local unmarried woman reportedly gave birth to a bizarre (ugly) baby covered with dense fur. Despite all the mother's attempts to hide the faces, word of this event spread throughout the village and agitated the locals. The rumor was that an "evil force" was somehow responsible for the occurrence. Witnesses were also located that swore to have seen some type of flying "snake" or creature, huge in size flying over the woman's house and entering through the chimney of the wooden structure.

After interrogating the unfortunate woman about her supposed "evil lover" she felt compelled to confess a bizarre story. She publicly decried that she was deeply sorry she had cohabited with the "snake" that visited her regularly at night, which upon entering her home transformed into human form (shape shifter?). After the confession the peasants decided that the child was indeed "satanic" in nature and a peasant court was convened which decided that the unfortunate creature should be drowned.

The whole village then gathered to carry out the sentence. They hollowed a hole in the frozen river and solemnly interred the hairy "monster." When the monster (or alien) child sank, the residents of the village crossed themselves with a feeling of accomplishment to their sacred Orthodox duty and went home totally relieved.

HC addendum.
Source: Gennadiy Nikolaev, *'Anomalous News'* Moscow, #20, 2005.
Comments: Was this unfortunate child some kind of hybrid?   Type: H?

* * * * * * *

Location: Island of Muck, Highland Region, Scotland.
Date: 1912.
Time: Morning.

   The two sons of a local man, Sandy MacDonald, aged about ten and seven, were playing on the beach when they found an unopened tin. As they were trying to open it, they saw a beautiful delicate looking little boy, a stranger to the island, standing beside them. He was dressed all in green. The boy invited them to come and look at this boat, and they saw a tiny vessel floating on the sea a few feet from the shore.
   A little girl three foot high, and a dog the size of a rat were in the boat, and the girl offered the children some tiny biscuits which they ate. After they inspected the boat, which was beautifully built with everything perfectly arranged, the green boy and girl said it was time for them to leave. They said goodbye to the two boys and told them, *"We will not be coming back here, but others of our race will be coming."*

HC addendum.
Source: Janet and Colin Bord, *'Modern Mysteries of Britain.'* Type: B?
Comments: Who are the "others of our race?"

* * * * * * *

Location: Near Gallipolis, Ohio.
Date: 1912.
Time: Morning.

   A man and his mother had been out picking berries in a wooded area when they noticed a dark cloud-like object descend overhead; it then followed them at treetop level. As they walked away they noticed a figure walking parallel to them, apparently observing them. The figure was dark in color with wide shoulders, a large bulky head, and no visible neck. The woman screamed and the figure looked at them emitting a growling sound. They both ran away and looked back to see both the figure and the dark cloud gone.

HC addendum.
Source: Janet and Colin Bord, *FSR* Vol. 25 #3.   Type: C?

Location: Cologne, Germany.
Date: 1912.
Time: Afternoon.

The young witness, Ernest Dickhoff was alone in his bedroom when he felt a strong urge to look behind him. He then saw two strange beings, sitting on his bed. This appeared to be man-like, but seemed to be naked. After a short duration the beings suddenly vanished in plain sight.

HC addendum.
Source: Denys Breysse, Project Becassine.   Type: E
Comments: Must be one of the earliest "bedroom visitation" cases on record. Is unfortunate that a more detailed description of the entities is not available.

* * * * * * *

Location: Barranco de Badajoz, Tenerife, Canary Islands, Spain.
Date: 1912.
Time: Afternoon.

Several laborers working at the bottom of a local ravine saw the rock wall suddenly collapse in front of them exposing an immense passageway. At this point the workers also saw three strange beings, described as being totally white in color. As the three figures attempted to approach the laborers and according to local lore, the two workers, in a panic, ran from the area towards a nearby Civil Guard post in the town of Guimar.
Another version of the incident claims that the two laborers in fact communicated with the three white beings and were told exactly where to excavate in order to find water. Both versions are circulated in the region and the debate is lively.

HC addendum.
Source: http://www.revistamisterios.com/Revistas/Revistas070.htm
Translation by Albert S. Rosales.   Type: E

Location: Currickbilly Range, New South Wales, Australia.
Date: 1912.
Time: Night.

"A huge man-like animal" in southeast New South Wales approached surveyor, Charles Harper and his two assistants, his fierce hunting dogs retreated whining and one of his assistants fainted and "remained unconscious for several hours."

HC addendum.
Source: Tony Healey, *'High Strangeness in Yowie Reports.'*   Type: E

* * * * * * *

Location: Codigoro, Ferrara, Italy.
Date: 1912.
Time: Night.

A man was returning home when he saw a glowing sphere in the distance. Arriving at his home, he saw the object hovering just above the ground and in front of him. The man; recalling old, popular beliefs; thought that it was the "spirit of the dead," and he raised one arm, shouting loudly towards the phenomenon. Suddenly the man felt a sort of "slap" to his face, so strong that he fell to the ground. At the same time the sphere departed from the location with a wobbling motion. Later, the man noticed something resembling the imprint of a "skeleton hand" on his cheek where he received the slap.

HC addendum.
Source: Maurizio Verga, *'When Saucers came to Earth.'*   Type: F?

* * * * * * *

Location: Banks of the River Volga, Russia.
Date: January, 1912.
Time: Night.

Mr. V. Dychkin and his friend were driving during a snowy night in separate sledges along the banks of the river. Dychkin's friend was driving ahead and he was following him. Suddenly they encountered two "strangers" standing alongside of the road, and Dychkin invited them to seat on the sledges. The two strange looking men convinced Dychkin not to continue home because of the storm, but to turn to the nearest town and spend the night there. Though Dychkin knew that there weren't any towns in the area, he drove against his will in the direction where the men told him.

One of the men then pointed and yelled out, "Look, there is the town!" Dychkin looked and to his amazement saw a beautiful scene; something resembling a huge strange "city" was located on a flat plateau, illuminated by thousands of lights. The lights were positioned in a "fantastic" arrangement; he had never seen anything like it. Convinced in the reality of his vision, Dychkin turned in the direction of the lights without hesitation. His companion followed and soon approached him. Suddenly both men were seized by incredible fear and rushed towards the road, never seeing where the two strangers had gone. Dychkin looked back in the direction of the lights but was surprised to see only the night gloom and darkness.

HC addendum.
Source: *Rebus* magazine, St. Petersburg, 1914, German Mikhailov, *NLO* magazine #50. Type: G?
Comments: The lighted "city" could have been a giant spacecraft but also the possibility of parallel worlds cannot be overlooked.

* * * * * * *

Location: Velikaya Dolina, near Novorossiysk, Russia.
Date: Summer 1912.
Time: Daytime.

Witnesses saw in the blue sky the appearance of a "white circle." Within this circle appeared a large cross and some clouds. Then the clouds parted and then appeared what resembled "warriors in helmets." These began to fight with each other. Eventually the clouds became denser and covered the whole scene, the circle vanished and again there was only blue sky.

HC addendum.
Source: Mikhail Gershtein ufo_miger@mail.ru quoting witness' letter.
Type: X?

Location: Kingsland, Auckland, New Zealand.
Date: July 16, 1912.
Time: Night.

The police are investigating a 'ghost' scare at Kingsland. Several women and girls encountered a horrible figure in white, making strange noises. (No other information). Nervous persons are afraid to leave their homes after dark.

HC addendum.
Source: *Thames Star* (NZ) Vol. XLVII #10301, July 17, 1912.   Type: E?

* * * * * * *

Location: Elm Creek, Manitoba, Canada.
Date: August, 1912.
Time: Night.

"Residents of sobriety and truthfulness residing in Elm Creek in the southern portion of this province, affirm and are prepared to take oath that five weird lights are seen nightly in a field in the immediate vicinity of the town. For the past week they have been seen every night shortly before 12 o'clock and each night the number of people going to see them has increased.

Those lights are five in number and hover over a wheat field close to the ground. Men of reputation say they have walked around them and that they move from place to place but never go far from the center of the field. One man braver than the rest managed to get close enough to them to see the time by his watch in their brilliancy, but the sensation was so weird he took several days to recover his shattered nerves.

Search has been carefully made by daylight but nothing unusual has been seen in the field and the whole countryside is wondering and propounding theories, but it remains the big mystery of the territory and people from surrounding towns have come to see the strange lights. One man says that he saw what resembled the outstretched arms of a man of huge proportions surrounded by the lights which always stay a certain distance apart.

Indian legends have been handed down in the Canadian Northwest about "Wendigos" which haunt certain sections and another legend is to the effect that lights are seen at the spot where some Indian crime has been committed. These stories are about the only explanations which the people of Elm Creek can give and these they do not believe. It is probable that the lights are due to "Ignis Fatuus" or "will-o-the-wisp," as is commonly termed, due to the decaying vegetable matter giving an inflammable gas. Imagination usually produces the other effects."

HC addendum.
Source: Kay Massingill in Magonia Exchange, quoting the *Winnipeg Tribune*, (Manitoba, Canada), August 2, 1912.　　　　　Type: E?

* * * * * * *

Location: Escalante, Spain.
Date: August 11, 1912.
Time: Night.

Claudio Rey Castillo was coming home late one night when suddenly everything around him was illuminated like daytime. The light seemed to emanate from something that descended from the sky at high speed. The witness stepped back and turned around and was confronted by a huge man-like figure. It resembled a giant man that emitted intermittent flashes of white light. He could not see any features on the humanoid, which seemed to float just above the ground.

The humanoid was all white in color and moved slowly back and stopped right under the entrance to the local church. At this point the witness noticed that the figure must have been some 3.30 meters in height. Armed with a knife he moved towards the figure, which suddenly seemed to "tremble" and raised his arms up showing the palms of its hands. It then drifted back and disappeared into the darkness as the horrified witness watched.

HC addendum.
Source: Iker Jimenez, *Enigmas Sin Resolver* II.　　　　　Type: E
Comments: Other sources give the year as 1914.

* * * * * * *

Location: Bolton Abbey, Yorkshire, England.
Date: August 18, 1912.
Time: Before midnight.

Upon reaching the top of the stairs in the Rectory, the Marquis of Huntington found a strange monk-like figure standing at the doorway of his room. "There was a hood over the head and he was dressed in a long garment like a dressing-gown. The hood and shoulders seemed to be gray, but lower down the color was black or brown." The Marquis, only a boy then, ran to fetch the Rector but could not find him. By the time he returned, the specter had vanished.

HC addendum.
Source: Michael D. Winkle, *the Anomalist* #10.　　　　　Type: E

Location: Proskurov, Podolsky region, Russia.
Date: December 24, 1912.
Time: Evening.

The mayor of the village of Vyhilevka was walking towards Proskurov when he saw a dimly lit "machine" on a nearby field. He came closer and saw two men standing next to it, who seemed to be wearing military uniforms. The mayor asked the men who they were and where they were from but received no reply.

The men then chased the witness and caught him dragging him inside the "machine," despite his protests. In the air the "pilots" asked the mayor numerous questions but he refused to answer. Soon the object landed and he was released near the city of Bar, 60km from Vyhilevka. The "machine" then disappeared in an unknown direction.

HC addendum.
Source: Mikhail Gershteyn. Type: G?

* * * * * * *

Location: Caldwell, Idaho.
Date: December 29, 1912.
Time: 8:20 p.m.

"Several Caldwell citizens and farmers in this vicinity were startled last night by the sight of a rapidly moving aircraft, traveling down the Boise Valley and passing over the city. The aerial stranger was first sighted by the motorman and conductor on the Idaho Traction company car which arrives here, via Middleton, at 8:20 p.m. They and Roy Smith, who is employed in a local candy kitchen and who happened to be a passenger on the car, watched the aeroplane in its flight due south in the face of a brisk wind until it disappeared in the darkness. The machine was visible for about 10 minutes and was seen by several people. It is estimated that it was traveling at a rate of about 70 miles an hour.

In describing the nocturnal visitor today Roy Smith said: "My attention was called to the craft by the conductor on the Interurban car as we were crossing the Boise River Bridge about a mile from town. The powerful headlight carried by the machine was searching the ground in an apparent effort to locate a suitable landing place. The machine was no great distance from us and I could distinctly see the framework of an aeroplane and what appeared to be a man in the driver's seat."

Miss Harriet Cupp of this city another who saw the strange craft is quite positive in her declaration that it was an aeroplane. "When I first saw the machine it was to the north of the city and was traveling southward rapidly," she stated. "The headlight was visible for several minutes and only disappeared from view as the driver swerved into a more southerly course. I could hear the faint throb of the engines and am confident that it was an aeroplane."

G. W. Emery, a local merchant, states that he saw the airship about 8:20 last night and that it was traveling almost due south. He watched it for about 10 minutes and is positive that it carried at least one and perhaps two men.

Speculation is rife as to the identity of the air navigator and the appearance of the aeroplane is a topic of general discussion here today. Some credence is placed in a story to the effect that the airman is Silas Christofferson, the Oregon aviator, who gave an exhibition in Caldwell during the Canyon county fair. Christofferson, who was one of the stars at the aviation meet held at Tanforan Park in California last week, suddenly disappeared from the field with his machine. The birdman ascended at 4 o'clock Friday afternoon, ostensibly to give an exhibition of fancy flying. Heading his machine northward he disappeared and no trace of him has since been found.

HC addendum.
Source: Idaho Statesman (Boise, ID) December 31, 1912.	Type: A?

* * * * * * *

Location: Nuriootpa, South Australia.
Date: Circa 1913.
Time: Unknown.

A farmer discovered a metallic landed object on a field and was "zapped" by a humanoid (not described) which appeared from within it, leaving a lasting paralysis in the witness. No other information.

HC addendum.
Source: Darryl Tiggeman, Adelaide, citing Colin Norris.	Type: B

* * * * * * *

Location: Las Hurdes, Spain.
Date: 1913.
Time: Evening.

A peasant walking along a local valley called "Valle De Sapu" found his way blocked by a short stocky little man wearing a dark tight-fitting leather like outfit. For a few moments both witness and humanoid stared at each other, then the witness attempted to walk by but was prevented from doing so each time by the little man that would block his path.

Soon a struggle ensued and the witness felt the humanoid's skin and noticed that it was very rough and cold. At one point the witness managed to hit the humanoid on the head with a large piece of hard bread, the being then stepped back and shot upwards inside a beam of light and into a large circular moon-like object.

HC addendum.
Source: J. J. Benitez, *La Quinta Columna* (The Fifth Column).   Type: B

* * * * * * *

Location: Off Pentland Firth, Orkneys, Scotland.
Date: 1913.
Time: Afternoon.

The crew of a fishing vessel claimed they had seen a mermaid rising from the waters of the Pentland Firth. The creature rose to a height of three feet above the waves and was described as being like a woman with a shawl draped around her shoulders. According to the crew this sighting was their third encounters with the mysterious sea-woman.

HC addendum.
Source: Orkneyjar Folklore.   Type: E

* * * * * * *

Location: Chevroux, France.
Date: 1913.
Time: Night.

A young man walking through a wooded area on his way to join an army unit heard noises and felt a presence behind him. Upon turning around he saw a 3-meter tall human-like figure approaching him taking great strides. Terrified, the young man ran away from the area and did not look back.

HC addendum.
Source: SOS Ovni Database.   Type: E

Location: London, England.
Date: 1913?
Time: Unknown.

At the WC1 (Greater London), Old Chambers, Lincoln's Inn (no longer standing) Charles Appleby was found dead in his room there, with large claw marks on his arms and neck, the door and windows were locked from the inside. Witnesses outside the building who could see into his room through a window said they could see the man fighting a shadowy bird-like creature, though it was at least the same size as Appleby.
Reports of the creature continued for a while afterwards, and one team of investigators, who put down chalk dust during their stakeout recording finding large claw marks in the powder the following day.

HC addendum.
Source: http://paranormaldatabase.com/reports   Type: X

* * * * * * *

Location: Killary Harbor, Ireland.
Date: Late February, 1913.
Time: Unknown.

A Mr. Collins was aboard his yacht when he saw a strange "aeroplane" like object approaching from the sea. It suddenly ditched into the water near the shore. Collins then approached the craft, which was now apparently at the shore. He saw three occupants apparently working on the object. Two were tall, heavy set, blond-haired and light complexioned.
Thinking they were or German origin he asked if they needed any help in German. One of the men responded in French, claiming he could not understand, and then in no uncertain terms told the witness to leave the area. Collins quickly left and did not see the craft depart.

HC addendum.
Source: Nigel Watson.   Type: C?

Location: Beningbrough, Yorkshire, England.
Date: February 21, 1913.
Time: 9:00 p.m.

John Ripley and T. Clarke were dredging in the River Ouse between Beningbrough and Linton Docks when they observed a cigar-shaped aerial object with a central bulge, which hovered low and revolved. There were three wheels on one side of the object and another in the rear. There was a boxed-in portion where they could see a pilot. The object carried a brilliant searchlight on its side and made a strange humming sound. It disappeared about 2230 and reappeared at 0400 the next morning, disappearing at 0530 toward Easingwold.

HC addendum.
Source: David Clarke citing *Yorkshire Evening Post,* 24 February, 1913.
Type: A

* * * * * * *

Location: Near Motihari, Bihar, India.
Date: May, 1913.
Time: Various.

The Englishman's Champaran correspondent writes: Rather a strange thing is happening in this district just now. About ten or twelve days ago a small "mela" (gathering) was held at a place called Arraraj near the Tarkaulia indigo factory about nine miles from Motihari and vague reports came in that all the people who had come there had bolted in fear of something, and were collected round about Arraraj. First I heard that fire or a fiery being had descended from the heavens and was hovering about the place where the 'mela' takes place, but these were only native reports on which I placed no reliance, and thought nothing more of the matter, believing it to be a silly scare.

Since then, however, the scare has spread, and is rapidly coming down country. The native version of the affair is that a light will be seen in the distance resembling a man carrying an ordinary lantern. This light eventually becomes two lights, or three lights and generally appear in the vicinity of a village. Someone calls the attention of the other villagers to the lights and they are given the impression that they are having a visitation from ghosts or whatever they like to think of them.

They then collect and go out and approach the lights, which become more numerous covering a fairly large area, until there may be 20, 40, 60 or 100 lights. Then when they get quite close to any one light it disappears and nothing remains for them get hold of. In several cases villagers have tried to surround one of these lights. They have collected and formed a ring round it, armed with sticks but when they close in, it is said the light disappears and there is nothing to be found in the middle of the circle. Those who have seen the light at close quarters say that they thought they could make out the figure of a man, but only dimly, but that the man had no head. Some people say that the lamps are carried by a pair of hands and arms having neither body nor head.

At first it was thought that this was all a scheme of a band of dacoits (armed robbers) to frighten villagers and then loot the villages, but this business has now been going on for nearly a fort night and no looting has been reported from Arraraj. It has travelled gradually south about 40 miles, and is still travelling at this pace towards Sutamarhi. Once past it does not return. The natives are much frightened in the village where it takes place and in others where it is expected to arrive. The lights are seen on the same night in many villages, often far apart as far as 10 to 20 miles so the advance seems to cover a large front.

There have been very heavy west winds in this district this year, which have caused many bad village fires, some large villages being nearly gutted. I have heard of only one case where the fire was put down to these mysterious lights, but I expect that the fire took place from an ordinary cause and had nothing to do with the other. No damage of any sort or stealing has been reported as the result of the lights. (The rest of the narration is unreadable).

HC addendum.
Source: Kay Massingill in Magonia Exchange, citing *The Times of India* (1861-current) New Delhi, India, 17 May, 1913.   Type: X?

Location: Cova da Iria, Fatima, Portugal.
Date: May 17, 1913.
Time: Noon.

Three children were collecting their sheep about noon when they saw a flash in the sky. Later a white bright figure appeared near a tree. The entity resembled a beautiful female. A powerful bright light surrounded it. It appeared to be 12 to 15 years old, was about 4ft tall, and was wearing a tight skirt, a coat, and a cloak. Her head was covered by "something" hiding the ears and hair. Her eyes were dark.

She was carrying a string of beads around her neck and a ball of light at the waist level. She had appeared to come from the sky and vanished in stages. She did not execute any facial movements and her feet did not move while walking. She also spoke without moving her lips. Moved her hands briefly, turned back to the witnesses when leaving. This contact lasted for 20 minutes.

HC addendum.
Source: Joaquim Fernandes, Fina D'Armada.   Type: E or F?

* * * * * * *

Location: Badlands area, Montana.
Date: July, 1913.
Time: Unknown.

J. L. Buick and another prospector were startled by a small brown man saying; *"Peace be with you, my friends."* Sitting on a patch of sand was a silvery-round object nearly 100ft in diameter, with central dome and a small conning tower; no wheels underneath. Around it were other small men in brown picking flowers, pebbles, etc, and some mining a rock out-crop. The occupant told the witnesses he was from another planet, which had secretly been keeping tabs on Earth for over a hundred years; they had learned English via spies working in a US circus. The craft rose silently and then took off.

Next day it came back, and they were given a tour inside and were told; "gravity is only a different type of magnetism," so it can be controlled by an electromagnetic drive. They can do 9000 mph, and have artificial gravity inside the saucer. Rockets, they were told, had failed for space travel.

HC addendum.
Source: Witness' letter to Donald Keyhoe on Sep 24, 1956.　　Type: G

* * * * * * *

Location: Cova da Iria, Portugal.
Date: July 17, 1913.
Time: Afternoon.

The witnesses; three young shepherds, had another encounter with an entity supposed to have been the "Holy Virgin." A noise like thunder was heard before she appeared. When leaving, a noise like a rocket could also be heard.

HC addendum.
Source: Joaquim Fernandes.　　Type: E?

* * * * * * *

Location: Alcocer near Valencia, Spain.
Date: August 8, 1913.
Time: Afternoon.

According to news reports, the village of Alcocer was practically wiped out and the surrounding country ravaged by an 'aerolite' of great size. Shortly after noon there dropped from a cloudless sky a great lurid ball of fire, a deafening series of detonations like a thousand rifle shots resounded through the still atmosphere and, scattering tongues of flame in all directions, the heavy mass buried itself in the earth. The surrounding country was set on fire and within an hour nothing but blackened masses of smoldering cinders remained of farmhouses, haylofts, trees and gathered crops of hay, wheat and olives.

The whole population of Alcocer was at the moment attending a requiem service in the church, some two miles distant. But for that circumstance, the loss of life would have been terrible. As it was, five persons were seriously burned, one of them succumbing to his injuries the same evening. At the moment the aerolite fell at Alcocer a terrific thunderstorm, which was accompanied by a rain of stones some the size of oranges and weighing nearly two pounds, burst over the neighboring villages of Benavides and Cuartil. The ground was covered in places to a depth of five inches by these stones. A pungent odor of sulfur pervaded the locality for hours after the phenomenon.

HC addendum.
Source: Fabio Picasso post in Magonia list quoting *Los Angeles Times* August 10, 1913. Type: X

* * * * * * *

Location: Cova da Iria, Fatima, Portugal.
Date: August 17, 1913.
Time: Afternoon.

The three children heard a noise like thunder and lighting and a noise like "a thousand bees." While the entity spoke to the three children, a strange white smoke cloud formed over the tree where the entity appeared. Several colorful clouds were also seen in the sky, and daylight became darker than usual. The temperature went down and a quite pleasant smell was felt. Several objects were seen in the clouds, strange small balls hovered over the trees. The entity moved over "stairs of light." The sheep apparently felt a tranquilizing effect.

HC addendum.
Joaquim Fernandes. Type: F?

* * * * * * *

Location: Smolenskaya region, Russia.
Date: 1914.
Time: Unknown.

A local family living in a cabin in a remote area of the woods in this region of central Russia experienced a frightening encounter. They saw what appeared to be a strange fog or mist with sharp edges descend from the sky into a nearby meadow. Both witnesses; a woman named Nastya and her husband Demyan (a forester who worked in the area) saw the strange fog descend in the same place where their two children; a girl named Anastasiya and a boy named Herman, had been playing. Moments later, the fog suddenly zoomed up and vanished into the sky (the fog was apparently camouflaging some type of object).

The two children were now nowhere to be seen, and despite desperate attempts, they were never found; they had dissolved into thin air. Being Christian Orthodox, the parents began to pray, but later concluded that their children had been taken away by "wood goblins." In 1918, the family moved to the Krasnogvardeyskiy area of Crimea, Ukraine.

HC addendum.
Source: Andrew Zabava (Janefarlz) Ukraine.   Type: G
Comments: Appears to have been a permanent abduction.

* * * * * * *

Location: Borisovo-Romanovskiy, Alexandrovskaya volost, Russia.
Date: 1914
Time: Unknown.

Two workers of this hamlet saw something "strange," black, round and shaped like a vat or a deep circular craft flying low over the ground, and both witnesses distinctly saw two "men" sitting inside the object, in something like a cabin, in the opposite side of it, to the left and right of the direction of flight. The strange object was flying at an altitude of about 64 meters above the earth. The object quickly flew away and disappeared from sight.

HC addendum.
Source: Mikhail Rechkin, Omsk, "Crystal Pearl of Russia," Vol. 2, Moscow, 2005.   Type: A

* * * * * * *

Location: Pawtucket, Rhode Island.
Date: 1914.
Time: 3:00 p.m.

The witness; Hans M. Schnitzler, was sitting on his lawn, between his home and a low picket fence. Across the street there was a little white church with granite posts surrounding it and iron pipes running through them. Suddenly he heard a musical humming sound. At first he thought it was the clock (old pendulum clock that he was holding). He turned his head and across the street in front of the church about 25 feet from him hovered a strange object.
According to his recollection, it was about 30 feet wide and about 10 feet high. It stayed there motionless. The ship was gray in color. It had a gradual dome on top with a sharp radius coming down to a flat. The dome was about two thirds the width of it. The bottom was slightly

domed with a shaper radius going to the outer edge. The center of the dome, he thought, was about one half of the total height. As he watched; an opening appeared like two convoluted sliding doors from the center out, making an opening about four feet wide.

Two little people walked out and filed to each side of the door, walking on the flat of the ship, then two more etc, until they were eight abreast. At the time, he thought that the humanoids were children; he remembered they had arms and legs. The shape of their heads was round but he couldn't recall the faces. Then suddenly, they sang in a beautiful harmony. They sang loud and clear; a melody over and over again as if they wanted him to familiarize himself with it.

When they stopped singing, the doors opened again and they all filed back into the ship in the same order. The craft then went up slowly then gradually disappeared over the church. He later spoke to his parents about what he had seen. His mother told him (in German) that he had probably been dreaming, but his father told him that his grandfather had experienced something similar in the Black Forest in Germany.

HC addendum.
Source: Witness letter, *CUFOS Associate* newsletter Vol. 3 #6.   Type: B

* * * * * * *

Location: Santiago del Estero, Argentina.
Date: 1914.
Time: Evening.

A short dwarf-like female entity wearing shiny "flashy green clothing" chased a young child persistently in a wooded area. A similar entity pursued a young girl at another local ranch.

HC addendum.
Source: Fabio Picasso, *'Small Entities in Argentina.'*   Type: E

* * * * * * *

Location: Martilandran, Caceres, Spain.
Date: 1914.
Time: Night.

One night a local by the name of Juan Martin, known also as "el Tiu Mona" was, along with several other locals; involved in the slaughter of pigs to prepare for the coming celebrations. However when everyone sat down to enjoy the feast, they realized that they had run out of bread. The nearest bakery was located in the village of Nuñomoral located about 7 kilometers away. No one felt like walking in the dark that long of a distance except for Martin who gracefully volunteered to fetch the bread. He made it to the bakery without any incidents and obtained a large loaf of bread. However, on the way back to Martilandran, something strange happened.

Upon arriving at a location known as "Valle del Sapo," a "little man," more similar to a child than anything else, wearing a strange dark outfit, suddenly blocked his path. To Martin it seemed like an eternity as he faced off with the strange little creature standing in front of him. On two occasions he spoke to the creature, but not received no answer, so he continued his journey following the path that led him to the "little man."

Once Martin was very close to the creature it suddenly jumped up in the air and grabbed Martin by the neck; squeezing with unexpected strength. As Martin attempted to fight back he was horrified when he touched the skin of the creature, as it was very rough just like the trunk of an 'oak tree.' At one point Martin struck the creature on the side of its head with the large and hard loaf of bread. This caused the little creature to release its grip on Martin, it then, without any means of propulsion, rose up into the air and disappeared into a "bright moon" that illuminated the area like daylight.

Upon returning to the village all he managed to say to the others before collapsing was; *"If not for the bread!"* He seemed incoherent for the next several days and suffered from a high fever. From that day on he never ventured out at night and whenever he had to cross the "Valle del Sapo," he did so only accompanied by other locals.

HC addendum.
Source:http://www.looculto.260mb.com/ovnisenespana/ovnisenespana.htm   Type: B?

* * * * * * *

Location: Chanco, Maule Region, Chile.
Date: February 15, 1914.
Time: 6:00 p.m.

Published newspaper reports describe a "bolide" like object that crossed the firmament from west to east; leaving behind a white smoky trail that took about 15 minutes to dissipate. The event was also observed from Argentina in which witnesses reported a "celestial object" that emitted a large plume of white smoke from its rear, which remained visible for a long time. Witnesses thought that whatever it was had crashed into the Pacific Ocean or Chile.

A local witness; 104-year old Juana Anduar, only 14-years old at the time, remembers that the classes were dismissed early and everyone stopped what they were doing to watch the strange spectacle. Anduar remembers seeing an object approaching from the west in the shape of a modern "airplane fuselage." It flew diagonally emitting a tremendous noise.

The frightened witnesses could see what appeared to be flames behind the object. The object apparently impacted into an isolated area in the forest, quickly producing a large fire. According to reports, searchers failed to locate a crater or any signs of the object. Some in the area speculate that the object remains buried underground.

HC addendum.
Source: Josep Guijarro, *Año Cero* #10.   Type: H?
Comments: Is this one of the earliest UFO crash reports?

* * * * * * *

Location: Lajoumard, Limousin, France.
Date: March, 1914.
Time: Evening.

A farmer, now deceased, was returning to his farmhouse at twilight when he chanced to see, atop a nearby hill, a round luminous object. It was green in color, hovering just above the ground. When he was about 100 to 200 meters away, he saw several beings of small stature emerge from the machine, stroll about briefly, and then disappear once again inside. The object then took off in a spiral, or zigzag, trajectory, and then streaked off at very high speed. He spoke to his family of the incident and asked that they never speak of it to anyone else. It was only after his death that the incident was revealed.

HC addendum.
Source: Joel Mesnard and Jean Marie Bigorne.   Type: B

* * * * * * *

Location: Quitman, Mississippi.
Date: April 20, 1914.
Time: Night.

It's beginning to look as if the days of the "wampus" are numbered. At least that is what the (blacks) about here declare. A strange something passed over the black section of Quitman last night just before the moon went down. Many saw it and swear that it was a flying dog. It gave a yelp or so as it cleared the valley like a bolt of lightning and the blacks vow that a dog-shaped form and the flapping of wings could be plainly seen.

Lights went out quickly and a barricading of doors started simultaneously with the first sight of the thing. The blacks insist that the thing was a "wampus proof" dog that has sprung up to outwit the doings of a strange animal that bleached the yards and commons of the black section with the skeletons of 102 dogs by actual count during the high waters of last spring.

When seen, the 'wampus proof thing' was flying in a northeasterly direction. Various controversies have arisen over the probable course of the thing's flight. Most of the blacks allow that it was making for Marion Alabama, where the "wampus" was last heard of.

HC addendum.
Source: *The State Paper*, South Carolina, April 21, 1914.   Type: E?

* * * * * * *

Location: 2.5 miles W of Farmersville, Texas.
Date: Early May, 1914.
Time: 10:00 a.m.

Silbie J. Latham, then 13 or 14, had gone to the fields with his two older brothers Sid and Clyde. Two dogs, Bob and Fox, accompanied them. They were "chopping cotton" when they heard the two dogs start up a "deathly howl." The three boys walked about 75 feet to a fencerow where the dogs had something cornered. Clyde got there first and turned to the other two and said, *"Boys, there's something in there. It must be something kinda bad."* Then he said, *"Boys, it's a little man!"* Silbie looked and saw a little man some 18 inches high, just standing still, staring toward the north.

He was green all over and either naked or with a frogman's type outfit on, green in color. There was a hat with a wide brim on the back of his head, but it was all of one piece with the rest of the body. He said nothing and did not even acknowledge the dogs, by now worked up to a frenzy. Right after the three boys arrived, the dogs finally attacked the being, killing it. They told their folks but no one believed them; they went back to the site several times that day, but after that they never returned.

HC addendum.
Source: Ted Bloecher.   Type: H

Location: Blida, Algeria.
Date: Summer 1914.
Time: Night.

Right before the declaration of war (WWI), a French settler was walking back home from the fields after turning on the irrigation valves, when he watched a large luminous sphere flying over the fields and then land silently only a few meters from his location. Afraid, the witness quickly hid behind a hedge and was able to see several short figures exit the sphere. The figures wore helmets and light-colored combination suits.

These spread about on the field moving very quickly appearing to collect samples from the ground. After a few minutes, the short figures re-entered the landed sphere, which then took off and quickly disappeared from sight. The next day, other neighboring farmers reported that they had seen a luminous sphere flying over the fields the night before.

HC addendum.
Source: Le Forum De L'Ufologie, France.   Type: B

* * * * * * *

Location: Hamburg, Germany.
Date: June, 1914.
Time: 4:00 a.m.

05 oder 06.1914, Hamburg
(c) MUFON-CES

Gustav Herwager, who worked in a bakery at the outskirts of Hamburg, had gone outside at 4 in the morning when he observed a cigar-shaped object a short distance away, hovering close to the ground. It was illuminated from within and was surrounded by a halo of light. A series of illuminated windows were arranged along its rim. Four or five little "humans," at most 1.20 m tall, and all of them wearing the same kind of suit, stood next to the object.

When they noticed the witness, they rapidly ran towards the spaceship and entered it by means of a ladder. After the ladder was withdrawn, the sliding door closed noiselessly. The object rose vertically without making a sound and disappeared. The witness died in 1933, but his children submitted the report to the publisher of the *UFO-Nachrichten* (UFO News) where it appeared in April 1962.

HC addendum.
Source: Jacques Vallee, *Passport to Magonia*, quoting *UFO-Nachrichten* issue No. 68. Type: B

* * * * * * *

Location: Spike Island, Cork Harbor, Ireland.
Date: June, 1914.
Time: Afternoon.

The witness was walking along a path located next to the sea, absorbed in her memories with her eyes mostly on the ground. She happened to look up when she was about five yards away from the wall of a local doctor's house and saw something bizarre. A strange figure was looking over the wall across the harbor to Cobh. She walked a few more steps nearer before she realized what it was, and then she became rooted to the ground with fear. It was not ten paces away and she could see it only too clearly.

It must have been a very tall creature that was looking over the wall, because she could almost see it to its waist; and the wall was at least five feet high. It was in the rough shape of a human being; that is, it had a head and shoulders and arms; though she did not see the hands, which were behind the wall. Except for two dark caverns, which represented the eyes, the whole thing was of one color; a sort of glistening yellow. As the wall was parallel to the road and on her left, the thing was looking past her; across the little road and straight across to Cobh.

As the witness stood petrified, the thing began to turn its head very slowly toward her. At this point the young witness heard a voice in her ear; "If it looks straight at you, Eileen, you will die." Her feet seemed to be anchored to the ground by heavy weights, but somehow she managed to turn and run. She ran into a nearby cottage about 15 yards away. Her next memory was of Mrs. Reilly (the owner of the cottage) sponging her face with water, as she shook all over with shock and terror. She told Mrs. Reilly that she had seen something dreadful in the Doctor's garden. Mrs. Reilly told the young witness that she was not the first to see it and would not be the last.

HC addendum.
Source: Dermot Mac Manus, *'The Middle Kingdom.'* Type: E
Comments: It has become painfully clear that there exists in our midst terribly entities with boundless powers, we must tread lightly upon encountering them.

* * * * * * *

Location: V'jukhino near Strizhov, Russia.
Date: August 2, 1914.
Time: Daytime.

Two local peasant females were in a field when they noticed two strange figures on a remote and isolated meadow. The strange couple was dressed in unusual "red suits" and moving near something grayish that lay on the ground. Both women became frightened and ran away from the area. Another peasant reported that something "big and dark" flew in the direction of the meadow. The object emitted a "rustling" sound as it flew over his head.

HC addendum.
Source: Mikhail Gershtein, Anton Anfalov. Type: C

* * * * * * *

Location: St. Didier sur Rochefort, Loire, France.
Date: August 4, 1914.
Time: 4:00 a.m.

A Mr. Perret was at home sleeping when someone tapping on his back suddenly awakened him. He turned and saw a luminous being the size of a 10-12 year old child. The being had a white glittering face and wore a very shiny outfit. The being had come out of his grandparent's bedroom; it went in the direction of the opposite wall and passed close to the bed, then looked at the witness and smiled.
He illuminated the room completely; the being then walked through the door and vanished. An afterglow remained behind for about 3 seconds. The frightened witness remained in bed.
It is said that on the night of September 8, 1914, at nearby Mont Verdun, a procession of "beings of light" climbed the steep slope, entered the old priory and disappeared inside.

HC addendum.
Source: LDLN #243. Type: E

Location: Asanova, Sarinskaya volost, Perm, Russia.
Date: August 7, 1914.
Time: Unknown.

In an area of south of Krasnoufimsk, there were mass observations of mysterious flying devices. The population became extremely anxious and local newspapers "The Ural Life" and 'Zauralsky kray" reported about the events. On the above date a strange flying device landed near the village of Asanova with two unknown persons onboard. The local clerk shot three times at the uninvited visitors, but without result. The Bashkirs (people of Bashkir nationality) who saw the two "men" close enough reported that they were dressed warmly (details remained unclear).

HC addendum.
Source: *Zauralsky kray* newspaper, Russia, August, 1914.   Type: A?

* * * * * * *

Location: Hatloryille, Pennsylvania.
Date: August 8, 1914.
Time: Night.

Three respectable residents of Hatloryille have been telling of strange pictures seen by them in the sky on the 8th of August. Harry Hudleson was returning from Nescopeck when his attention was attracted to the sky and, he says, he was startled to see a picture of an immense house, filled with children dressed in white, with a black band on the arms of each. As he stood looking, the children came out of the house in columns of two, dividing at the door, with each column going in an opposite direction. He says he was not dreaming and the sight was to plain to be mistaken.

Later he learned that Mrs. Ruth Lutz, a neighbor, also had seen an immense house in the clouds. The effect was that of a picture thrown on a screen. Miss Pearl Puirsel, knowing nothing of the experiences of the others, made known that she had seen the form of an angel outlined in the heavens.

HC addendum.
Source: Kay Massingill in Magonia exchange group quoting Hawera and Normanby Star, NZ Volume LXVIII, 6 October, 1914.   Type: A or E?

Location: Georgian Bay, Ontario, Canada.
Date: Late August, 1914.
Time: 5:00 p.m.

William J. Kiehl, 18, with seven other people and a deer, watched a strange machine floating in a cove, with five little men in light brown clothes and square helmets taking a hose out of the water. When one of these went into the craft, Kiehl could see inside "a light green cone" with "some kind of net in the center and some pipe in front." The vessel was gray and looking like dented lead, perhaps 15ft high, with a silver band around it. It emitted multi-colored flashes, then (although one little man was still hanging on outside) it rose about 12ft. After pausing while water drained from its "square looking" bottom, it took off silently, trailing white vapor.

HC addendum.
Source: Letter to J. A. Hynek.   Type: A

* * * * * * *

Location: Alastaro, Finland.
Date: End of August, 1914.
Time: About noon.

A 10-year old boy; Arvo Kuoppala, was sitting in the living room of a farmhouse with his grandmother, Maria Falt, when suddenly it became dark outside like an eclipse of the sun, and a loud blowing noise could be heard. Then a bright wall of light came from the east and soon after a large shining globe became visible.

The globe approached the house and stopped outside the window, after which, an oval window opened on its side through which the top part of two male beings could be seen. The larger one of the beings was in the middle of the oval-shaped window, the second was more to the side but also well visible. Their heads were large in comparison to their bodies; the faces were broad and angular, but the eyes appeared friendly.

The being that was standing on the side was more midget-like and looked "ugly." Arvo became terrified by the thought that the men could come in through the window, but his grandmother assured him that they would not, that they only had "something" to say. The larger humanoid now began to smile and started to speak. His lips and face moved as if he was speaking but no voice was heard. Arvo exclaimed with excitement, *"He is talking; he is saying something!"* and immediately after, the creature ceased talking and the face abruptly disappeared inside the globe, although no movement could be seen when the oval opening closed.

After a moment a loud "thump" was heard, and then a bright flash and the object rose to into the sky and vanished towards the west with great speed. The observation had lasted only some minutes, but Arvo felt tired and went immediately to sleep, waking up later in the evening. His grandmother seems to have anticipated the event and she later told Arvo that the strangers were not from heaven, but from a distant place, and the globe was intended to travel short distances and that it had come from a "sky" ship to which it had also returned.

Of the beings she said that they had large heads and were much more intelligent than humans, but somehow were related to us, and visited now and then. It seems clear that she had a lot of information about the humanoids and she claimed to have made an observation by herself years earlier (no details on that).

HC addendum.
Source: Heikki Virtanen, Finland. Type: A

* * * * * * *

Location: Caerphilly, Wales.
Date: September, 1914.
Time: Afternoon.

Two persons, Mr. Uden and Mr. Hopkins, recall they were wandering on a mountainside after school on their way home, when they suddenly encountered a widespread mist at the edge of which were two small humanoid figures totally white all over. They advanced towards the children who became frightened and fled. Both beings wore abnormally tall hats, rather like those worn by chefs, and had piercing eyes.

HC addendum.
Source: Rupert Drew. Type: E

* * * * * * *

Location: Greytown, South Africa.
Date: September, 1914.
Time: Evening.

A farmer encountered a machine resembling a biplane while walking home across the veldt. Nearby were 2 pilots paling water from a stream. There were few, if any, viable planes in the country at the time.

HC addendum.
Source: *FSR* Vol. 8 #3. Type: C?

Location: Hurtsugly, Harahusovskiy area, Astrakhan region, Russia.
Date: September 23, 1914.
Time: 3:30 a.m.

A witness named Vasiliy Alexandrovich Sokolov; a contractor for stone works, had stopped to spend the night at the small village. After drinking tea, early in the morning he continued on his journey. He went to the yard, harnessed his horse, but did not get far away when a bright star-like object suddenly appeared in the sky. The object began increasing in size, descending from its high altitude, moving in a declining trajectory.

Soon he began to make out a cigar-shaped body, outlined in a bright light. The cylinder was brown in color, with a bright light on the front. The half-moon was shining and the stars were visible, and the sky was completely cloud free. Then the witness saw a kind of "suspended boat" under the cigar-shaped object; it was about 7 times smaller than the cigar-shaped object. The shadows of several men could be seen in it. In total there were six "men." Five of them were sitting and one was standing, as he looked higher than the rest.

The witness did not see the figures move or hear any sound. The object was seen in front of him towards the village of Harahusy. After seeing this the witness became afraid and ran to the yard, yelling at those present to switch the light of the room off and calling the Tatars there to come outside and watch the object. Then a beam of light projected from the cigar-shaped object, flashing like a thunderbolt, which lit a square on the ground and temporarily blinded the witness.

At this very same moment the cigar-shaped object turned perpendicular to the previous direction of flight with its front lighted section pointed towards Astrakhan. The light became dim and decreased in size. During the turn of the object a fast moving device was noticed on the stern section of the craft. The witness saw the object for about 10 minutes.

Then the object turned and flew northward vanishing from sight. Sokolov was convinced that he had seen some kind of foreign dirigible. An official inquest was conducted by the chairman of the Kalmyk Province, B. Krishtafovich. Authorities in Saint Petersburg had been worried about possible German dirigibles penetrating Russian territory.

HC addendum.
Source: Mikhail Gershtein, *'Mystery of the Astrakhanian Steppes,'* *'Crossroads of Centaurs'* #2, 1999. Type: A

Location: Portland, Oregon.
Date: October 7, 1914.
Time: 20:00-22:00

"A real sure-enough ghost at large on Portland's streets? But read what Patrolman Ben F. Hunt, a prosy policeman, says in his report for the "first relief" last night:
"People living in the vicinity of Tenth and Columbia Streets report the appearance every evening between the hours of 8:30 and 10 o'clock of a tall man in black coat and stiff hat who vanishes into thin air when approached. This mysterious person is said to appear regularly at the southwest corner of the intersection of these streets."
The policeman goes on to say that no one has been able to come close enough to this specter to describe him minutely, but that the "spook's" appearances are causing much alarm in that neighborhood.
"He must have some hole to hide in," comments the policeman but he fails to say what need a regular ghost would have of a place to hide when a mysterious disappearance is supposed to be a spook's long suit."

HC addendum.
Source: *Oregonian* (Portland, Oregon) Tuesday, Oct 8, 1914.   Type: E

* * * * * * *

Location: Near Cochabamba, Bolivia.
Date: December 6, 1914.
Time: 3:47 a.m.

David Mendiola Vilchez; an elderly man, was living in an isolated area near a cemetery when, one night while sleeping, claims he heard a noise which he eventually compared to that of an airplane; turbine engine coming from outside. Going out to investigate, he saw a large gray metallic cigar-shaped craft that appeared to be encircled in "electricity," descending in a nearby field.
Approaching the area, he was suddenly surrounded by a white bright light and found himself inside the craft surrounded by several "monstrous" beings which he described as very tall and thin, with huge eyes. Their skin appeared to be covered in a sort of "disgusting" mucous substance or cartilage-like material; he claims that their legs resembled that of octopi. He also revealed that he was examined by the humanoids but does not recall any additional details. There is a possibility of some missing time.

HC addendum.
Source: Lucy Guzman lucy@ovni.net   Type: G

Comments: Very early abduction tale if true. Apparently the witness passed on the details of his encounter to his children and then them to his grandchildren.

* * * * * * *

Location: Montes de Leon, Leon, Spain.
Date: Late December, 1914.
Time: 5:30 p.m.

Independent witnesses living on the outskirts of this city reported seeing two identical, tall thin figures that carried something on their backs resembling rucksacks. Both humanoids were about two meters in height and walked in unison along a path. They seemed to be joined together by one of the arms. Both wore tight-fitting green-colored shiny coveralls. At one point both figures suddenly rose into the air and disappeared into the distance.

HC addendum.
Source: Iker Jimenez, 'Encuentros: La Historia de Los Ovni en España.'
Comments: Translated by Albert S. Rosales. Type: E

* * * * * * *

Location: Sant Agata di Puglia, Italy.
Date: 1915.
Time: Unknown.

An undocumented report stating that several locals captured a "little green man." No other information.

HC addendum.
Source: Giuseppe Stilo. Type: H?

* * * * * * *

Location: Cornwall/Devon border, England.
Date: 1915.
Time: Daytime.

Witness saw a small man dressed in black "strutting about." Shortly afterwards, he shape-shifted into something like a black, long, furry "roll." Minutes later, she came upon two more roundly-shaped pixies who were apparently operating a two-man saw; but it was invisible. She stumbled on stones in the path and the beings vanished. Inspecting the site, she noticed that one of the two pixies must have been either airily lightweight or suspended in the air, as there was nothing but a gorse bush under it.

HC addendum.
Source: *Fortean Times,* 1993.   Type: E
Cmments: Date is approximate.

* * * * * * * *

Location: Fatima, Portugal.
Date: 1915.
Time: Various.

Another local resident; Carolina Carreira, reported encountering a strange entity which appeared to her inside a cone-shaped beam of light which would gradually approach and retreat from her. This cone or beam of light seemed to emanate from a strange cloud that would drift against the wind above the area. She told investigators years later that she had heard about 'the other rumors' in which the young shepherds encountered other entities including the Holy Virgin Mother.

HC addendum.
Source: Miguel Pedrero, *Año Cero* XXI Nr. 05-238.   Type: F?

* * * * * * * *

Location: Jicotea Las Villas, Cuba.
Date: 1915.
Time: Late evening.

Two men were patrolling the edge of a sugarcane field on horseback when suddenly, as they neared a bend on the trail, the horses stopped and would not move; snorting as if in a panic. The men then noticed what appeared to be a small white sack-like "bundle" on the ground near the trail. Both men had the impression that whatever it was, it was a "living" thing. The bundle began approaching the now terrified horses.
One of the men that was armed with a pistol fired several shots at the thing. Both men were then astonished to see that the "bundle" seemed to become larger every time it was shot at. When it almost as large as the horse, the men panicked and fled the area on foot, leaving the horses behind. The next day both horses were found wandering the fields apparently unharmed.

HC addendum.
Source: Story told to me by my grandmother Aurora on several occasions. Type: E

* * * * * * *

Location: Near Wann, Oklahoma.
Date: 1915.
Time: Night.

A young man named Crum King, who lived southeast of Wann, was returning home from a dance one night when he saw something near the gate of his house. "It was about five or six feet tall and it stood with its arms stretched out," King recalled in 1975. "It was about four feet wide in the chest and hairy all over. It was like a bear or something, but it stood up like a man." Terrified, King fled; he told no one of the strange encounter.

HC addendum.
Source: Jerome Clark and Loren Coleman, *'Creatures of the Goblin World.'* Type: E

* * * * * * *

Location: Cabeco, Portugal.
Date: April, 1915.
Time: Afternoon.

The young shepherd; Lucia Abadoro, along with Maria Rosa Matias, Teresa Matias and Maria Justino were walking along a hill when they saw suspended in the air, over some nearby trees, a figure resembling a statue made out of snow. The rays of the sun seemed to shine right through it given it a transparent appearance; it resembled a person wearing a white sheet; no eyes or hands could be seen.

HC addendum.
Source: Enrique De Vicente, *Año Cero*. Type: E

Location: Sulitjelma, Norway.
Date: Summer 1915.
Time: Unknown.

The witness saw a dark, bell-shaped craft descend and land, apparently behind a nearby hill. Two short humanoids emerged from behind the hill and walked towards the witness, one stopped and smiled. The humanoids had long wavy dark hair; gray skin and the heads were big in comparison to their body. Both wore dark brown overalls. The humanoids then walked behind the hill and shortly thereafter, the bell-shaped craft rose and disappeared.

HC addendum.
Source: Ole Jonny Braene, Pre-1947 UFO Type incidents in Norway.
Type: C

* * * * * * *

Location: Near Panovo, Totemskiy area, Vologda region, Russia.
Date: Summer 1915.
Time: Daytime.

A young boy; Pafnutiy Senyukov, was pasturing some cows several kilometers away from the village and was sitting under a tree watching the cows peacefully graze. Suddenly, with a loud howling sound, the cows rushed out of the field. Some ran to a nearby copse and others to the river. When Pafnutiy looked towards the sky he saw a strange cloud that seemed to appear from nowhere; the cloud then seemed to become concentrated and get denser in the middle.

Gradually, the cloud became a strange round object, like "a sphere made out of pastry" of a very large size. The object descended and began to hover low, just above the grass. Then inside the object, something resembling "a peapod" seemed to open up on the surface of the craft (resembling an elongated segmented door). A beam of light was projected from this opening and then an awful looking "scarecrow" like creature traveled within the beam of light to the ground. Then a second such creature appeared, slipping down the beam of light, in the same manner as the first.

The terrified boy rolled himself into a ball after seeing the "scarecrow like creatures." He first thought that he was having some type of terrible vision so he jumped to his feet and yelled out some curse words and cracked his whip onto the ground; apparently in a futile attempt to scare off his "vision." But it had the opposite effect, the entities turned toward him and at this point the boy could see them better. The entities seemed to have flat bodies, elongated like a slab of cardboard, thin, with long arms.

Instead of normal heads they had something resembling "buckets.' Moments later something resembling "fog" or a mist began flowing from the humanoids, immediately the boy was knocked down to the ground, having the feeling of being pressed down by a powerful current of air, he couldn't move a muscle. Then both "scarecrows" returned to their sphere, the elongated segmented door closed and then the object zoomed up into the sky, disappearing in seconds, leaving only lighted specks in the air, like snowflakes that stayed for a while and then melted away. The boy mentioned his experienced in the village but was not believed.

HC addendum.
Source: Georgiy Markovich Naumenko, *'Extraterrestrials and Earthlings: Testimonies and Contacts,'* Moscow, 2007. Type: B

* * * * * * *

Location: Kazan region, Russia.
Date: September, 1915.
Time: Evening.

Local people heard and saw an object similar to a dirigible; a huge balloon with a motor roaring in the air and with spotlights shining down. Also reported were a cigar-shaped object with a fin that hovered over a village and six humanoid shapes in a "boat" under the object's "belly."

HC addendum.
Source: Phillip Mantle and Paul Stonehill *'UFO-USSR.'* Type: A

* * * * * * *

Location: Linakjula, Kihnu Island, Estonia, USSR.
Date: October, 1915.
Time: Evening.

Tiju Vezik from nearby Nada Estate was on her way to the local post office in order to mail some correspondence. Only the moon lighted the plain. As she approached the opening of the fence surrounded by overgrown weeds at the Koidu Estate in order to get onto the road, she suddenly noticed three strange entities near some houses. These were apparently males of colossal height and in dark clothing.

The three huge figures moved soundlessly and quickly under the moonlight, parallel to the road near two women that seemed unaware of their presence. The three entities moved single file, like soldiers and at times would stop and briefly bend down and then continue on their strange procession. They crossed the field which was about 100 meters wide and disappeared under the pine trees. The stunned witness noticed that their heads touched the lower branches of the pine trees, thus making their height about 4 meters. Fearing that the entities might return, the frightened witness returned to her home.

HC addendum.
Source: Yuri Linna, Estonia and Mikhail Gershtein, Saint Petersburg.
Type: E

* * * * * * *

Location: Aldeburgh. Suffolk, East Anglia, England.
Date: 1916.
Time: 11:55 a.m.

Mrs. Agnes Whiteland had gone upstairs just before the midday dinner, and opened a casement window and looked out to see who might be on the road. Having looked both ways and noticing that nobody was in sight, she was about to step back when something urged her to look again.

A little above the level of the house, at a height of about 30ft., eight to twelve men appeared, on what seemed to be a round platform with a handrail around it. This they gripping tightly. She could see them so clearly. They were wearing blue uniforms and little round hats, not unlike sailors' hats. She heard no sound from the machine as it came off the nearby marshes. It turned a bit, and went over the railway yard, to disappear behind some houses.

The time was close to 12 o'clock noon. When she first caught sight of this platform with men on it coming towards her, at about roof height; it seemed to have come over the Marsh Gate. This was a five-barred gate with a smaller one beside it for the footpath, and a few railings with a fairly large house on the left as seen from where she was at the bedroom window.

The thing came straight along the road, and then when she thought it was going to pass her house (one of the terraced black of six), it suddenly turned away at right angles from her and went between the Railway Hotel and the sheds on either side of the railway yard. The shed opposite the house was maybe 23 to 25 ft. high; it was two stories, and hay was stored in the upper part, and the thing just cleared its roof, from what Mrs. Whiteland said.

She says the number of men was between 8 and 12, and she is certain it was nearer 12, as they stood around on this circular platform, holding tightly on to the handrail. The rail was of brass, and a second rail, also of brass, was at the height of the men's knees. As she was trying so hard to take it all in, she cannot say of what material the platform seemed to be made. She says, 'It made me think of a bathing-raft.' These were the type of rafts used in the sea at that time, about 12 feet across and six-sided, so that people could dive off them. She thought that the thickness or depth of the 'platform' was about 12 to 12in. The men were dressed in blue, with round blue hats (round without any stiffening) pulled tightly on to their heads. They stood shoulder to shoulder looking straight outwards, with ordinary faces like us, but staring straight ahead.

She kept wondering what was making the thing move, and looked up in the sky and then at the men and then in between their legs to see if there was an engine there in the middle, but she could see nothing there. There was nothing in the middle, just a hollow, with the men around the sides. She says there was no sound at all. 'It just came along straight, not up or down or anything, till it turned away and over the top of the roof of the shed and away over the railway-station yard and straight towards Aldeburgh Lodge and the trees ¼ mile away. It kept getting smaller, and went behind the trees or the house. If they had not been in the way. She would have seen it go right out to sea. The whole occurrence lasted for about five minutes or so, as she says the platform moved as fast as a man can run.

HC addendum.
Source: Gordon Creighton, *FSR* 15 # 1 quoting the *Daily Mirror*, August 8, 1968.
Comments: Illustration courtesy of David Sankey.   Type: A
Additional details:

Figure 1. Agnes Whiteland and grandson.

The single biggest problem was being able to determine when exactly this incident took place. According to Agatha, it was mid First World War, which would make it 1916. What a shame we didn't have a date to work to, although we took note of what Alfred had said with regard to him starting school at three-and-a half years of age, which could have meant an earlier period of, say, 1914 but one's impression is that it this had been the case surely Agatha would have remembered it as pre-war rather than more likely to have occurred during the War.

The fact that no rope, or securing wire, was seen by the witness appear to have been forgotten by many, who were adamant that Mrs. Whiteland had seen an Airship; a conclusion no doubt drawn from numerous reports of Airships having been seen in 1909, five years before the First World War, airships that were, by the way as we understand, only capable of short flights of 20 minutes or so; hardly capable then of flying over England and certainly not capable of making sharp turns in the air, as pointed out by Mrs. Maitland.

In a letter written to Mr. C. Grove by Charles H. Gibbs-Smith - the Aviation Historian at the Victoria & Albert Museum, during 1968; then regarded as the leading authority on aeronautical history in the UK, he was to state categorically, quote: *'There is not the remotest possibility that what Mrs. Whiteland saw was anything to do with Zeppelins!'* and enclosed a copy of an observation device, as used by the airships, which according to him, *'was used when the airship was flying above cloud cover, never suspended near the ground, since they could be easily attacked by gunfire. There are many other reasons why the platform could not have been hanging from the Zeppelin. As you point out, a turn of 90 degrees would have been impossible. I find your remarks about the thickness of the rope required to support such a platform as great interest.'*

According to Douglas H. Robinson in Giants in the sky: a history of the rigid airship (G.T. Foulis, 1973: ISBN 0-85429-145-8) cloud cars or spähkorb were used solely by German Army airships between 1914 and 1917. He describes them as follows: *'A small streamlined nacelle hanging in clear air half a mile below the Zeppelin and connected by telephone with the control car, it enabled an observer to direct the airship hidden in the clouds above. With its steel cable and winch driven off one of the airship's engines, it weighed over half a ton'.* (p.361) the cloud car had been designed by Oblt. Z.S.d.R. Lehmann and his executive officer Freiherr von Gemmingen, Count Zeppelin's nephew. Robinson states that the cloud car was overrated because of its appearance in films after the war and that there was only one raid in which it was used for its specific purpose. The naval service rejected the car on account of its weight.

Army airship operations were officially terminated in June, 1917, by the O berste Heeresleitung when incendiary ammunition used by the Allies and the increased accuracy of Allied interceptors made them obsolete. All remaining German Army airships were handed over to the German Navy so that they could be used for training. We learnt the East Coast of England was attacked soon after midnight on the 16th of April, 1916, by two Zeppelins flying over Norfolk. Both airships were seen coming from Lowestoft, heading South-west towards London, where they dropped bombs at Malden, thirty miles from London.

A dispatch to the London Daily Chronicle tells us an aircraft; apparently a zeppelin; was seen over Dagenham at midnight, having come from over the sea and proceed at a rapid rate, towards East Mersea, where bombs were dropped at Lowestoft. Three raids were carried out on the 31st of July, 2nd August and 8th August 1916, all made during the late evenings. On October 16th 1916, England was again under attack by Zeppelin Bombers. On this occasion, one of the airships was shot down in flames over London.

The authorities had ample warnings of the Airships after the Dutch authorities had telegrammed England. Notices were then sent to Police Stations of some of the East and South coast towns, notifying them of possible 'aerial visitors.' Mrs. Whiteland said it was summer but could it have been spring? Unfortunately, while there may always be some confusion as to when this happened, there is no confusion as to the time; midday, which means we should rule out the above Airship attacks as being responsible.

Again, common sense dictates the German Airships would never fly during the day, as this would render them vulnerable to attack either by the RFC; the Army's Royal Flying Corps., or the Royal Naval Air Service (RNAS), although nine Airships did make a daylight raid on the 13th January, 1916, intending to attack Liverpool but made a mistake and dropped bombs over Tipton, causing damage and loss of life.

We scoured the Internet trying to find just one report involving a sighting of some of the crew of an airship suspended from an observation platform, (known as a sub cloud car) known as 'spahkorben' and eventually found a reference contained in a book 'Zeppelins of World

War 1 by Wilbur Cross, when during a raid over England the winch mechanism used to lower and raise the sub cloud car (weighing nearly half a ton) was damaged leaving the observer dangling below (on a rope allegedly to be several thousand feet in length). As it began its journey homeward the Zeppelin was unable to maintain its height due to previous damage and was forced to descend and deposit its cargo onto the ground, where the observer scrambled out, and was arrested two months later in the Sussex area, unfortunately Wilbur Cross does not identify the name, date or location of where this incident took place, although we were able to identify it as being from the LZ90, found near Colchester on the night of the 2nd/3rd of September 1916, the damaged winch was found near Bury St Edmonds. According to the Imperial War Museum the car which is on display in the museum is 4.3meters long and 1.16m wide and weighs 54 kilogram.

We were to discover the cloud car or sub cloud car was essentially a small cigar shaped one man observation platform mainly used by the German Army Schutte-Lanz airships constructed of wood, as opposed to the Naval Zeppelin which were made of aluminum, the use of the German Army Airships were generally discontinued by 1916, which tells Us whatever Agness saw was certainly not likely to have been any airship Or sub cloud car, bearing in mind, that there appears to have been only One raid over England involving the lowering of a cloud car. (As above) So strictly speaking for this present time this was a UFO, as opposed to Having any connection with a German Zeppelin or cloud car. (Sources as above in addition thanks go to Rebecca S. Hawley, Imperial War Museum and Cardington Airship Museum)

* * * * * * *

Location: Fatima, Portugal.
Date: Early 1916.
Time: Unknown.

The young shepherds (involved in numerous events) on one occasion saw what appeared to be a 'transparent cloud' containing what appeared to be a human figure inside of it. On another occasion they saw a light flying over their heads and inside of it they could see a short child-like figure. No other information.

HC addendum.
Date: Miguel Pedrero, *Año Cero* XXI #05-238.   Type: A?

Location: Lake Superior area, Wisconsin.
Date: February 29, 1916.
Time: 4:30 a.m.

Dock workers observed what one called a "big machine 50 feet wide and 100 feet long," pass rapidly overhead. It had three lights, one on each end, and one in the middle and carried a long rope or cable trailing below. Three men were visible inside of it.

HC addendum.
Source: Jerome Clark, 'The Unexplained.' Type: A

* * * * * * *

Location: Near Hines, Wisconsin.
Date: March 3, 1916.
Time: Evening.

F. A. Porter, a farmer residing near Hines, today reported to the sheriff that last evening a large 'aeroplane' landed in a field adjoining his farm home. When he went out to investigate, one of three men met him and asked him to keep away. According to Porter the aeroplane rested in his field for a half hour. In then sailed away in the direction of Superior.

HC addendum.
Source: Kay Massingill in Magonia Exchange groups quoting Aberdeen American (Aberdeen SD) Sunday, March 5, 1916. Type: C?

* * * * * * *

Location: Cabeco near Cova da Iria, Portugal.
Date: April, 1916.
Time: Noon.

Three young cousins were in a field when they felt a strong gust of wind. They then saw a brilliant light, hovering above some olive trees and within the light they could see a white figure resembling a crystal statue with rays of the sun coming through it. They described the figure as resembling a very handsome young man, which then approached them floating in mid-air, telling the children not to be afraid. He said he was the "angel of peace" and told the girls to play and to sacrifice themselves. He gave two of the children something to drink and something resembling "piece of bread" to Lucia, the main witness.

When the figure disappeared, the children remained paralyzed; repeating the same prayers over and over and did not recover until sunset. The second encounter with the "angel," occurred on a hot summer day that same year. The entity suddenly appeared to them, calling to them and demanding that they pray fervently and to "make sacrifices" in their daily lives. The children remained paralyzed during the encounter. Only at dusk where they able to move again, they refused to speak about the encounter among themselves.

HC addendum.
Source: Enrique De Vicente, *Año Cero*.   Type: E

* * * * * * *

Location: Stavanger, Norway.
Date: April 16, 1916.
Time: Unknown.

Several children playing outside witnessed a black cloud appear overhead; it had a bright red light behind it. Suddenly an angel-like figure that appeared to be carrying a cross became visible next to the cloud. The children also saw a message in red letters of a religious context.

HC addendum.
Source: Ole Jonny Braene.   Type: A?

Location: Cookham Dean, Berkshire, England.
Date: Summer 1916.
Time: Daytime.

A young girl had been picking blackberries in a field and was startled to see a short thin human like figure, dressed in brown and wearing a pointed cap, dash out of one of the bushes. The being had a scraggly beard and appeared solid as far as the waist, but his legs were transparent and shadowy. The being quickly ran away disappearing from sight among the bushes.

HC addendum.
Source: David Lazell, *Fortean Times* #71.   Type: E

* * * * * * *

Location: Alwernia, Poland.
Date: Summer 1916.
Time: Midnight.

Soldier Boleslaw Lesniakiewicz had decided to spend the night at a ruined brickyard when around midnight a strange voice and the sounds of a little bell jingling woke him up. He got his rifle and stepped out of the brickyard. His horse was acting very uneasy. Suddenly he noticed a big, white dog-like creature, which slowly came closer and closer. Overcome with fear, he shot at the dog. At the same time a bright flash of blue-violet light illuminated him and he lost consciousness. When he woke up it was high noon. His horse was covered in strange foam. He suffered from strong headaches in the next two weeks.

HC addendum.
Source: Robert K. Lesniakiewicz.   Type: E?

* * * * * * *

Location: Cova da Iria, near Fatima, Portugal.
Date: July, 1916.
Time: Daytime.

The "Angel" that the three children had seen that spring suddenly appeared and demanded to know why the children were not praying continuously. The Angel insisted that the children pray and offer sacrifices continually. Lucia Abadoro asked how the children were to make sacrifices and the Angel told them to sacrifice everything that they possibly could. The children were left paralyzed and regained their senses only when evening descended. The children did not discuss the matter.

HC addendum.
Source: George Mitrovic, *'Strange and Mysterious Great Britain, Ireland and Europe: 1800-1977.'* Type: E?

* * * * * * *

Location: Adrian, Michigan.
Date: August 13, 1916.
Time: 2:00 a.m.

Mrs. W. H. Clark of North Scott Street tells of witnessing an unusual sight early Sunday morning; this being nothing less than that of an airship carrying two or more people which passed over the city.

Mrs. Clark telling her story to a Telegram reporter, said she had been unable to sleep and had gone downstairs about 2 o'clock, deciding that she would write a letter to her daughter. Her attention was attracted by a flash of light outside, and she peered out of the kitchen window to see an aircraft of some kind. It was moonlight, she said, and the craft was plainly visible carrying two or more bright lights. Although she could not see close enough to make out what kind of an airship it was, she said that she could make out at least two or more figures which moved about on it.

The airship, she said was visible 20 to 30 minutes coming out of the northwest and disappearing in the southwest. It was so plain that there was no chance of it having been some other sort of phenomenon, she declared. Investigation failed to find anyone else who saw the mysterious craft.

HC addendum.
Source: *Daily Telegram*, Adrian, Michigan, August 15, 1916. Type: A

Location: Cova da Iria, near Fatima, Portugal.
Date: October, 1916.
Time: Daytime.

Lucia Abadoro and her two cousins were at the Cova da Iria when the Angel reappeared and gave the children communion. The influence of the Angel seemed to overtake the witnesses so that they were practically deprived of the use of their bodily senses.

HC addendum.
Source: George Mitrovic, *'Strange and Mysterious Great Britain, Ireland and Europe: 1800-1977.'* Type: E?

* * * * * * *

Location: Puyko, Ob' River, Yamal-Nenets Province, Siberia, Russia.
Date: Sometime before 1917.
Time: Evening.

Teacher Marfa Senkina was staying with Khanty people in this local village, located on the Ob' River. When she asked why their dogs were barking ferociously on several nights in September, she was told the "Zemlemer" was about. One night she saw it, about 8 feet tall, glowing eyes, walking swiftly outside and confronted by barking dogs. When one attacked, it picked up the dog and hurled it through the air.

HC addendum.
Source: Dmitri Bayanov, *'In the Footsteps of the Russian Snowman,'* Moscow, 1996. Type: E

* * * * * * *

Location: Jyrinvaara, west of Kurkijoki, Karelia, Finland (now Russia).
Date: Between January and Easter, 1917.
Time: Unknown.

A lone widow, by the name of Anni Lattu, 44, was living in her little house about 6km to the west of the Kurkijoki Church, reportedly disappeared for some days, and the villagers thought she had gone to visit her daughter. But when she came back, she had an amazing story to tell.
A large machine, like a big wash-basin, had landed beside her house and from it; small creatures, which Anni later called "devils," came down by a ladder-like protrusion. Somehow she could understand a little of their language. She was not willing to follow them, but she was taken

aboard by force, and they traveled very fast. Everything was shown to her and there was a lot of wonder. The machine was shining inside and made no noise. Anni said that the devil flew her "over the world and even between the stars."

Anni kept to her story, but many said that she must have had a fever and had hallucinated it all. Anni did not agree and added that onboard the machine there were many little men who moved about very quickly. Anni was also known in the area for her clairvoyant and palm-reading abilities.

HC addendum.
Source: Heikki Virtanen, Nordic UFO Newsletter No 1/1988, pages 3-4 also UFO Research of Finland, 1985, *Annual Report*.
Type: G

* * * * * * *

Location: Peñascosa, Albacete, Spain.
Date: 1917.
Time: Afternoon.

The Alguacil family was working in a field when they saw a large metallic, hat-shaped object descend to the ground and land on four legs nearby. Two men exited the object and briefly walked around the area. They were described as very tall, blond-haired and appeared to lack 'mouths,' wearing metallic gray outfits. The men never communicated and refused food offered to them by some of the locals. According to the witnesses, the object and the strangers remained in the area for two days and then vanished. The family claimed to have seen a symbol resembling the letter "H" on the side of the object.

HC addendum.
Source: http://www.planetabenitez.com/prensa/ummo07.htm Type: B

Location: Over Western Belgium.
Date: Spring 1917.
Time: Early morning.

   German Air Force Ace Peter Waitzrik and the famed Baron Manfred von Richtofen were flying a mission over western Belgium when an object with undulating orange lights suddenly appeared in a clear, blue sky directly ahead of their Fokker tri-planes. Both were terrified and assumed it was some type of US aircraft (The US had just entered the war).
   The Baron immediately opened fire and the thing went down like a rock, shearing off tree limbs as it crashed in the woods. Then two little bald headed occupants climbed out of it and ran away. Waitzrik described the craft as silvery in color about 40 meters in diameter and resembling a saucer placed upside down. The two bruised but otherwise unhurt occupants ran into the woods and were never seen again. At the age of 105-years old, Waitzrik recently broke his silence and confessed the details of this incident.

HC addendum.
Source: Peter Waitzrik.   Type: H?

* * * * * * *

Location: Cova de Iria, near Cabeco, Portugal.
Date: May 13, 1917.
Time: Afternoon.

   The three children from the previous sighting at Cabeco, saw another flash of light in a clear sky at Cova da Iria, (Cave of Saint Irene). There was a radiance streaming from a globe hovering above a three foot tall tree. Within the globe was a small person with a luminous robe and a face of light. A feminine voice said "Don't be afraid, I am from Heaven. I am here to ask you to come here for six months in succession on the thirteenth day at this same hour and then I will tell you who I am and what I want and afterwards I will return here a seventh time."
   The person asked them to say the Rosary every day and to pray for peace. Only Lucia Abadoro and one other child heard the voice. The third only saw the being. Adults refused to take the children seriously but word spread.

HC addendum.
Source: George Mitrovic *'Strange and Mysterious Great Britain, Ireland and Europe: 1800-1977.'*   Type: E?

Location: Guadalajara, Spain.
Date: Summer 1917.
Time: Afternoon.

A group friends had gone for a walk along the banks of the River Henares and one of them, a Miss. Pimentel, became separated from the group and sat down to read a book near the river. Soon she began hearing loud shouts and laughter that attracted her attention. Thinking that it was her friends, she looked up and saw several small humanoids floating just above the waters of the river, this strange group was apparently the source of the commotion. Miss. Pimentel called her friends over but when they arrived, the little men had already vanished, however they were able to hear distant laughter fading away into the distance.

HC addendum.
Source: Lo Oculto, *'Ovnis en España.'* Type: E

* * * * * * *

Location: Fatima, Portugal.
Date: June 13, 1917.
Time: Evening.

The Virgin again appeared to the young shepherds. At first a sound like a thunderclap was heard and a 'white fluffy cloud' appeared in the sky, from which the Virgin descended on a beam of light.

HC addendum.
Source: Miguel Pedrero, *Año Cero* XXI #05-238. Type: F

* * * * * * *

Location: Cova da Iria, near Fatima, Portugal.
Date: July 13, 1917.
Time: Afternoon.

The shepherd children were back near the tree and the cave. There were now 4,500 witnesses who heard a buzzing or humming sound as well as a decrease in the glow of the Sun as well as its heat. A small whitish cloud appeared over the tree and there was a loud noise at the lady's departure. The children were shown a vision of Hell and were told that there would be apparitions of lights in the sky and that the war was going to end and that if people did not stop offending God, another and worse war would start during the reign of Pope Pius XI (who died in 1939).

When you see a night illuminated by an unknown light, know that this is the sign that God is giving you that he is going to punish the world for its crimes by the means of war, famine and persecution of the church and of the Holy Father. To prevent this the apparition asked for the consecration of Russia and if Russia were converted then there would be peace. If not, then Russia will spread her errors throughout the world.

HC addendum.
Source: George Mitrovic, *'Strange and Mysterious Great Britain, Ireland and Europe: 1800-1977.'* Type: F

* * * * * * *

Location: McPherson County, Nebraska.
Date: August, 1917.
Time: Afternoon.

The witness (involved in other encounters), a young girl at the time, was lying on the grass resting and gazing into the clear sky, when suddenly to the right of her, she noticed a white cumulus cloud. Where this cloud came from so quickly she will never know but as she stared at the cloud in amazement, a silvery object slowly glided in behind it for protection. She was certain she saw 'faces' peering at her from the windows as it slipped into the white mist.

HC addendum.
Source: *Flying Saucers* magazine, February, 1958. Type: A

* * * * * * *

Location: Cova da Iria, near Fatima, Portugal.
Date: August 13, 1917.
Time: Afternoon.

Eighteen thousand people gathered at the Cova da Iria. The children were not there though as they had been kidnapped and jailed by a local official who had decided to end the 'nonsense.' The crowd of people heard a clap of thunder followed by a bright flash. A small whitish cloud formed around the tree where it hovered for a few minutes before rising and melting away.
The clouds in the sky had turned crimson red and then changed to pink, yellow and blue. There was colored light like a rainbow on the ground. The clouds around the sun were reflecting different colors onto the crowd and some witnesses saw falling flowers. One witness stated that he saw a luminous globe spinning through the clouds.

HC addendum.
Source: George Mitrovic, *'Strange and Mysterious Great Britain, Ireland and Europe: 1800-1977.'* Type: F

* * * * * * *

Location: Aljustrel, near Fatima, Portugal.
Date: August 19, 1917.
Time: 4:00 p.m.

The children were released from the jail and were tending sheep near Aljustrel when the temperature suddenly dropped, the sun became yellowish and the colors of the rainbow filled the neighborhood. These colors were also seen by adults in the vicinity. There was a bright flash and a glowing light settled about a tree near the children where the entity, clothed in gold and white, stood in the center of the glow.

The witnesses fell onto their knees and feasted their souls in rapture. The entity or Lady as she was called, asked the children to make sacrifices for sinners and after ten minutes she went to the east with a roaring noise.

HC addendum.
Source: George Mitrovic, *'Strange and Mysterious Great Britain, Ireland and Europe: 1800-1977.'* Type: F

* * * * * * *

Location: Near Hamilton, Montana.
Date: Late August, 1917.
Time: Early morning.

Residents of Helena declare an airship has been circling above this city, between midnight and early morning, of recent days.
Three weeks ago, residents of Western Montana reported a similar ship which is said to have taken fire and fallen into a swamp, near Hamilton. There is no clue to the identity of these weird air visitors and if the federal authorities know anything, they remain silent.

HC addendum.
Source: Kay Massingill in Magonia Exchange list quoting *Grand Forks ND Herald,* September 1, 1917. Type: H?
Comments: Previously unknown crash of an early unidentified craft?

Location: Berlanga, Badajoz, Spain.
Date: August or September, 1917.
Time: Early morning.

Right after dawn a group of miners on their way to work saw near an old disused bull arena, a strange object shaped "like a table" on four legs and an illuminated turret. It was hovering close to the ground. As the men attempted to approach the object it flew up and disappeared in the direction of Berlanga. At the same time there were reports of numerous animals and livestock found dead and bloodless in the area.

HC addendum.
Source: Los Oculto, *'Ovnis en España.'* Type: X

* * * * * * *

Location: South Jutland, Denmark.
Date: September 1, 1917.
Time: Afternoon.

A wrecked airship this afternoon passed across the southern part of Jutland from the North Sea, and disappeared over the Kattegat. Several steel ropes with iron hooks were dragging behind the airship so low that they tore down telegraph wires, trees, and roofs of houses, and killed and injured many domestic animals. Great damage was done at several places. A man was observed in the car.

HC addendum.
Source: Kay Massingill in Magonia Exchange, quoting *Aberdeen Journal*, Aberdeenshire, Scotland September 1, 1917. Type: A

* * * * * * *

Location: Cova da Iria, near Fatima, Portugal.
Date: September 13, 1917.
Time: Afternoon.

The crowd at the Cova da Iria numbered thirty thousand, including two priests who had come specifically to establish the falsity of the event. At noon the sun got dimmer although there were no clouds in the sky. Thousands of witnesses cried out; "There she is; look." A globe of light was seen advancing slowly from the east and came towards the children and settled on the tree. A white cloud formed and out of the empty sky there was a fall of shiny white petals that became smaller and smaller as they neared the children and had melted away completely before reaching the witnesses.

The children saw the Lady in the center of the globe and there was a dialogue. The promise of a miracle on October 13th was repeated. Then the radiant globe rose and disappeared into the sun. One of the priests stated that the globe was a heavenly vehicle that carried the Mother of God from her throne above to this forbidden wasteland.

HC addendum.
Source: George Mitrovic, *'Strange and Mysterious Great Britain, Ireland and Europe: 1800-1977.'*   Type: F

* * * * * * *

Location: Near Youngstown, Pennsylvania.
Date: October, 1917.
Time: 12:30 a.m.

John Boback, 17, was walking along the railroad tracks between Youngstown and Mt Braddock when he saw a saucer-shaped object with a platform and rows of lights, sitting in a field 30 yards to his left. He watched the object for one or two minutes until it took off with a high-pitched sound, rising gradually like a slow plane. Its size was that of an average car. The top of the object was a dome with elongated windows, through which figures could be seen.

HC addendum.
Source: Orvil Hartle, *'A Carbon Experiment.'*   Type: A

* * * * * * *

Location: Grays, Essex, England.
Date: October, 1917.
Time: 9:30 p.m.

Hundreds of persons of this little riverside town, who emphatically assert that for several nights past, at about 2130, while the afterglow of the sun suffused the sky, three unmistakable apparitions, angelic in form, have appeared in the heavens with wings outspread, immediately above the training-ships in the river. At first it was thought the supposed angels might be aeroplanes, but this theory was dispelled by their stationary attitudes and the absence of the familiar sound of aircraft.

Eye-witnesses stated that they could neither believe nor deny the evidence of their senses. Nor were they inclined to regard what they have seen as merely fantastic shapes formed by the clouds. One said, "I am neither a dreamer nor a believer in spiritual phenomena, but at the same time I plainly saw three figures outlined against a rainbow which answered in all respects to Gustave Dore's pictures of celestial beings." One witness claimed that he could read the word 'peace' in a sort of halo over their heads.

HC addendum.
Source: *The Strait Times Singapore*, 10-27-1917, also August 25, 1917, Dundee, Perth, and *Fife's People's Journal*, Angus, Scotland.   Type: E?

* * * * * * *

Location: Cova da Iria, Fatima, Leiria District, Portugal.
Date: October 13, 1917.
Time: Afternoon.

Three young shepherds (Lucia, age 10, her cousins, Francisco and Jacinta Marto, nine and seven, respectively) were gathering together the sheep that they were herding. Strangely, they were drawn to the sky, and as they looked up, they saw a brilliant white globe. Soon after, a mysterious being, which they believed to be the Virgin Mary, appeared. "The wonderful lady looked young. Her dress, white as snow and tied to her neck by a gold band, wholly covered her body. A white cloak, with a golden edge, covered her head."

HC addendum.
Source: Joaquim Fernandes.   Type: E?

* * * * * * *

Location: Near Cambroncino, Spain.
Date: Early November, 1917.
Time: Late evening.

Local pig farmer; 39-year old Nicolas Sanchez Martin, known by his nickname of "Colas," was returning home accompanied by two local women; Maria Iglesias and her sister Pepa, after selling some of the hogs at a nearby market. Near an isolated field all three noticed a strange light floating above the nearby river. Concerned, the two women decided to return and to continue no further, but Nicolas continued on with his donkey and armed with a machete.
As he attempted to cross the river, the strange light flew in his direction and apparently waited for him on the other side of the river, floating just above the ground. Undaunted, Nicolas and his donkey crossed the river but immediately afterward, the strange light blocked

their path. It seemed that every time he attempted to move a certain direction, the light would block him. Somewhat annoyed, Colas grabbed his machete and yelled at the light to leave or he would "make it leave."

At this, the light flew towards the donkey, scaring the poor animal, which Colas had to almost drag away from the area. The light finally vanished, but Colas remained almost in shock and breathless. Soon Colas, a healthy and strong man, became deathly ill, and during the following nine days, remained bedridden in wrenching pain; he died finally on the ninth day. The attending physician Don Victor Sanchez Hoyos attributed his death to sudden pulmonary edema, but Colas' family was convinced that the strange ball of light had caused their loved one's demise.

HC addendum.
Source: *'Ovnis en Las Hurdes,'* Leyendas.   Type: F
Comments: If the light did indeed caused the death of Nicolas Sanchez Martin, how did it caused such a death, what kind of lethal energy did it emanate? One is reminded of the tragic death of the Brazilian farmer in 1946 again after encountering a mysterious light. I must emphasize, "Tread lightly in the presence of the unknown."

* * * * * * *

Location: Eastbourne, Sussex, England.
Date: 1918.
Time: Night.

At the Claremont School, novelist Pamela Frankau reported seeing a little "albino" dwarf that ran around her bedroom floor and escaped via the landing, fading from view.

HC addendum.
Source: http://www.paranormaldatabase.com   Type: E

Location: El Santo, Las Villas Province, Cuba.
Date: 1918.
Time: Afternoon.

    A boy playing along the backs of a local river heard a noise and saw over a nearby field; a large object resembling a "Mexican Sombrero" coming down for a landing. After the object landed, a large 'door' opened and several tall man-like figures wearing dark diver's outfits emerged and briefly walked around the surroundings. They then gathered at the entrance of the craft and boarded the craft.
    After a few minutes, he heard a loud buzzing and the object took off, disappearing at high speed towards the ocean side (North). The boy reported that at the site of the landing he found some strange 'papers' which resembled the wax paper currently used to wrap Ritz crackers (at least that was something the witness was able to compare it to, when he was interviewed in 1998 at age 90). It is not known what he did with the alleged 'wax paper.'

HC addendum.
Source: Direct from researcher Hugo Parrado Francos.   Type: B

* * * * * * *

Location: Wrangell, Alaska.
Date: 1918.
Time: Daytime.

    A German gold prospector, half-starved, made his way back to Wrangell from a northern mining camp, looking for food and provisions. The story goes that he sat down to pick new sprouts of fireweed plant to eat, which was mixed in a scraggly field of berries. He ate what his stomach could tolerate and fell asleep, curled up in a bed of grass with the warm sun on his back. He claimed he was awakened by someone talking nearby.
    Excited to have company and needing direction to the settlement, he crawled around a high bramble of berry thorns to see who was there and meet his company. He said he saw a bush-woman sitting on the ground, feeding a smaller one berries by hand; it was sitting inside the circle of her huge legs. The prospector watched only a short time in fear of the giantess but heard the bush-woman talk to the smaller one in Indian language.

HC addendum.
Source: Alice Petermann to grandson 1947, stories by Elwood Petermann
http://www.bigfootencounters.com/stories/wrangell/htm   Type: E

Location: Windsor, Ontario, Canada.
Date: Early March, 1918.
Time: Night.

Scores of Windsor residents, including members of the police force, stoutly affirm they witnessed a startling phenomenon last Thursday night in the form of an angel who appeared surrounded by a circle of flaming red, in the western sky. Following as it does, reports from France that soldiers have seen Joan of Arc and St. Michael leading them into battle, as well as the apparition of the angel of Mons, the experience of the Windsorites is attracting more than ordinary attention.

Patrolmen on duty Thursday night, skeptical over reports received over the telephone, walked out where they could view the section of the sky in which the phenomenon was reported. They declared they beheld the blood red circle high in the heavens though the angel's figure, if it had been there, had disappeared. Another member of the police force, however, is authority for the statement that he previously saw the angel, circle and all.

Many Detroit residents declare they, too, had seen the angel in the red circle, a striking coincidence with the experience of the Windsorites. All descriptions of the apparition agree that it was far too bright, vivid and well defined to have anything to do with the aurora borealis, which was faintly visible Thursday night from this part of the continent.

HC addendum.
Source: Kay Massingill in Magonia Exchange, quoting *The Bridgeport Telegram*, Tuesday, March 12, 1918, Bridgeport, Connecticut.

* * * * * * *

Location: Near Heshbon, Indiana, Pennsylvania.
Date: March 18, 1918.
Time: 5:00 p.m.

A big government observation balloon landed in Blacklick Creek, near Heshbon, on Monday evening about 5:00 o'clock. In the basket of the craft was a suitcase, camera, map and other equipment, and an identification tag of F. G. Keansen. The pilot was missing and last night no information as to his whereabouts had been learned. There are many suppositions as to the fate of the man who occupied the basket, but nothing definite is known.

Sherriff H. A. Boggs was notified of the aerial visitor and drove to Heshbon on Monday night and brought the balloon home with him yesterday morning, and it was on exhibition in front of the Court House the greater part of the day. The balloon is believed to have come from a training camp in Ohio.

HC addendum.
Source: Kay Massingill in Magonia Exchange, citing *The Indiana Progress*, Indiana Pennsylvania, Wednesday, March 20, 1918. Type: X?

* * * * * * *

Location: Dundee, Scotland.
Date: April, 1918.
Time: Night.

A curious phenomenon, says the *People's Friend*, has been witnessed at Dundee, where a number of people saw the gleaming shape of an angel in a bright cloud form. The figure was clearly discernible for some little time; afterwards fading slowly amid a wonderful glow. A few days before, Popular Science Siftings contained an article explaining the visions seen above Przemysl during the assaults by the Russians in March, 1915.
It is believed that the visions were devised by Austrian scientists to stimulate the Austrians in the belief that they were under Divine protection, while the superstitious Russians fell on their knees and prayed instead of fighting. The vision took the form of the holy picture, a Virgin and Child, in the Church of Czestochowa; a painting which is familiar to all Russians.
It is suggested that the Przemysl vision was projected on low lying clouds by means of a "stereopticon" operated from an aeroplane. This outfit could be carried easily by a biplane, and would show a picture with 185 feet diameter at a distance of 1000ft.

HC addendum.
Source: Jerry Brown in Magonia Exchange quoting *Fielding Star*, Volume XIV, Issue 3511, April 6, 1918. Type: E?

Location: Mt. St. Lawrence, Washington.
Date: July, 1918.
Time: Unknown.

"Mountain devils" supposedly attacked a miner's cabin at Mount St. Lawrence near Kelso. Allegedly these hairy creatures, which stood seven to eight feet tall, *could make themselves invisible.* Unfortunately that is all we know about this alleged episode.

HC addendum.
Source: Jerome Clark, and Loren Coleman, *'Creatures of the Goblin World.'* Type: X?
Comments: Date is approximate.

* * * * * * *

Location: Fontainebleau, Quebec, Canada.
Date: November, 1918.
Time: Night.

18-year old Maria Dion was returning home from a dance, and as she walked along a wooded area, several short 2-foot tall green-colored figures suddenly appeared and began chasing her. The creatures were very quick despite their size. She noticed that the beings wore what appeared to be helmets and uniforms, which she later compared to modern day 'astronauts.' Somehow she was able to elude the little men.

HC addendum.
Source: Donald Cyr, Quebec, Canada. Type: E

* * * * * * *

Location: (Undisclosed location) Western Australia.
Date: 1919.
Time: Unknown.

A lone traveler going down an isolated road came upon a man working on a strange silvery object. The traveler approached to offer his assistance when the man looked up startled and pointed something at the traveler that knocked him unconscious. When he woke up, the stranger and the silvery object were gone.

HC addendum.
Source: Jerome Clark, *Strange* magazine #10. Type: C

Location: La Rua (Evgliers) and Le Cros, Herault, France.
Date: 1919.
Time: Morning.

Mr. Manonviller; 12 years old at the time, together with another lad was busy collecting mulch for the cows in the barn when they saw two entities walking with a "staggering" pace. The entities were about two meters in height and each one had "a glowing light" fixated to a belt.

HC addendum.
Source: Jean Sider quoting personal communication from Joel Mesnard.
Type: E

* * * * * * *

Location: Linaalv, Lappland, Sweden.
Date: 1919.
Time: Daytime.

Ragnar Byrlind and his brothers and sisters were inside the family's house playing games when their mother called for them to come to the window and look. About 400 meters away some sort of object was coming along the road. It was a dark gray object, longer than the timber Lorries of the present day. On what appeared to be a coach box, in the middle sat a figure and two others were running in front of it carrying flashlight-like implements in their hands.
The entities looked like human beings and wore some kind of headgear but it was impossible to discern any details at that distance. While the object was under observation by the witnesses, it suddenly released a light smoke and disappeared on the spot. The family investigated the area but found no traces.

HC addendum.
Source: Sven Olof Svensson. Type: C

Location: Greendale, South Island, New Zealand.
Date: 1919.
Time: Dusk.

A Mr. Church was returning from a rabbit shoot at his farm in Greendale; dusk was falling. He noticed, sitting in a creek bed, some two chains from him, a dull gray object. It was about fifteen feet across, elliptical in shape, and appeared to have a ramp protruding from its side. It was partially shielded from view by scrub. He started to move towards it, after watching it for some thirty seconds, and as he did so, the object shot skywards, making a distinct whirring sound.

HC addendum.
Source: Peter Hassall quoting *Spaceview* magazine #67, May, 1976.
Type: X.

* * * * * * *

Location: Branksome Park, Dorset, England.
Date: 1919.
Time: Night.

A Mr. Lonsdale was in the park when he suddenly became conscious of movement on the edge of the lawn. He then saw several little figures dressed in brown peering through the bushes. In a few seconds a dozen or more small people about 2ft in height, in bright clothes and with radiant faces, ran on to the lawn, dancing hither and thither. This went on for about five minutes. They were frightened away by a servant bringing tea.

HC addendum.
Source: Janet Bord, Faeries, *'Real Encounters with the Little People.'*
Type: E

* * * * * * *

Location: Near Tehachapi, California.
Date: 1919.
Time: Night.

While hoboing across the country, Mike Childers spent what he thought was a night in the woods near Tehachapi. When he awoke and set off on his way, he discovered that the year was 1934 and America had passed into the Great Depression. Childers made a small media splash as a modern day Rip Van Winkle but was never able to discover what happened to the fifteen years he'd lost. It wasn't until 1990 that the decrepit Childers began to have nightmares that hinted at forgotten memories. Having seen Dr. Denton Schaeffer on a tabloid talk show about repressed memories, he mailed Schaeffer a description of his experience and dreams (along with his collection of journal articles and news clippings about him from the mid-1930s).

Schaeffer interviewed and hypnotized Childers on thirty occasions before Childer's death in 1995 and was able to uncover a vivid tapestry of dark and horrifying memories in which Childers was taken beneath the ground by chattering alien creatures that surgically removed his brain and transported him to alien realms. The most disturbing part of this case is the medical evidence that Childers was subjected to extensive and inexplicable cranial surgery sometime during the 1920's.

HC addendum.
Source: *'World of the Strange; Close Encounters.'*   Type: G?

* * * * * * *

Location: East of Barron, Wisconsin.
Date: Summer 1919.
Time: About midnight.

Thirteen year old Harry Anderson, his family and some friends went for a drive in the family's new Ford Model T automobile. At about 2200 as they headed back to Eau Claire, the car's engine began running a little rough. Papa Anderson eased it to a halt on the southbound lane of Highway 25.

"We're running low on oil," he said, handing the oil can to his son. "Head on up the road, Harry, see if you can get some old farmer to lend you some." And so with the empty oil can swinging from his hand, Harry hiked down the darkened road. A roadside sign told him he was just outside Barron, about five miles west of Rice Lake. Seeing the roof of a farmhouse on the horizon, he took a shortcut across a cornfield. The farmer filled Harry's oil can for him, and, "as he was walking back, he saw twenty little men walking towards him in a single file.

They had bald heads and white skins, and wore leather 'knee pants' held up by braces over their shoulders." Startled, Harry ducked behind a red maple tree, staying out of sight as the dwarfish platoon marched by. His ears caught fragments of their conversation, mostly muttering and a quirky little song:

"We won't stop fighting
Till the end of the war
In Nineteen-Hundred

>   And Ninety-Four
>   Sound off—one, two
>   Sound off—three, four
>   Detail, one, two, three, four
>   One—two...three—four!

The column marched on into the forest, leaving Harry, in his own words, "heart pumping and terrified."

HC addendum.
Source: Jerome Clark.   Type: E

> * * * * * * *

Location: Near Webster City, Iowa.
Date: July, 1919.
Time: 11:00 a.m.

    A brother and sister who lived on a farm in the Webster City area, "heard a chirping-like sparrows feeding," the sister would testify, "We turned and saw a brown-green object beneath the tree near the creek about 75 feet from us." They ran toward it before noticing a figure wearing green-brown clothing that appeared 'stern-looking' and standing in the door (of the object) which had been lowered to the ground and had steps.
    He startled them by making strange guttural sounds; then they noticed a shorter figure in the same clothing, running toward the stream leading to the pond. He went very fast and dipped up some water in what looked like a tin about the size of a small soup can. He got the water despite the protests of the man in the door. The one with the tin can was smaller than the one in the door. The big one hustled the little one into the vehicle and the door slammed shut; it made a metallic sound when it closed.
    The vehicle rose straight up very fast. The top of the vehicle hit the tree limbs and broke a few small branches off; all of this without a sound of a motor. It rose straight up, and then went sidewise and over the hill with its three leg-like protrusions still down, no lights no sound. They followed up the hill, but it soon left them and it was out of sight. They went back to where it landed. The soil in a wide area where they had landed was covered with round spots that resembled cane marks.

HC addendum.
Source: Jerome Clark, *Strange* #10 citing NICAP files.   Type: B

Location: Near Castelfranca, Veneto, Italy.
Date: December, 1919.
Time: Various.

The great arsenal and powder stockpile in the castle of Godego, near the town of Castelfranca Veneto, is unguarded. The sentries who were posted there have fled in alarm at the repeated nightly visits of a strange spectral form.

Recently (according to the Milan correspondent of the Daily Express) a soldier was mounting guard over the magazine when a luminous human figure from whose head issued tongues of flame, appeared before him at a distance of about 20 feet. The sentinel gave the alarm and the entire guard team hurried to the spot. The specter had in the meantime vanished, but shortly after the arrival of the soldiers, it re-appeared. The whole company then fired rifles at the figure, which instantly dissolved into a great ball of fire, finally melting away into space.

The following night the apparition was seen once more. A Sicilian soldier of the guard approached the figure with a number of his companions, and an attack was made on it with the bayonet. Their furious thrusts, however, encountered no tangible resistance, and the phantom disappeared in a few moments in a fiery halo which was speedily dissolved in the atmosphere.

The consequence of the strange occurrence was that all the soldiers fled from the spot, leaving the depot, which was crammed with explosives, entirely unguarded. In the absence of the men, a dozen officers volunteered to act as sentries, pending an official inquiry into the affair.

Meanwhile four of the soldiers who were visited by the 'apparition' have gone out of their mind. They are now confined in the military asylum.

HC addendum.
Source: *Ashburton Guardian* (NZ), Volume XL, Issue 9187, December 22, 1919. Type: E

* * * * * * *

Location: Between Nowra and Huskisson, New South Wales, Australia.
Date: December, 1919.
Time: Evening.

"The Sun's South Coast correspondent describes the strange appearance of the animal, in a sworn testimony for the benefit of those who investigate psychic phenomenon accredited evidence only. He says;

Mr. George Dent, son, who drives the daily coach between Nowra and Huskisson (Jervis Bay), reports a strange experience on the Jervis Bay

Road. He was accompanied by a lady passenger, well known in the locality and of high repute, who directed his attention to a white object crossing the road some little distance in front of the coach. He describes it as a white fleecy cloud or a 'man of snow,' about the size of a large bear; seemingly wafted across the thoroughfare without touching the ground and it was clearly discernible some distance across a cleared patch in the paddock until it was lost to sight in the bush.

A resident of Nowra name Connolly, who claims to have varied experiences with the bear tribe in foreign countries was under the impression that it was a "white bear." He has seen the same species of bear gliding along and it would appear as if it had no legs." (!)

HC addendum.
Source: *Queensland Times*, Ipswich, Queensland (1909-1954) December 16, 1919. Type: E

1920-1929

Location: Bass Strait, Victoria, Australia.
Date: 1920.
Time: Various.

"The Navy submarine depot ship, the Platypus, was involved in the search for a missing schooner, the Amelia J., in Bass Strait. Mystery lights, thought at the time to be "evidently rockets," were observed. Two aircraft left the flying training school and aircraft depot at Point Cook to join in the investigation. One was piloted by a Major Anderson and the other by Captain W. J. Stutt; an instructor for the NSW Government Aviation School at Richmond; Stutt and his mechanic, Sargent Dalzell, were last seen by Major Anderson flying into a large cloud. Their plane and the schooner were never found."

HC addendum.
Source: Chalker, W. 1996. *'UFOs sub-rosa down under: The Australian Military and Government role in the UFO controversy.'*
Comments: Perhaps permanent abductions?

Location: (Undisclosed location) Quebec, Canada.
Date: 1920.
Time: Night.

A man was returning home one night when his horse began acting strangely. Then he spotted a circular UFO resting on the ground nearby. He said it was about 50 feet in diameter and 16 feet high, with a yellow light. The witness reported observing four or five small, humanoid figures moving quickly around the outside of the object, and said he heard "child-like" sounds coming from them. He then saw the UFO take off with a "machine-like" noise and what sounded like a rush of air.

HC addendum.
Source: Phillip L. Rife, *'It Didn't Start with Roswell.'*   Type: C

* * * * * * *

Location: London, England.
Date: 1920.
Time: Night.

At the Central Railway Station, a man in a white cloak was seen jumping effortlessly, back and forth from rooftop to the street below. No other information.

HC addendum.
Source: Spring Heeled Jack, London, England.   Type: E

* * * * * * *

Location: "Maori district" (Undisclosed location) New Zealand.
Date: 1920.
Time: Evening.

The witness had just finished hanging some clothing and had stepped out onto the verandah when she heard a soft galloping coming the direction of the orchard. She crossed the yard to get the pegs, and heard the galloping coming closer. As she stood under the clothesline she saw a little figure riding a tiny pony close beside her. It rode right under her uplifted arms. She looked around and found herself surrounded by eight or ten tiny figures on tiny ponies resembling dwarf Shetlands.
The little figure that had come so close to her, stood out quite clearly in the light that came from the window, but he had his back to it, and she could not see his face. The faces of the others were quite brown, the ponies were brown. They wore close-fitting dark jersey like clothing.

They resembled tiny dwarfs, or children of about two years old. Startled, the witness cried out and the tiny figures galloped away and disappeared into the distance.

HC addendum.
Source: Janet and Colin Bord, *'Faeries: Real Encounters with the Little People.'* Type: E

* * * * * * *

Location: Quemchi, Chiloe, Chile.
Date: 1920.
Time: Late evening.

    The two sons of the Muñoz family, 12 and 13 years of age respectively had gone fishing in a small boat on the Caucahue canal near their home. The fish were biting and it was getting late and it became night; their worried parents noticed that they had not returned yet from their fishing expedition. Concerned, the parents accompanied by several neighbors went out searching for the boys in their boats. At first they couldn't find them anywhere until they thought of going further out to sea where the golf waters met the canal.
    There on a small beach they found the overturned boat of the boys and their 12-year old son, apparently unharmed, the 13-year old was nowhere in sight. When asked what had occurred to his brother the 12-year old boy could only say that they suddenly felt a very strong wind dragging them out to sea and they saw what appeared to be a water spout twisting about 100 meters above the waters, the waters suddenly turned white and that was his last memory.
    Later he found himself floating next to his upturned boat, his brother nowhere in sight. Everyone was stunned since there had been no reports of inclement weather during the time. The oldest brother 'Nano' remained missing. They searched for him for a week and after a while they assumed he was dead, drowned. According to local tradition a wake for held for the child.
    However four years later, one afternoon Nano Muñoz suddenly appeared at the front door of his house, wearing the same clothing he had left with the same day he had gone fishing with his brother. The astounded parents could not believe what happened and attempted to ask Nano what had occurred and where he had been the past four years. However they were horrified to learn that Nano was now completely deaf mute and since he had never learn how to write he was never able to explain what had occurred to him.

HC addendum.
Source: http://ovnisseacercan.blogspot.com/2011/10/humanoides-en-la-patagonia.html   Type: X
Comments: Translated by Albert S. Rosales.

* * * * * * *

Location: Tuerin, Mongolia.
Date: 1920.
Time: Early morning.

Drug dealer and arms merchant John Spencer had escaped China on foot and was wandering in an exhausted state through murderous marshlands and nightmarish landscapes. Completely exhausted, tormented with hunger and racked by fever, he finally collapsed on the trail. Wandering Buddhist monks stumbled upon the near comatose American and carried him to the Lamaist Monastery at Tuerin. Soon he regained his strength relatively quickly.

The monks of the monastery were entertaining another guest from America at the time. This was scholar/businessman William Thompson, who had been at the monastery for some weeks, and who was known for his fascination with the religious beliefs of the Far East. It seems that, at his first contact with the recuperating John Spencer, Thompson must have spoken to him very enthusiastically about the monastery. For suddenly the one-time arms and drug dealer was very much interested in exploring his new surroundings, and nothing in the world could keep him in bed until he had made a complete recovery.

A few days after the initial meeting, Spencer was up and about very early in the morning. Poking around outside, tracing the wall of the Lamaist monastery, he came upon weathered steps leading down to a small metal door. Spencer was extremely curious by nature. He climbed down the few steps and gingerly opened the door.

He found himself in a spacious, brightly colored, twelve-sided room. The walls were decorated with drawings, which seemed to depict the constellations. He could recognize one of them. It was the constellation Taurus; under whose sign he had himself been born, and a representation of which he carried with him at all times, engraved on a medallion hanging around his neck. Spencer traced with his index finger one by one the outline of each drawing. As he came to the end of a drawing apparently depicting the Pleiades, the wall gave way beneath his finger and noiselessly opened into a corridor beyond.

His curiosity got the better of him. He advanced a few steps into the gloom. He could make out a faint greenish glimmer, apparently coming from a distance. Before following the glimmer, he pushed a large boulder into the open doorway, so that nobody could surprise him from behind and the doorway would remain open. He continued to make his way along the narrow, solidly constructed tunnel until he came to an intersection. Now he kept to the right at all times to avoid getting lost.

After several minutes, Spencer reached the end of the tunnel. A large hall opened out before him, in which the ubiquitous green light shone more strongly and more dazzlingly than ever. The light was so intense that he could see, without difficulty, along the length of one wall, 25 to 30 enshrined coffins standing in a row. Spencer had the impression that the shrines were floating one or two feet above the floor, but he was not afterward able to remember exactly. His thoughts were mainly of running to the rich treasures which he thought must be in or around the shrines, and of which he wished to disburden this quaint underground place of worship. He set to work without delay, noting happily in passing that the lids of the coffin were effortlessly easy to open. In the first three shrines he uncovered the corpses of monks who wore the same clothes as the monks he saw all around him in the monastery.

In the fourth coffin lay a woman in men's clothing; in the fifth a man whom he guessed was from India and who wore a red silk jacket. The corpses showed no signs of decomposition. It seemed to him, as he advanced along the wall, that the coffins had been there for a longer and longer time. They all had one thing in common, however: a complete absence of the treasure, which this inveterate adventurer was, with increasing desperation, seeking to discover. He went through each coffin with great thoroughness. In the third to last, there lay, perfectly preserved and clothed in white linen, the body of a male; in the next to last coffin there rested the body of a female whose ethnic origins he couldn't quite determine.

He lifted the lid of the coffin in the very last shrine. He could not believe his eyes. He was gazing at a small creature dressed in clothing that shimmered as if made of silver. The head was silvery in color, with huge closed eyelids and a very short stub of a nose. The creature did not seem to have a mouth. When Spencer leaned forward to touch the corpse, the huge round eyes suddenly snapped open. A sharp green light blinded the would-be plunderer. An immense, unaccountable terror seized Spencer. He slammed the coffin lid down. He flung himself away and ran screaming out of this gallery of the dead. Back in the main part of the monastery, he immediately sought out Thompson and related his experience to his fellow countryman.

The next morning upon investigating the room, in which Spencer found the passageway, nothing was found. A few days later; just after he had left the monastery; John Spencer disappeared without a trace. He was never heard from again.

HC addendum.
Source: Hartwig Hausdorf, 'The Chinese Roswell,' also Peter Kolosimo 'Timeless Earth.' Type: F or H?

* * * * * * *

Location: Crimean Peninsula, Ukraine.
Date: 1920.
Time: Unknown.

During the Russian civil war, a mobile Red Army group was moving along a local road in the rugged mountains of the Crimean Peninsula. There were a total of five soldiers including one woman. They were moving in a cart wagon and were armed with rifles and "Maksim" machine guns. Suddenly they noticed a lighted area on the side of the road and the stopped near the road, prepared their weapons and began to check the area. They soon came upon a strange dome-shaped object on the ground and several tall figures walking near the object.

The figures were described as dressed in a kind of armored suit, resembling chain-mail, The figures were about 2 meters in height, or taller. Thinking that these were foreign enemies, the group prepared to fire upon the strangers with their Maksim machine guns but were suddenly blinded by a bright flash of light and knocked down, losing consciousness. When they returned to their senses again, the object and the strange figures had disappeared.

HC addendum.
Source: Anton Anfalov, quoting 'UFO-Liaisons of the Universe,' Lugansk, Ukraine. Type: C

* * * * * * *

Location: Nulato, Alaska.
Date: 1920.
Time: Unknown.

Albert Petka died after fighting with a "bushman" that had attacked him on the boat where he was living. His dogs drove the "bushman" off, but the man later died.

HC addendum.
Source: John Green card-file, BC Archives. Type: X

Location: Ust Tsil'Ma, near Pechorla, Siberia, Russia.
Date: 1920.
Time: Afternoon.

A fifteen year old boy, along with six other boys and two adults were mowing hay by the Tsil'Ma River when suddenly two incomprehensible figures appeared on the opposite bank. One was small and black whilst the other was an immense height, well over two meters. The big one was gray and whitish and both began to run around a large willow tree. The whitish one would run off and the black one would chase it.

They were playing for several minutes and then they darted towards the river and vanished. The witnesses hid in a hut for one hour and when they got out they found large and small tracks. The large tracks had a clearly defined sixth toe and flat feet. The toes were not pressed together and spread outwards. Other villagers saw the creatures as well.

HC addendum.
Source: George Mitrovic, *'Strange and Mysterious Great Britain, Ireland and Europe: 1800-1977.'* Type: E

* * * * * * *

Location: Near River Arque, Cochabamba, Bolivia.
Date: 1920.
Time: Late night.

Several men were traveling in very rugged terrain on horses and donkeys and upon reaching the banks of the River Arque they set up camp and went to sleep. Late that night one of the men was awakened by noises outside the tent. Thinking it was thieves, he went out to check. Stepping out of the tent he was confronted by a small "man" who identified itself as a "Duende." Using perfect Spanish the small humanoid or "Duende" told the stunned witness that he needed fire.

Terrified, the man thought he was confronting the devil and told the short humanoid to leave, and this one promptly did, jumping into the nearby river. The man then lay down again and attempted to calm down and did not wake up his companions. Soon he felt someone throwing stones at the tent, walking outside he was suddenly seized by two short "Duendes" or humanoids who attempted to drag him away. The man screamed in terror awakening his friends who ran out to assist him, the two small humanoids then released him and both disappeared into the river.

HC addendum.
Source: http://greyhunter.alien.de Type: E

Comments: Was this an early abduction attempt? Translated by Albert S. Rosales.

* * * * * * *

Location: Near Krasnogorskoye, Altay region, West Siberia, Russia.
Date: 1920.
Time: Unknown.

Two military officers on special assignment in the area, T. Barabashin from the counterintelligence branch of the VChK (predecessor to the KGB) and I. Shifer, also a secret service officer, were performing a search in this remote area. Both men, riding on horses, had neared a mountainous gorge surrounded by thick forests when they suddenly stumbled upon an extraordinary scene; something that they had never seen before in their lives. They encountered a group of "humans" wearing dirty robes performing what appeared to be "slave" work, extracting ore from a nearby mine.

All the men were behaving in a strange manner, they all had expressionless glassy eyes and all moved around like zombies or robots, displaying a total lack of emotion, performing the arduous job in a totally monotonous manner. Over the group of men hovered in midair a tetrahedron shaped object. The object appeared small, the length of its lower section was no more than 60cm (it was evidently a non-piloted device). This object flew over the "work force" to different locations, descending and ascending, apparently observing everyone's movements very closely. After watching the incredible scene for a few minutes, both men hid behind a large stone amid some bushes, still observing the scene from a distance fearing exposure the whole time.

At this point the men could also now see several cigar-shaped objects hovering in the sky. These resembled large flying "barrels" about 20-25 meters long and approximately 5 meters in diameter. These objects were apparently securing the perimeter and guarding the entire area. The stunned observers could also see other flying craft; small oval-shaped machines, which flew about emitting bright beams of blue light. The beams of blue light were at times projected towards the ground. Somehow the men understood that these objects were some kind of "combat flying machines."

Deeper in the gorge, the men saw several other types of unknown machines; some pyramidal in shape and very tall, apparently dozens of meters in height; those were apparently the "main" flying craft. Near the large pyramid-shaped objects, Barabashin and Shifer saw a group of tall humanoid entities dressed in shiny metallic like outfits. They appeared to be doing something but because of the distance the witnesses could not tell exactly what they were doing. Afraid of being found out, both men left their hideout and quickly returned to their VChK office and reported their stunning discovery. But several days later when a heavily armed detachment was sent to check on the information they found nothing, nothing seemed out of place and they could see no traces. So both men were then accused of providing false data to superior officers.

HC addendum.
Source: Dr. Vladimir G. Azhazha, *'Underwater UFO,'* Moscow, 2008.
Comments: Who were those unfortunate forced laborers? Had they been permanently abducted by negative entities years before? What were they doing in that remote area of West Siberia? Type: C or G?

* * * * * * *

Location: Near Nontron, Dordogne, France.
Date: Summer 1920.
Time: 11:00 p.m.

On a Saturday evening, between 2300 and midnight, a group of young people was returning from a dance when they saw in the sky, above a little wood, a strange spectacle; a group of beings of small stature about in the air, and giving off "musical sounds." The young people could see their little legs move about, and noticed that surrounding the figures were a number of luminous balls that gave the group a "fiery aspect." According to the accounts of two of the group; Louise and Marie Grasset, they felt no fear at the strange sight.

HC addendum.
Source: Joel Mesnard and Jean Marie Bigorne. Type: E?

* * * * * * *

Location: Mattawan River area, Ontario, Canada.
Date: June, 1920.
Time: Afternoon.

Albert Coe from New York, was on a canoeing holiday in Ontario with his friend Rod. While he was alone one day, he heard a voice crying for help from below the rocks over which he was climbing. He said he located the source of the voice; a young man of human appearance who had become trapped in a cleft in the rocks. Coe said he rescued the man, who thanked him profusely and said that he had been fishing when he accidently stumbled into the cleft. He was described as handsome, blond-haired, young, and dressed in a strange, silver-gray suit.

The man told Coe that he had a small aircraft in a nearby clearing, and when Coe helped him return to it, he realized that it was unlike anything he had ever seen; a 20 feet diameter disc, resting on three landing struts. The alien had Coe swear not to say anything and opened a hatch in the underside of the craft and climbed in; it then took off with a high-pitched whine. Coe further claims that six months later he received a short note requesting a lunchtime meeting at a certain hotel in New York City. It was signed, "Xretsim." (i.e. 'Mister X' spelt backwards)

Coe went to the hotel, and met again the young man he had rescued; although this time he was dressed in an ordinary suit. At lunch the young man said that he was part of a survey team charged with monitoring Earth's scientific progress. His race, he said, comes from planet Norca in the Tau Ceti star system, that begun to dehydrate and 14,000 years ago, forcing the inhabitants to migrate to another system. They explored our solar system and chose it as their new home.

According to Zret, 243,000 Norcans embarked on the journey of colonization in 62 huge spacecrafts, that all fell into the sun because of a navigation error, except for one which crash-landed on Mars, killing 1,300 of its 5,000 passengers. The survivors colonized Mars, and then moved on to Venus and Earth, where they founded Atlantis and Lemuria. Zret went on to state that the Norcans now live mainly on Venus, although they maintain several research bases on Mars. Coe claimed he maintained contact with Zret and other Norcans for the next sixty years, meeting them on average once a month.

HC addendum.
Source: Albert Coe, *'The Shocking Truth,'* 1969. Type: G

* * * * * * *

Location: Hot Springs, Arkansas.
Date: July, 1920.
Time: Night.

"The Path of a meteor seemed to be from the southwest, slightly northeast, and many who saw the meteor believe they saw on it the figure of a human. Others say there seemed to be the figure of a person under the meteor."

HC addendum.
Source: Kay Massingill Magonia list quoting *Colorado Springs Gazette-Telegraph*, July 12, 1920, which quotes the *Hot Springs Arkansas Sentinel-Record*, unknown date.
Comments: Clearly not a meteor. Type: A?

Location: Near Bethel, North Carolina.
Date: September, 1920.
Time: Afternoon.

During the local cotton harvest, 14-year laborer Nicora B. and her family were out in the fields plucking the white balls from the cotton plants and stuffing them in their trailing tote sacks when they saw something large flying over the farm. They described it as an object resembling two pie pans placed together lip to lip. The silvery object zigzagged across the sky and came to rest in the field in front of the witnesses.

Two little bald white men got out and pointed short stick-like implements at them. They were the size of little boys but their faces seemed older. One of the little bald men began digging and poking in the dirt with something like a shovel and put some dirt into a bag. He then took a small plant and placed it in the bag also. Both little men then backed up one after the other and entered the pie-pan shaped object, still pointing the sticks at them as they walked backwards. Presently the UFO took off and zig-zagged back in the direction it came.

HC addendum.
Source: *UFO Roundup* Vol. 7 #28, and *Filer's Files*.   Type: B

* * * * * * *

Location: Pechyeniha, West Yaroslavl Province, Russia.
Date: 1921 or 1922.
Time: Unknown.

A local villager nicknamed "Pechyonyi" had been sensing or hearing strange vibrations in the ground on a regular basis, coming from the area under his wooden cabin. These usually began suddenly. On one occasion, several small-sized entities entered his house. They had gray-greenish faces, big slanted dark eyes, and hoofed legs. The strange visitors told him (in bad accented Russian), "Leave this place, you cannot stay here, there is too much traffic and it cannot be changed." After that his cattle began dying and his wife became sick also. In a short period of time he left the area.

HC addendum.
Source: Valeriy A. Kukushkin, Yaroslavl UFO Group, *'Chimeras of the X Location,'* Anton Anfalov.   Type: E

Location: Dassen Island, Western Cape Province, South Africa.
Date: 1921.
Time: Unknown.

An animal with a fish-like tail and a woman's head and breasts was seen by a fisherman at Dassen Island, off Western Cape Province.

HC addendum.
Source: George Eberhart, *'Mysterious Creatures.'*   Type: E

* * * * * * *

Location: West Yaroslavl Province, Russia.
Date: 1921.
Time: Unknown.

   A local resident encountered several humanoid beings that came to his house. They were definitely nonhuman, shorter than average height, with greenish-gray skin, and hoofed legs. They told him that they had been planting lime-trees (lindens) in the area for some time now but it had been unsuccessful. The trees were always damaged by different causes.
   So they asked him to plant the trees for them. They gave him numerous saplings and told him that they had brought them from very far away, that he should take care of the trees, he was promised money for his labor. They indeed gave him money and also blue vitriol (copper vitriol) for the same purpose. The humanoids explained to the witness that a long time ago they had crashed in the area, and four of their people had been killed. So, according to custom, trees, specifically lime trees must be planted in that area to honor the dead.
   They later added that they had brought the saplings from the area of Chernigov or Bryansk. The witness did what he was told. After the encounter the witness neighbors noticed his strange behavior and he confessed to them what had occurred.

HC addendum.
Source: Valeriy A. Kukushkin, Yaroslavl UFO Group, *'Chimeras of the X Location,'* Anton Anfalov.   Type: E

Location: Hertfordshire, England.
Date: 1921.
Time: Daytime.

A man was driving down a rural road with nothing going on, when he spotted a roadside tree stump up ahead. Sitting on the stump was a small (18" high) round-face being with a pointed cap which slouched over to one side. Before being able to secure a better look, the being was no longer there.

HC addendum.
Source: *Fortean Times*, 1993. Type: E
Comments: Date is approximate.

* * * * * * *

Location: Charters Towers, Queensland, Australia.
Date: 1921.
Time: Unknown.

An Aboriginal woman named "Delma" claimed she had been abducted by "six, 7ft tall male beings dressed in strange clothing" on a dirt road out from Charters Towers. She was only 19-years old at the time and remembers being dragged into bushland where there stood another man in the same clothes with a phone-like apparatus into which he spoke in some weird language. At this a large round, brown-colored flying machine appeared above them from out of nowhere and it was house-size. It landed with little sound and she was dragged screaming into it.
   Delma recalled; "I couldn't understand all the machinery inside and was terrified as the men held me down on a table; their faces looked yellowish, Asian-like, with narrow eyes. I was injected by one of them with a needle on the end of a long tube attached to a large box and became drowsy before I fell asleep."
   The room she was in was dimly lit and she doesn't remember much now as she woke up, naked, her clothes piled beside her on the floor of a bright blue, oval room into which she had apparently been taken while asleep. She had barely dressed when a round door about 6ft in diameter slid open and she quickly escaped out onto open ground near where she had been captured. The flying craft rose with a "whooshing" sound and flew high into the air, then shot off to the west at unbelievable speed. She told an informant years later.

HC addendum.
Source: Newsletter of the Blue Mountains UFO Research Club, Jan, 2012. Type: G

Location: Marseilles, Bouches du Rhone, France.
Date: Summer 1921.
Time: Afternoon.

"In 1921; a very hot year; I was playing one day among the hills of the North Canal. I was eight years old and I loved to lose myself in the moonlike landscape made by excavation, and from the First World War. Suddenly, two beings, wearing a sort of pliable helmet, literally leaped out from between some acacia trees. Without preliminaries, they dragged me toward what I thought was an oddly shaped tank. They took me up into the machine, without my being able to resist. I should say, without my being able to want to resist.

I suddenly began to cry; and I don't know whether that moved them, but after a while an opening appeared in the ceiling of the cabin, and in a few seconds I found myself on the ground. However, I had to walk most of the afternoon until I found myself near the road I had left five minutes before. When I got home that night, my parents treated me like a little liar, and no one believed me. I can now hardly add much detail to the machine, or its cabin. Doubtless, I was too astounded.

I only remember two details; there were square or at least rectangular portholes. The cabin had a kind of soft couch that I sat on." I seem to recall that their helmets appeared metallic. I don't recall any anatomical details, except that the two beings were very tall and very slender."

HC addendum.
Source: Joel Mesnard and Jean Marie Bigorne. Type: G
Comments: Classic early abduction report.

* * * * * * *

Location: Piedra Grande, Honduras.
Date: August 1921.
Time: Unknown.

A young girl called Emeteria Garcia was repeatedly visited by a fairy or goblin that would not let her sleep. The strange being that she called "Manuel," even went to the extreme of punching one young man in order to keep him away from her. The fairy manifested itself in a number of ways reminiscent of a poltergeist, such as by playing the guitar; invisibly, of course; and writing complex mathematical square root equations on the blackboard. Before a priest successfully exorcised Manuel, Emeteria said that she had been abducted by the being and taken to fantastic faraway places by it. Sometimes she would be found dazed and alone in unlikely and dangerous spots, including on cliff-tops.

HC addendum.
Source: Chris Aubeck, *'Return to Magonia.'*   Type: G?

* * * * * * *

Location: Mount Shasta, California.
Date: August, 1921.
Time: Night.

Elberta Payne was lying sick at her grandmother's home when she saw two large black "furry creatures" with large eyes, watching her through the bedroom window. Almost immediately she recovered from what was thought to have been typhoid fever.

HC addendum.
Source: Peter Guttilla, *'The Bigfoot File.'*   Type: E

* * * * * * *

Location: Eastbourne, NSW, Australia.
Date. December, 1921.
Time: Various.

"Eastbourne is being troubled, or entertained by a "ghost" mystery. A strange apparition has been seen several times gliding along the Crumbles, near the fisherman's huts, and across Fisherman's Green. As the place is within 800 yards of the spot on which Irene Munro was murdered, some of the local residents accept the theory that the spirit of the murdered girl is abroad by night; but one of those who has seen the "ghost" says it was a male figure.

It was first seen in the half-light of a December morning by Mr. Richard Prodger, a fisherman, who says he was walking towards the huts when an apparition, clothed in a long black gown, suddenly rose from the ground in front of him. As he moved forward, the ghostly figure went ahead some distance. When he stopped, the ghost stopped also.

"It was wearing a thing like an Ulster cap that reached down to the ground" he says. "It did not walk; it glided along. It wore also a big round hat. Three times I stopped and the ghost stopped, too. It continued in front of me right across Fishermen's Green, and then suddenly sank into the ground and disappeared. I walked to the spot, but saw no signs of the ghost. If I had not been loaded down with boat-hooks, I should have gone for it."

The same apparition has been seen by Mrs. Goldsmith, caretaker of the Fishermen's Institution, adjoining Fishermen's Green. She says the ghost was white and luminous. She was walking near the huts, when the strange figure emerged from between two of them like a white cloud. She stopped, trembling with fright, when just as suddenly, the apparition disappeared; "vanished into nothing."

Bolder spirits are making nightly visits to the spot, in an effort to run the strange visitor to Earth. Mr. Prodger is certain that the figure looked like a man who hanged himself in a house close to the huts and thinks it is only natural that he should return to his old home at Christmas time. On the other hand, Mrs. Goldsmith is equally sure that Irene Munro walks the Crumbles every night, while a girl who saw the ghost on her way home one night, says she could "see right through it" as it glided along and vanished through the side of a hut. More superstitious people dare not face the desolate waste after dark."

HC addendum.
Source: *Cairns Post* (Queensland), Monday, March 6, 1922.   Type: E?

* * * * * * *

Location: Tuna, Sweden.
Date: 1922.
Time: Evening.

Rita Raninger (involved in other encounters) watched a metallic disc-shaped object on the ground at close range. Several man-like figures wearing tight-fitting dark frogmen's suits were seen milling around the craft. It is said that after the object left, metallic traces were found on the ground. No other information.

HC addendum.
Source: UFO Information, Sweden.   Type: C

* * * * * * *

Location: Near Aracariguama, Brazil.
Date: 1922.
Time: Night.

In a wooded area, Emiliano Prestes saw a strange entity described as tall, man-like and resembling a bipedal wolf-like creature. The witness threw a rock at it and it ran into the brush quickly, disappearing from sight. The witness was the brother of Joao Prestes that in March 1946 died under bizarre and mysterious circumstances after being struck by a strange beam of light from the sky.

HC addendum.
Source: Pablo Villarubia Mauso. Type: E

* * * * * * *

Location: Near Lincoln, Nebraska.
Date: 1922.
Time: Night.

A man witnessed a large circular object land near his home; an eight-foot tall being emerged from the object. The witness, a deeply religious man, was sure the creature had to be the devil himself. *"Get thee behind me, Satan,"* he said, turning his back on the being in a symbolic Christian gesture. At that moment, he saw a second disc descending from the sky. It hovered above him, as if to protect him.

The witness heard voices coming from this object, which he recognized as quoting from the bible. As if in response to the sacred text, the tall being hurried off on foot. The witness followed the tracks it left to the spot where the creature's disc had landed. He felt that his religious interpretation was confirmed when he discovered that the tracks, which resembled hoof marks, passed straight through a barbed wire fence. The fence had been burnt through and was still very hot.

HC addendum.
Source: Chris Aubeck, *'Return to Magonia.'* Type: B or F?

* * * * * * *

Location: Between Welch and Blue Jacket, Kansas.
Date: Early February, 1922.
Time: Unknown.

"Dug out of a coal mine 200 feet below the surface; a strange stone image rests today in the home of Sam Jenkins, a miner living between Welch and Blue Jacket, across the Oklahoma line. Is it the petrified remains of a pre-historic man; the likeness of the first American caveman? Or is it merely a strange freak of nature in molding the human image during the formation of the coal strain?

The image is of black rock. Jenkins digging coal in the end of a drift mine, uncovered it. It is a trifle more than the average human size, showing a deep barrel chest, heavy-muscled arms and legs and a big well rounded head, with flattened forehead and features and powerful wide jaws. The neck is thick and short, the head almost nestling between the huge shoulders. The image is imperfect, for there are no hands or feet.

Before discovering the image, Jenkins, working along the vein of coal, unearthed the footprints of some huge pre-historic animal. The prints were perfectly formed in the shale and were in the same location where remains of a prehistoric animal were unearthed a few years ago. Hundreds of persons have flocked to the miner's cabin to look at the strange image. The image has the appearance of a man squatting, as sitting before a fire."

HC addendum.
Source: Kay Massingill in Magonia list quoting *The Miami Herald* (Miami FL) February 5, 1922. Type: X

* * * * * * *

Location: Hubbell, Nebraska.
Date: February 22, 1922,
Time: 5:00 a.m.

A hunter; William C. Lamb, was following mysterious tracks when he heard a crackling noise followed by a high-pitched sound and realized that a circular object was flying overhead. He hid behind a tree and saw this object, now brilliantly lighted, land in a hollow. Soon afterward a "magnificent" flying creature at least 8ft tall appeared that landed like an airplane and left traces in the snow. It passed by the tree and disappeared; Lamb followed the tracks for 5 miles before giving up.

HC addendum.
Source: Jacques Vallee. Type: C?

* * * * * * *

Location: County Donegal, Ireland.
Date: April, 1922.
Time: Early morning.

During the Irish civil war, soldier Lawrence Bradley came to a cave; the foliage at the entrance of which was burned. Soldiers sheltering inside said they had been awakened in the early morning by a 'whirring' sound, and fired at an object. The object fired jets of fire at the cave. As the soldiers emerged; the object, circular and metallic, was beginning to ascend.

HC addendum.
Source: INTCAT quoting FS Menace, Watford and *South Herts Post* April 30, 1964. Type: X

Location: Timber Lake, South Dakota.
Date: April, 1922.
Time: Afternoon.

Trapped by a blinding Dakota sleet storm without food or shelter, two Indian guides, John Stands On His Ear and his brother Joe, discovered one of the most mystic caves in America, brilliantly lighted from no apparent source of power, with walls carved with fascinating figures of Indian bells and fairies.

Like the poor little maiden in the dream books which every child has red, the Indian brothers were fighting a losing battle with the terrific storm. They turned loose their horses and sought shelter among the banks of the sluggish Missouri River; their clothes were wet and torn. Aimlessly they groped through the underbrush for a dry spot to rest their weary bones. They stepped into a hole; the hallway of fairyland but didn't know it.

John offered to lead the way. Down and down he crawled through the dark narrow passageway with Joe close at his heel. Suddenly they beheld an immense room, lighted like the mirrored stag of a Broadway cabaret. It was at least a mile long, half as wide and forty feet high. Near the entrance, as though thrown carelessly down by ancient warriors who had no use for them here, were large metal axes and spears with hilts of bone. On the south wall, near which was the opening from the outer world were startling drawings of great beasts, birds and reptiles such as had never been seen in pictures by the wandering men.

On this wall down toward the center of the great room was the life size painting of a woman seated in a 'throne' mounted on a strange looking beast. So marvelously had the artist wrought that the pictures seemed to stand out from the wall and for a moment the men were dominated by the feeling that they were standing in the living presence of a regal personage of mother age.

The features of the woman were fair and strikingly beautiful. Her light brown hair hung loose, cape-like garment of mixed blue and gold. The beast resembled a horse the head and the hoofs were cloven twice forming three blunt toes. Long the men gazed upon this masterpiece of an ancient mural artist and then turned to look upon the strangest and most startling thing yet disclosed. Near the center of the great room was long stone table surrounded by about twenty chairs of like construction and in each chair, the upright mummified body of a human; the remains of a prehistoric people of giant stature.

In the center of the table rested a huge bowl and on each side of it were two or three decanters. Each of the mummified bodies were smote with blood. Suddenly, from them came freezing moans and terrifying shrieks as though a million lost souls were voicing their lamentations. The men were no longer curious as to the furnishings of this age-old banquet hall. Their only desire on Earth was to again get on the outside of it and it is not unlikely that they straightened the hole some in making their exit from a place where they insist they would have had a view of the infernal regions had they the courage to remain. What they witnessed and heard were probably the products of the combined working of electricity and air currents but their views are so self-satisfying that it would be a shame to disabuse them were it not for the fact their assistance is needed if others are to have the privilege of visiting the most wonderful place.

When they emerged into the storm, they had but one thought in mind, and that was to travel the shortest route to the point farthest removed from where they were. They were picked up on the open prairie the next forenoon by another Indian, nearly dead from exposure, and taken to their home. All efforts to induce the men to assist in again locating the entrance to this cave of wonders having proving fruitless. They shake their heads and say that it is the earthly abode of the Evil Spirit and that misfortune might befall them if they again sought to find it.

HC addendum.
Source: *Aberdeen Daily American*, April 15, 1922, Magonia listing.
Type: X

* * * * * * *

Location: London, England.
Date: April 16, 1922.
Time: Night.

In 1922, a giant bat-like creature had been seen in the vicinity of West Drayton Church. An old man who claimed he had seen the giant bat twenty-five years previously, maintained that it was the spirit of a vampire who had murdered a woman to drink her blood in Harmondsworth in the 1890's. No one took the oldster's tale seriously.

Then, on the 16th April, 1922, so began a series of attacks on the general public which bore all the marks of a blood-sucking assailant. Several people witnessed a tall black creature with wings (similar to Mothman) flying around a church. They said that it went into the church cemeteries and ran around the graves. Two policemen chased it and it led out an awful scream and flew away. For a short period, the bustling metropolis of London was on vampire alert.

It was 6:00 a.m. and a local clerk was walking to work, heading down Coventry Street. Suddenly he was accosted from the shadows by an unseen form which bit him in the throat. The man collapsed unconscious to the floor, and awoke in Charing Cross Hospital where he told the surgeons of his grim encounter. His tale seemed too farfetched to the doctors, they believed he'd been stabbed in the neck. Then, just over two hours later, another attack took place. A second man rushed to the hospital and had the same encounter to speak of as blood trickled from his throat. He'd been attacked by an invisible predator at exactly the same spot.

As the hospital staff attempted to solve the mystery, during the late evening another man was attacked, his throat punctured by an unseen assailant at exactly the same spot; the turning just off Coventry Street. The police could not fathom as to what had happened and the press was quickly to lap up the grisly rumors that a vampire like attacker was on the loose, with the *Daily Mail* reporting on the sinister encounters.

A reporter boldly and yet sarcastically asked the police if a vampire could be on the loose, and the officer replied nervously, "That's all!" and left the conference. As hysteria rose in the area, there was a rumor that the police hired a vampire hunter, where he chased the being and stabbed him in the heart with a stake. The corpse being taken to Highgate Cemetery; soon after the attacks stopped.

HC addendum.
Source: http://www.thothweb.com/article201.html and http://www.bloodylexicon.com/monsters/coventry-street-vampire/
Type: X?

* * * * * * *

Location: Blackstone, North Carolina.
Date: May 20, 1922.
Time: Unknown.

"A party composed of Mr. and Mrs. W. L. Thomas, Charles, Walter L. and Edmund Thomas, Misses Graves and Ella Satterfield and Taylor Long left here in automobiles early last Sunday morning for Blackstone to see the fallen 'meteor,' but returned however, stating that the nearer they locality, that had been described by the press, that the meteor fell they found upon inquiring of the neighborhood people that they knew nothing of the event and they returned home without ever locating the much talked-of area.

It is reported by others who claim to have been near, that stranger than the meteor itself, is an old man of unearthly appearance who stood near the scene immobile, neither speaking or apparently looking at the throngs of curious sightseers. The superstitious believing that he came down with the precipitating meteor."

HC addendum.
Source: *Greensboro NC Daily News*, May 22, 1922.   Type: E?

Location: Rannoch Moor, Scotland.
Date: Summer 1922.
Time: Evening.

James Halliday was enjoying a leisurely holiday and all the benefits of the unexpected "Indian Summer." Halliday had stopped briefly to catch his breath on lonely Rannoch Moor when he heard heavy footsteps clumping across the moorland path towards him. Thinking that it might be a shepherd or a gamekeeper, he glanced around. Then the footsteps stopped; and Halliday saw that there was nobody there. But even as he stared, he heard them again, growing louder and coming with every second that passed.

Although Halliday could see for miles back along the path, there was nobody in sight. He turned and ran down the hillside. By then he was so petrified with fear that he did not dare look back for fear of what he might see. And all this time, the ghostly feet pounded rapidly after him. Just when they were almost upon him, Halliday stumbled and slid down a gully. Then the footsteps halted.

Anxiously, not knowing what to he expected to see, the hiker looked around and back up at the path. This time there was somebody there. To Halliday's horror the most grotesque looking man he had ever seen was standing a few yards away, grinning evilly at him. It was a man with a large head shaped like an egg, out of all proportion to the size of his body. As the man walked past him, Halliday, horrified by the hideous sight, almost fainted for fear that the creature might lumber closer to him.

Twilight was falling as Halliday, too terrified to do anything else, trudged along the path behind the distant monstrous figure. Although the apparition glided on effortlessly, Halliday floundered among the rough clumps of heather and stones, and shook all over with fear in case the man turned and came back towards him. A ghostly white mist had begun to creep down from the mountain tops above the path which now took a slight incline towards a large gray boulder some distance ahead.

When the apparition reached this rock, he walked into the rock and disappeared. Presently as he emerged from the mist-shrouded mountain side, Halliday saw the lights of Rannoch Station ahead of him. He went to the village inn, where in the dining room, he joined the hotel's only other guest for dinner. Later that same night, Halliday apparently encountered the same eerie figure sitting on a parapet on a small bridge.

HC addendum.
Source: John Macklin, 'Challenge to Reality.'   Type: E

Location: Detroit, Michigan.
Date: Summer 1922.
Time: About 10:00 p.m.

Mrs. Irma Hinz was walking home from a movie with a young friend when the two teenagers saw a large disk-shaped object hovering over a vacant lot on Dragoon Avenue. The sky suddenly lit up and the object descended to the height of a large tree and slowly revolved as it hovered, around the perimeter of the bottom of the object were rectangular windows, lit from within; seated at these windows were approximately 20 entities that were seen only from the shoulders/neck up. They were bald headed, with eyes set close together, and they were staring intently at the young couple.

No other features were observed, Mrs. Hinz and her date watched for several minutes, but left quickly when they became frightened. Although Mrs. Hinz told her parents at the time, her mother tended to believe it was a "vision" of some kind. She recalls her date's name was William O'Brien.

HC addendum.
Source: Ron Westrum and Ted Bloecher. Type: A

* * * * * * *

Location: Chippewa County, Michigan.
Date: June 1922.
Time: Early morning.

"Famer folk of Chippewa County are in an uproar over the remarkable "miracle" rescue story told by D. K. Brown, for three generations a local farmer and noted as one of the most devout men in Michigan. Brown recently became lost in the wilderness near his house and asserts he was rescued after the manner of the Children of Israel of biblical times, by a God-sent light which appeared in answer to his prayer; after darkness had settled and he had given up hope of ever getting out of the forest alive.

The story is endorsed by his wife who is also noted for her religious faith and who led the searching parties. Other members of the posse also tell of seeing the "light." Such evidence is given the story by farmer folk that they have held a religious revival in which farmers and their families within a radius of 25 miles came. According to Mrs. Brown's story, it was a Sunday morning and they were bringing the cows home by diving them in front of a buggy. An automobile horn frightened the animals into the bush. Brown got out and started to round them up. He did not reappear and the posse was gathered by the pastor's son, who went to church, held a short prayer and then brought the men to the scene. The party searched all day Sunday and at night heavy thunder showers came up and they had to quit until the next morning and continued throughout the night. Here Brown takes up the narrative:

"Night came and I found I was in a thick swamp amidst spruce and elder trees. Then it began to rain. I fell in spring holes over his knees and I got faint and tired. It kept raining. I gave up all hope of help and then I remembered the Thirty-third Psalm. This poor man cried and the Lord heard him and saved him out of his troubles. I caught a sapling to hold myself in the heavy rain and cried out my prayer.

I had hardly finished when I noticed an opening in the dense underbrush. This opening appeared to open the way toward a light. It was not fire, but appeared to be more like the northern lights. "Then I noticed a white object which appeared like a seagull's wing. There was no head body or tail attached to these wings, but the light seemed to radiate from this. This object seemed to move and slowly rose from the ground and circled.

For a long time I followed; more than a mile I should say, and then came to a thick brush. The light passed over and into this and the thick brush, soaking wet, began to burn. I stood beside it warming and crying myself. I looked again and the winged fire I had been following had disappeared, but I was sure God had led me to a spot where I would be found. Just then a voice at my elbow said, *"Why Brown, what are you doing out here at this time of night?"* It was H. O. Blixt who spoke. I went around the fire and there under a tent were six men who had ventured into the forest to search for me."

HC addendum.
Source: Kay Massingill, Magonia Exchange, citing the *Evening Gazette* (Port Jervis, N. Y.) June 07, 1922. Type: X

* * * * * * *

Location: Lake District, England.
Date: June, 1922.
Time: Evening.

Theosophist Geoffrey Hodson claimed to have had a "psychic" vision of a creature he called a "Deva" on a hilly area. He described seeing a huge, brilliant crimson, bat-like thing, which fixed a pair of burning eyes on him. The form was not concentrated into the true human shape, but was somehow spread out like a bat with a human face and eyes, and with wings outstretched over the mountainside.

As soon as it felt itself, to be observed it flashed into its proper shape, as if to confront the witness, fixed its piercing eyes on him and then sank into the hillside and disappeared.

HC addendum.
Source: Michael D. Winkle, quoting Hodson, *'Faeries at Work and at Play.'*   Type: E or F?

* * * * * * *

Location: Targowek, Warsaw, Poland.
Date: June or July, 1922.
Time: Afternoon.

The main witness was taking a stroll with his brother-in-law and aunt when they saw something descending from the sky and at the same time emitting a whistling sound. The startled witnesses were sure it was going to crash but somehow the object managed to stop in mid-air at about 6.5ft to 10ft above the ground. The object resembled an enormous slightly flattened sphere; something like two plates connected together by their upper rims. It looked like it was made out of aluminum, kind of silvery but also somewhat gray metallic in color.

The witnesses stood at about 330-500ft away from the object. The main witness noticed that both sections of the saucer were separated by a sort of rotating ring. The other parts of the craft remained motionless. Soon the rotating section stopped and he saw something resembling a frame; probably a section of the craft's windows. He got the impression that the crew of the object was observing the stunned group of observers.

The witness was convinced that the craft was going to land and they "would be invited onboard" but moments later the craft shot up at an angle of circa 45 degrees, followed by a loud blast and it vanished into the distance.

HC addendum.
Source: Bronislaw Rzepecki and Krysztof Piechota.   Type: A?

Location: Mont Pelvoux, Massif Des Ecrins, France.
Date: July 13, 1922.
Time: Morning.

My friend Charles Artrois has sent me the following curious letter. From every point of view it seems to me to be sufficiently interesting to justify its publication:
"...Last summer I had a curious adventure which was so incredible that I have hitherto hesitated to tell you about it. Ever since I have been wondering whether the events that I am about to relate were actual facts or nothing more than a series of hallucinations. I have not even mentioned them to a single friend for fear of making myself ridiculous. But these events have made such an impression upon me and all the details are so clearly imprinted on my mind that I have decided to tell you about them.

Possibly someone of our friends may be able to refer the incident to some actual occurrence which is within his personal knowledge. It is the question of the disappearance among the mountains of a climber on July 22, 1922. I have myself been quite unable to obtain any news of such an event, but then of course, the man may have come from a distance without anyone being aware that he was in the region where I met him. However, here are the facts; they are as clear to me now as on the day when they occurred.

During the morning of July 13, 1922, I made an unaccompanied ascent of Mont Pelvoux. In spite of my solitude, and in defiance of all sound mountaineering principles, I had made up my mind to try to follow the ridge which dips steeply to the north of the Pointe Durand and then, if the ridge became impracticable, to make my way across the wall overhanging the Glacier Noir. Those who have seen the grim wall connecting the Ailefroide with Mont Pelvoux will remember that it is one of the most sinister and imposing precipices in the Alps. Never expose to the rays of the sun, the blackness of the wall is relieved only by sheets of 'verglas'(a thin coating of ice on rock) and step ribs of rock, like knife blades, separated by icy chimneys.

Reaching the Pointe Durand quite early I gave myself up to the enjoyment of the truly wonderful weather. There is a great joy in lying alone in the sunshine on a summit of 4,000 meters. One feels the pride of a sovereign surveying from the roof of his palace, all the fair country which he has conquered. Then a great restfulness banishes all else. Not a sound reaches to this height, and lying at full length upon the rock one's breast seems filled with a sense of life and freedom.

But it would not do to remain too long in this condition of delicious torpor. The Glacier Noir which I had planned to reach before nightfall was far below, and the ridge which I hoped would lead me thither seemed to take a sudden and uncompromising dive into nothingness. A start was soon made. There was no difficulty at first, but I was soon at the upper edge of a narrow chasm, to the bottom of which I had to climb over nasty steep slabs. I was now no longer in the cheering sunshine and the resulting chill in the air made me settle to my task in more serious mood.

Following the ridge but a short distance further I was brought up by a steep gendarme. However, it was surmounted without much difficulty, but the further side proved so vertical that a descent had to be made by the western face. On the slabs of the face it seemed much safer to make use of a doubled rope. So, looping it over an apparently firm knob of rock I proceeded to climb down, depending from time to time entirely on my support from above.

All seemed going well when suddenly my knob of rock must have coma adrift. I fell! A momentary feeling of terror. My breast heaved and my hands convulsively clutched the rope. I tried to open my horrified eyes. Then nothing more. I must have struck my head against the rock. When I came to myself I found I was on a narrow cornice, which had providentially checked my fall almost as soon as it had commenced. My head was aching severely and my hands were covered with blood. Soon I began to look about me.

My astonishment can be imagined when I saw a man coming along the cornice towards me. He was a short man wearing a large cape which at first almost hid his face. He advanced slowly, making his way carefully along the narrow ledge. He was close enough for me to make out more of his features, a broad brow and large and deep set black eyes. These dark and somber eyes affected me most curiously and seemed almost to fascinate me. He did not utter a single word, but, taking one end of my rope, he secured it round his waist. So great an influence had he already established over me that, without demur, I tried on to the other end. He silently pointed out the way and began to descend. Mechanically I took in the slack of the rope, passed it around a rock, and 'payed' it out as he advanced.

On the way down we met with no serious difficulties. The rock was dry and the angle not particularly steep. We had been going for perhaps an hour when my companion signaled to me to look at a small cloud capping the summit of the Pointe des Ecrins opposite. Then he went on at a faster pace. I soon saw that we should be caught: a storm was about to burst.

Only a few minutes later a huge yellow cloud came surging up behind the Pic Salvador Guillemin. In a moment it was on us, disgorging a hurricane armed with sheets of hail. So strong was the wind that we had to claw hold of the rocks to avoid being blown off. There we remained unable to stir, our brows glued to the rock, seeing nothing and hearing only the uproar of the hurricane and the crash of the stones falling on all sides of us. My cap was snatched from my head and lost in the mist.

Little by little the wind decreased, but snow began to fall in its place and the rocks became covered. A move had to be made and we started down again. The mantle of snow grew deeper and deeper, my feet kept slipping in the hidden and icy steps, and my hands were too frozen to grip the holds. Our progress was slower. Suddenly we were held up by a vertical wall of rock falling away directly under our feet. Anxiously we diverged first right and then left, trying to find a way down, but finally stopped on a narrow terrace on the very edge of the abyss.

All at once m companion began to show symptoms of most feverish excitement. He made wild and meaningless gesticulations, and then suddenly stood stock still and seemed to transfix me with wide staring eyes alight with madness. He pointed at the abyss with outstretched arms. His intention was plain even to my disordered imagination; thither he meant to go. Plunging forward he leapt into the gulf. Fascinated, I was about to follow.

Just in time my sanity returned and my mind rebelled against the mad act. I threw myself back and snatched the rope round a projecting rock. There was a terrific strain, then nothing more. The rope had broken. A hollow sound reached me from below and, leaning far over, I saw through a rift in the clouds, a body sliding rapidly down the slopes of the glacier. Struck with horror and quite powerless I was afraid to move. Time has passed.

The snow is abating, the mists open out and then disappear. The sun has set behind the mountain. Night is falling. It is too late to make another start. There is nothing for it but to find a safer place in which to sit and wait. Night is now supreme, a fine summer night with the clear sky of high altitudes, full of countless twinkling stars, a night silent, freezing and endless.

During one of these intervals of wakefulness I fancied I saw a glimmer of light below me. I leant over the edge and was able to make out plainly one, two, three lights, one following the other over the glacier in the valley bottom. No doubt a late party coming down from the Col du Temple. I seemed unable to take my eyes off these three little flickering gleams.

On they came, slowly, making numerous zigzags to avid the crevasses. They were just below me; now they should reach the corpse of my companion. I was just going to call to them when aw the lanterns stop. Then they began to swing to and fro, like censers, and to my stupefaction and horror, the notes of a chant came floating up to me; "*De profundis clamavi...*" I seemed to see these travelers of the night wind a rope round the body of the dead man and lower him into a crevasse. Then pieces of ice were heaped into the cleft.

I clearly heard the noise of the ice blocks striking the walls of the crevasse, and each blow resounded like a passing bell. The somber voices went on, "*Requiescat in pace...*" Then once more silence, a silence even more mournful than the chant. The lights resumed their journey; they were soon lost to view behind a rocky spur.

Succumbing to faintness and fatigue I later fell asleep, once more to be roused only by the dawn of the morrow. Torpid in brain and limb, the sun, already covering the Pointe des Ecrins, decided me to move. Looking downwards I could see no sign of my companion and could find no practicable route.

There was nothing for it but to retrace the whole of the steps traversed the previous day. The ascent of the wall, still covered with fresh snow, proved not only difficult but dangerous. Once the summit was reached the descent of the other side was without incident. I passed through Ailefroide without passing, and at once turned towards the Glacier Noir and walked up it as far as the point at which my companion had fallen. There I saw nothing. Nothing but virgin expanses of snow, slopes of black ice, and gaping crevasses.

I turned back to Ailefroide. With calmer mind I tried to puzzle things out as I walked. I passed in review all the details of my adventure, details so incredible as to suggest those of a nightmare. Were these extravagances nothing but hallucinations? Finally, I came to the conclusion that I must have been dreaming; but the details are so clear, so clear, I do not know what I am to believe."

HC addendum.
Source: Bruno Mancusi in Magonia Exchange, quoting Rene-Lucien Rousseau, *L'envers des contes: valeur initiatique et pensee secrete des contes de fees,* Dangles, Saint-Jean-de-Braye, France 1988.   Type: E?

* * * * * * *

Location: (Undisclosed location) Czechoslovakia.
Date: September 19, 1922.
Time: Night.

After observing a hovering circular object in the sky, the witness sees a bright blue flash and experienced a four hour memory loss. No other information.

HC addendum.
Source: http://www.ufo.cz/zare/seznamy.htm   Type: G?
Comments: Unexplored abduction event?

Location: Braeraich, Scotland.
Date: 1923.
Time: Unknown.

A mountain climber descending on the slope of the mountain heard footsteps behind him; he turned and was terrified to see a huge gray man-like figure with pointed ears, long legs and feet with talons. The witness ran away from the area.

HC addendum.
Source: Graham J. McEwan, *'Mystery Animals of Britain and Ireland.'*
Type: E

* * * * * * *

Location: Near Mount Erie, Illinois.
Date: June, 1923.
Time: Afternoon.

Norman Massie was 10-year old when he went out to take his horses into a pasture. As he led his horses through the gate, he observed an object with lights all around it nearby. He walked to within 50 feet of the object and noticed five men onboard the craft. He described the men as about 4ft tall with blond hair. As he got closer he could hear them talking. One of the men sat on a chair, and the others referred to him as "Commander."

The other men made trips back and forth into the object. Massie then overhead one of the men tell the commander that the repairs had been made. The object was described as metallic and standing on three legs. It had a dome on top with holes in it. The top of the object resembled melted glass. The object then rose up and hovered and the tripod legs telescoped up into the belly of the craft, which went straight up then shot away towards the west at high speed.

HC addendum.
Source: Len Wells, *Evansville Courier*.   Type: A & B

Location: Barcelona, Spain.
Date: August, 1923.
Time: Night.

Jacques B. Bley, the 12-year old son of a Barcelona industrialist, suffered from "lympathy-pathological obesity; and could make no progress in school. One August night he felt an irresistible impulse to go to the terrace of his house, overlooking the sea. Then "in the sea appeared delta-shaped vehicles, of massive and metallic appearance." Three of them came to rest on the terrace; "their dimensions oscillated between 6 and 10ft."

One of them "opened up like a fan" and there emerged a man about 4ft tall, whose face only was visible, the rest of his body being hidden by a mantle apparently covered with diamonds, beneath which could be seen a "shining" knitwear garment clinging to the body, "hardly touching the ground with his feet," and told him that they had "taken him under their protection" and that he would now become strong both in body and intelligence. He gave the boy something resembling a large square piece of chocolate and told him to eat it.

Then the man re-entered his vehicle, and it went off into the sky toward the north at a high rate of speed. Jacques ate the "chocolate;" it tasted of tar, and the flavor remained all day. Within the next three years he was transformed into a young athlete with an exceptional physique.

He performed as a gymnast in a circus, and became an intrepid mountain climber. At one time during the civil war, he survived a fusillade by three hired killers, who fired revolvers at him at a range of 12 feet until their guns were empty; none of the bullets touched him. Later in life, living in Andorra, he became an enormously successful executive, and developed the faculty of "psychic surgery" with his bare hands. At the age of 61, he was still physically a young man.

HC addendum.
Source: Antonio Ribera. Type: B

* * * * * * *

Location: Otter Cliffs, Mount Desert Island, Maine.
Date: Autumn 1923.
Time: 11:00 p.m.

At the US Navy compass station, the radio operator on duty was monitoring a violent electrical storm when a lightning bolt hit the cable outside the building. The bolt went through the transmission key and landed inside the man's abdomen. A fiery light seemed to shine from the witness's stomach as a soft light went through the station roof, which then formed a field of light that surrounded the now paralyzed witness and extended into a seven foot radius.

Suddenly there were three flashes of light and three majestic looking men appeared standing in front of the witness. They wore shining robes and were smiling. Each bowed at the witness without speaking. The three men described as having very fine features, with light cream textured complexions and extremely bright eyes. They wore soft form-fitting boots.

The being to the left of the witness pointed his finger at the fiery ball of light on the witness abdomen and in a flash of light it leaped into the being's hand that then tossed it to the being next to him, that then tossed it to the third being who threw it into the copper mesh screening of the station, the fiery ball went up in a shower of sparks and disappeared. All three men then smiled, bowed again, and disappeared in three flashes of light.

HC addendum.
Source: Shirley C. Fickett, *Alternate Perceptions* #28, quoting Ray Fowler. Type: E

* * * * * * *

Location: Mount Leinster, County Carlow, Ireland.
Date: November, 1923.
Time: Afternoon.

The witness was on her way to bring home her father's cows and she had quite a distance to go along the narrow twisting lanes, thick with mud in places, that led to the field of rough sparse grass at the foot of the mountain where the cows were. Having arrived at the field, she opened the gate and stood back to let the cows through. Usually they would all be crowded round the gate, anxious to get in and out of the cold and damp and away from the scanty autumn grass to the warmth and good feeding of the byre. But now only four cows stood close to the gate, the other three being in a group twenty or more yards away.

Having let the first lot pass, she stepped into the field to get the other three, but they came on at once, so she waited by the ditch to let them go by. A gray one led them, a favorite of hers, and it was not more than four or five paces from her when a little "fairy" appeared from its far side. He looked fresh and young, perhaps of her own age, and he moved quickly as if he were in a hurry thought not a desperate hurry. He passed close in front of the cow, which tossed her head, making a pass at him with its horns. As it did so he looked round at it, in what seemed to her a friendly and possessive way, and gave it a light tap on the nose with a switch of sally or osier which he carried in his right hand.

He then glanced quickly but intently at the girl, whom he almost touched, and then, walking up to the ditch, he took a long step across it and disappeared right into the bank. He seemed to walk into the solid earth with the same ease that an ordinary human being would walk through a bead curtain. She described the entity as about four and a half feet tall, he wore a black cap turned up in front, which was rather like a sou'wester but neater, of much finer material and more closely fitting, a bright red coat, which was buttoned up in front, and on his legs buff trews, which seemed rather tight.

HC addendum
Source: Dermot Mac Manus, *'The Middle Kingdom.'*　　　Type: E

* * * * * * *

Location: Dunwich, Suffolk, England.
Date: Pre 1924.
Time: Various.

In an area known as the "red stile" between Dunwich and Heveningham a pale phantom figure described as wearing a white veil, or having black patches around the head has been seen. One brave man touched the entity, and went numb down his right side. A large black hound-like creature was also reported in the area, and a clanking chain heard.

HC addendum.
Source: http://paranormaldatabase.com/suffolk/　　　Type: E?

Location: Dade City, Florida.
Date: 1924.
Time: Daytime.

Ultra-Terrestrial Pod

Mrs Evelyn Wendt, when a small girl, was playing in the schoolyard. "The first thing I remember is that this egg-shaped thing was on the ground, and this bright light was shining in my eyes. Then the light went out, a hatch opened and little people emerged. I think they were robots; they were smaller than I, and resembled animated flowers with faces where the bud would be. They were carrying a weapon of some sort to the school's science building. I was told they were going to stop the work that was being done in the science building; they said if the work continued, they would destroy the place.

Later I heard the place was a shambles. There seemed to be a man with the little people. The conversation wasn't real talking; when they were going to leave, they asked if I wanted to go, but I said, *"no."* They promised to come back for me in 35 years, but nothing happened. The saucer was leaden looking and very pockmarked, then when it started up, its molecules expanded and it turned silvery bright. It went straight up, hovered, and then disappeared."

Not surprisingly, Wendt's memory of the incident was not entirely clear after the fifty years that had passed since the day. She recalled that "there seemed to be a man with the little people," but not much else. There was some telepathic communication and they invited the girl to go with them in their craft, but she said she didn't want to. "They promised to come back for me in thirty five years, but that was up a long time ago and nothing happened that I know of."

HC addendum.
Source: Timothy Green Beckley, *'Book of Space Contacts,'* 1981, citing
Stephen Putnam. Type: B

* * * * * * *

Location: Near Honolulu, Hawaii.
Date: 1924.
Time: 4:30 p.m.

At "the sand island in Honolulu," third grader Sidro L. Basa, 8, was catching crabs alone, when he saw a canoe arrive, about 100 yards away, with three little children and a dog. Puzzled at seeing no adults, he went up to one whose back was turned and asked, *"Where's your mother?"* The "child" turned around, showing a face that was adult, old, and wrinkled. Frightened, Sidro "fled for dear life."

HC addendum.
Source: *Amazing Stories,* 1946. Type: E

* * * * * * *

Location: Quero, La Mancha, Spain.
Date: 1924.
Time: Afternoon.

The witness was standing near a local rural church when he saw a short humanoid figure about 1.20 meters in height wearing a tight-fitting green-colored coverall, it had its arms and legs in a rigid position and approached to within 2 meters of the witness. The humanoid seemed to have both feet together and, resting on some type of circular platform that apparently propelled him above the ground. On his hands he carried an object or control panel that seemed to operate the floating platform.

The humanoid, which had human features, disappeared silently into some distance fields.

HC addendum.
Source: Iker Jimenez, 'Encuentros: Historia de Los Ovni en España.'
Type: E

* * * * * * *

Location: Wigan, England.
Date: 1924.
Time: Various.

Several times the witness saw in a field of daisies seven or eight pairs of little people dancing, suspended about three feet off the ground. They were dressed in brown with long pointed caps and pointed feet. They sported impish grins; one fairy was different in that she was dressed in a shiny pink beautiful gown and had an aura of pink about her.

HC addendum.
Source: *Fortean Times,* 1993.   Type: E
Comments: Date is approximate.

* * * * * * *

Location: Yekaterinoslav, Ukraine, USSR.
Date: 1924.
Time: Early morning.

The three daughters of a Soviet Army Captain Andriychuk, simply vanished. Captain Andriychuk was of Russian desent and very little is known about him, except that he traveled a lot. A farmer that lived near Captain Andriychuk's house said that he saw the Captain's daughters walking towards the woods maybe 2 hours before sunrise. Intrigued, he followed them at a distance. After walking for 30 minutes he described seeing "purple and red lights and mist" through the trees. He got closer and saw the two girls entering what he called "a floating bright windmill-like plane." He also reported seeing five creatures as small as children but with a "much older face."
According to him the "windmill" then flew very slowly "into the stars" until he could not tell them apart. According to the farmer, he ran to Captain Andriychuk's house to warn him about the event. Upon arriving, he knocked on the door but nobody answered. He then entered the house and found the Captain and his wife dead on their bed; their faces "were peaceful," as if they had died during their sleep. All their animals (three

dogs, one horse and two goats) were dead as well. On the kitchen table there was a letter or note (not signed) with the handwriting that matched Sofiya, one of the daughters. It stated (in part); *"We are going to the school on the Moon, with our friends."*

HC addendum.
Source: Dante Di Santori, *'Book of Alien Races.'*   Type: X?

* * * * * * *

Location: Savasse, Drome, France.
Date: 1924 (or 1925-1926).
Time: Evening.

Ms. X (her name known to investigators) deceased in 1969; at the time the witness was living on an isolated farm near Montelimar, between Savasse and Condillac. The habitation had no electricity. One evening while knitting by the chimney glow, she was attracted by a light coming through the window. Once outside, she then saw at the end of the dirt road 150 meters away and between two poplars, a ball with a beam of light shining down. She was able to distinguish shadows moving in that light and coming her direction. Then suddenly the whole phenomena disappeared.

HC addendum.
Source: UFO-Informations (Newsletter from the Association of friends of Marc Thirouin) No. 34.   Type: B?
Comments: Intriguing that the phenomena "suddenly disappeared." Did something else occur that the witness never remembered?

* * * * * * *

Location: Coast of Margate, Durban, South Africa.
Date: April, 1924.
Time: Afternoon.

"Strange Battle witnessed on the coast of Africa."
"H. C. Balance of the Margate Estate here was walking along the seacoast when he saw two whales battling for life against a strange sea monster whose head reared up 20 feet above the surface of the sea. Ballance watched while the monster killed both whales and exhausted, floated ashore on its back. Balance remembered an appointment and went home, but returned to the beach next morning and found the monster stranded and unconscious. He measured it and found it was 47

feet long with a tail 10 feet long and 2 feet wide and instead of head, a trunk like an elephant's, but resembling a pig's snout at the end.

The monster was entirely covered with snow-white hair 10 inches long. For ten days it remained on the beach, apparently resting. The natives saw it refloat itself and swim off in a southeasterly direction.

HC addendum.
Source: *Dansville Breeze*, Dansville, NY, April 16 or 18, 1924.   Type: X?

* * * * * * *

Location: Gem, West Virginia.
Date: May, 1924.
Time: Afternoon.

A farmer outside Gem in monster haunted Braxton County reported seeing an 'airplane' crash in a forest. Planes were a very rare sight in those days, especially in West Virginia, and a crashing plane was big news. According to the farmer, the plane was very odd in that it didn't seem to have any wings, didn't make any noise and seemed unusually large. "As big as a battleship" is the way the farmer described it. A party of men, including the local sheriff and local newsman John Cole systematically searched the woods. Within hours they found the wreck in a small clearing. According to Cole;

"We weren't the first ones there, though. There were already five or six men in the clearing. Some of them were dressed in black business suits, neckties and all, and that seemed damned silly in that neck of the woods." Others were dressed in coveralls of a funny color; some kind of very shiny material. They were talking among themselves in a rapid-fire foreign language when they found them. They got real excited when they saw the search party. The men in coveralls ran into the wreck; like they were trying to hide.

Some of the men in the search party were carrying guns and one of them said to Cole, *"By God, they're spies!"* and he raised his gun. The strangers were all small, just a little over five feet tall, and they all looked like Orientals, with high cheekbones, slanted eyes, and dark skin. One of them spoke English. He told the men nobody was hurt, that everything was all right. He said he would call on the sheriff later and make out a complete report. There wasn't much they could do. No crime had been committed. Nobody was hurt.

According to Cole while he was looking around he spotted a 'little thingamajig" on the ground. He picked it up and decided to keep it. He doesn't know why he just didn't turn it over to one of "foreigners." He put it in his pocket. They all finally went away, leaving the foreigners to fuss with their contraption. It didn't look like much of a flying machine.

It face, Cole didn't think it could fly at all. It was like a fuselage of a modern plane, with windows and all. But it didn't have any wings, tail or propellers. And like the farmer said, it was mighty big. According to Cole at least seventy five feet long, it filled the whole clearing.

He went back home in Weston and went right to bed. He was pretty tired from all the day's hiking. About three a. m. somebody started pounding on his door. He got up and looked and there was an army officer standing there. He was dressed in one of those broad-brimmed hats they used to wear, with those leg wrappings and all. It was a U.S. Army uniform, but except for his clothes he looked just like those foreigners from the airplane. Slant eye, dark skin, but he was maybe a little taller. *"You picked up something today,"* he said. *"We need it back."* Cole was half asleep and at first he couldn't think what he meant. Then he remembered the metal 'thingamajig" It was still in his coat pocket. Cole went and got it.

"Is this what you mean?" He asked him. He didn't answer; he just grabbed it and walked off without a word. He didn't, seem to have a horse or a car. Cole shuffled back to bed. But the next day he started wondering about it. How had the supposed officer managed to track him down? A couple of days later he went back to those woods and found that clearing. It was empty. The grass and bushes were all crushed down where the airplane had been but there was no other sign of anything or anybody. After the Army 'officer' came by, Cole figured that maybe it was a secret Army deal of some kind and he thought it was better to leave it alone.

HC addendum.
Source: John A. Keel, *Saga* 1975 UFO Annual, and *'The Eighth Tower.'*
Type: H, C or E?

* * * * * * *

Location: Near Peñascosa, Albacete, Spain.
Date: Summer 1924.
Time: Afternoon.

Rogelia Juarez Barba, her husband Domingo Martinez Alarcon and several other field workers were on their way to nearby field outside of town when they all spotted an object descend from the sky landing near a ranch called "Ramoncillos," within the Cerro de Cruz valley. The craft was described as rounded, spherical in shape with a metallic surface very smooth and shiny that emitted an intense silvery glow. It was the ground supported by four metallic legs. There was a small door from which two men both over 2 meters in height emerged; both wore tight-fitting silvery suits and loose-fitting caps.

Some of the witnesses claimed the men seemed to lack mouths, other sources reported that the men were blond-haired with large slanted eyes. Apparently the object and the strange beings remained on the ground for two days (!) and seemed to be studying the local field workers and shepherds. On several occasions when locals attempted to approach the men, these would re-enter the object. After two days the object rose up into the air emitting a sound similar to that of a 'deflating bicycle tire.' On the ground, the workers found a strange ground indentation similar to a large letter "H" about 5-6 meters in longitude.

HC addendum.
Source:http://www.looculto.260mb.com/ovnisenespana/ovnisenespana.htm
Comments: Translated by Albert S. Rosales.   Type: B

* * * * * * *

Location: Northern Iraq.
Date: July 24, 1924.
Time: Unknown.

Lieutenant W. T. Day and Pilot Officer D.R. Day
Missing July 24th 1924 - Never seen again!

Both temperatures and tempers were blazing in the summer of 1924, in the Middle Eastern desert. In the area then known as Mesopotamia, the Arabs were fighting and the British were trying to keep a hand on the situation. On July 24, Flight Lieutenant W.T. Day and Pilot Officer D.R. Stewart took off in their single engine plane for a routine, four hour long reconnaissance flight over the area. When the fliers failed to return, a search party was sent out after them.

The next day their plane was found; in perfect condition. The craft had not been shot down. Moreover, gasoline was in the tank and the engine turned over as soon as it was started. But where were Day and Stewart? And why did they land in an area of barren desert. Looking for clues the search party noted boot marks where the officers had jumped out of the plane. Their footprints showed that the men had left the plane and walked along, side by side for about 120 feet. Then, while still standing next to each other, the men simply stopped; and vanished. A half dozen of desert tribesmen, soldiers in armored trucks and search planes never turned up a trace of the pilots, who seemed to have walked off the surface of the Earth.

HC addendum.
Source: http://library.thinkquest.org/C007446F/disappear.htm
Comments: Permanent abduction? Type: G?

* * * * * * *

Location: Denver, Colorado.
Date: August 29, 1924.
Time: Unknown.

A local woman; Mrs. H. C. Hutchinson, reported that she had received telepathic messages from the "Martians" on this day. Among the information she received from the "Elder Brothers," was the fact that they had come to Earth two million years before to establish a colony here. The main concern of Martian men was to find human women to make love with, as on Mars this is done by a process of 'parthenogenesis.'

HC addendum.
Source: W. Raymond Drake, *'Gods and Spacemen in the Ancient East,'* 1974, citing Robert Ernest Dickhoff, *'Homecoming of the Martians.'*
http://en.wikipedia.org/wiki/Parthenogenesis Type: F?

* * * * * * *

Location: Wilkowyje, Poland.
Date: September, 1924.
Time: 8:00 p.m.

Two brothers were sitting next to the main road between Mikolow and Tichy. It was around 2000 and it was getting dark. As they talked, one of them noticed a mysterious figure sitting on a stone about 2 meters away. The figure was that of a woman with a gray kerchief on her head. He didn't notice any facial features. She was motionless, sitting on the stone where a few moments ago nobody was seen.

The man realized that it was some kind of "phantom" and drew his brother's attention to her. Both men became afraid and slowly began walking away. After a while they reached their neighbor's house and told the occupants about the strange female sitting on the stone next to their gate. The house contained a family of about ten people and they were all having supper when the two brothers arrived, upon hearing about what the boys had seen they all went outside to investigate. The mysterious woman was still motionless, sitting on the stone.

Several persons then began gathering around her and began to surround her, wondering who she was and where she was from. One of the local men heard about the situation and grabbing a whip, he ran to the middle of the crowd and began swinging the whip at the "phantom" and shouting, *"What are you doing here?"*

Moments later the strange figure disappeared in plain sight as the whip struck the stone. It was the night of the full moon and everything was very clearly seen. As the entity vanished one of the boys noticed a shadow moving away, it was seen climbing a nearby fence and it resembled that of a "man" running away. It is said that the strange woman appeared there many other times and was seen once crossing the road.

HC addendum.
Source: P. A. Cielebias woe_@vp.pl   Type: E
Comments: Apparitional encounter?

* * * * * * *

Location: Cranagh, County Carlow, Ireland.
Date: November, 1924.
Time: Afternoon.

A young girl was standing by a farmyard gate, tending some cows when she saw a little man appear from behind one of the cows. He walked quickly and tapped one of the cows gently on the nose with a stick he was carrying. He walked by the witness, staring at her, and then walked straight into a bank of solid earth and vanished. He was described as four foot tall, young looking, and wearing a black cap, a red coat, and tight trousers.

HC addendum.
Source: Graham J. McEwan, *'Mystery Animals of Britain and Ireland.'*
Type: E

Location: (Undisclosed location) Saskatchewan, Canada.
Date: Winter 1924.
Time: Early morning.

In a rural area while doing some morning chores on her farm, a woman observed a little green-colored man walking around the brush. The entity was seen entering a small silvery ship, which took off at high speed.

HC addendum.
Source: John Brent Musgrave, *'UFO Occupants and Critters.'*   Type: B

* * * * * * *

Location: Flat Mesa, near Battle Mountain, Nevada.
Date: 1925.
Time: Afternoon.

Don Wood Jr. and another American landed in a two-seater plane on Flat Mesa in the Nevada desert. While walking about the top they noticed something coming in to land. It was round and flat like a saucer, and about 8ft across, with a reddish underside. It skidded to a stop about 30 feet away. They walked up to it and found that it was an animal-like thing; nothing they had seen before. It had a mica-like body, but no visible eyes or legs. It was hurt, and as it breathed the top would rise and fall making a half-foot hole around it like a clam opening and closing. A hunk had been chewed out of one side of the rim, from which a metal looking froth issued.

After a 20-minute rest, it started pulsating again, and grew very bright except where it was hurt. It tried to rise up, but sank back again. Suddenly the men saw a much larger animal, 30ft across, approaching. It settled on the smaller one with 4 sucker-like tongues. Then it grew too dazzling to look at and both rose straight up and shot out of sight in a second, at an estimated speed of 1000 miles an hour. They left behind an awful stench. The frothy stuff the little creature had "bled" looked like fine aluminum wire, and there was frothier, wiry stuff in a 30ft circle where the big creature had been. This material finally melted in the sun.

HC addendum.
Source: David Pratt, *'UFOs: The Psychic Dimension,'* also *Flying Saucers* magazine, October, 1959.   Type: E?

Location: Richford, Berkshire, England.
Date: 1925.
Time: Various.

Renowned horror writer H.P. Lovecraft secretly traveled to Richford and Berkshire to investigate a strange phenomenon that was occurring in the two towns. Lovecraft had been visiting friends in southern Vermont when he first learned about odd sightings in Richford.

Locals there were terribly afraid of a beast they had dubbed "the Awful." First spotted atop the Boright building at the corner of Main and River streets early one evening around dusk, the Awful, according to records of old, was a winged creature that resembled "a very large Griffin-like creature with grayish wings that each spanned ten-feet." The creature possessed "a serpent like tail that equaled its wing length" and "huge claws that could easily grip a milk can's girth."

Three men, workers at a local sawmill, were walking across the Main Street Bridge when they spotted the Awful perched on the building's rooftop staring menacingly down at them. One of the men was so petrified he suffered a heart attack on the spot and had to be carried home. For weeks afterwards his wife and children woke up in the middle of the night to hear him screaming in his sleep.

Two weeks later the Awful was seen flying about 50 feet above a Berkshire field near Lost Nation road. The creature it was said clutched a small, wailing infant in its gnarled claws, but most likely it was a small animal of some sort, a sheep perhaps. Over the next several weeks, numerous farmers around Richford and Berkshire reported seeing the Awful flying over their fields.

Farm wife Oella Hopkins was hanging wash out to dry in her yard when she looked up to see what her dog was fiercely barking at. Following the dog's nervous glare she saw the Awful perched on her porch roof gazing down at her. Terribly frightened, she ran into her house and hid under her bed, refusing to come out for hours. A year after the Awful was first spotted, sightings dwindled to a few each month. After 3 years, they stopped completely.

When H. P. Lovecraft returned to southern Vermont from Richford, he told friends he was convinced that the Richford locals he had interviewed were "not in the least mistaken about what they had witnessed." Lovecraft later wrote, "The Awful became ample sustenance for my imagination" and "over time the creature became the basis for many of my own fictional inventions."

HC addendum.
Source: H. P. Albarelli Jr.
http://www.thecountrycourier.com/index.php?option=content&_task =view&id=3463&Itemid=   Type: E

Location: Vila Belmiro, Santos, Brazil.
Date: 1925.
Time: 6:00 p.m.

The eight-year old witness was playing with some friends on the street in front of her house when they suddenly heard a strange buzzing sound and see a tall figure wearing silvery clothing that covered "him" from head to toe. The strange figure carried a metallic luminous "baton" in one of its hands. As the figure approached the playing children, they ran away from the area terrified.

HC addendum.
Source: Edison Boaventura Junior in UFOVIA, Brazil. Type: E
Comments: Translation by Albert S. Rosales.

* * * * * * *

Location: Edale, Derbyshire, England.
Date: 1925.
Time: Various.

A large black creature of unknown origin caused havoc here in the 1920's when it killed dozens of sheep. Though rarely seen, the creature was said to have a howl like a fog horn. Locals allocated the blame on a 'lycanthrope.'

HC addendum.
Source: http://www.paranormaldatabase.com/reports Type: E

* * * * * * *

Location: Port Burwell, Ontario Canada.
Date: Summer 1925.
Time: Night.

The witness woke up and felt compelled to go outside into the backyard; she then saw a large "train-like" craft approaching. It was emitting a loud whining sound. A light approached the witness and she recalled floating up into the craft. Several small gray beings with large eyes, set far apart took her gown off. The beings were slender with whitish gray skin, large heads, and bulging eyes and were wearing tight fitting satin like outfits. She is later floated up and apparently examined with various instruments. She was eventually released.

HC addendum.
Source: *Cuforn Bulletin,* May-June, 1988. Type: G

* * * * * * *

Location: Port Burwell, Ontario, Canada.
Date: Late summer 1925.
Time: Daytime.

The witness was lying on the grass outside when she saw a flat silvery disc land nearby. Several beings with wrinkled yellow skin came out. She was then apparently taken inside the craft and given a ride. The disc flew at a very high altitude and the witness was returned later.

HC addendum.
Source: Cuforn Bulletin May/June, 1988. Type: G

* * * * * * *

Location: Vanch District, Tajikistan, USSR.
Date: Fall 1925.
Time: Unknown.

Maj. General Mikhail Topilski; head of a scouting party ran across a group of "Golub-yavan" (Wildman of Central Asia) during a skirmish with White Russian guerillas in the Vanch District. The guerillas had taken refuge in an ice cave that the creatures apparently used as a shelter. One Wildman was shot and inspected by the party's physician. The dead creature was 5 feet 6 inches tall and looked much more human than apelike, though it was covered with dense hair except for its face, palms, soles, knees and buttocks. It had heavy browridges, a flat nose, and a massive lower jaw. The foot was noticeably wider than a human's. The soldiers could not take the body with them, so they buried it under a heap of stones.

HC addendum.
Source: George Eberhart, *'Mysterious Creatures.'* Type: H

Location: Edale, Derbyshire, England.
Date: October, 1925.
Time: Various.

"A creature "black in color and of enormous size" slaughtered sheep in this district, "leaving the carcasses strewn about, with legs, shoulders and heads torn off; broken backs, and pieces of flesh ripped off. People in many places are so frightened that they refuse to leave their homes after dark, and keep their children in the house."

HC addendum.
Source: Jerome Clark and Loren Coleman, *'Creatures of the Goblin World,'* quoting *The London Daily Express*, October 14, 1925.   Type: E?

* * * * * * *

Location: Near Ancud, Chile.
Date: 1926.
Time: Night.

The 18-year old brother of Marcelino Zaldivia was sleeping one night on the porch when he disappeared. He was not found until Easter week of 1976 when Marcelino, feeling nostalgic about his lost brother, visited their old home on the banks of the Rio Pudeto. There seated in the living room and dressed as he'd been half a century earlier, was his brother, now old and evidently demented. When Marcelino asked where he'd been all those years, the man replied only that he'd been on a 'boat' and implored him not to ask anything more. When a woman named Elena Vera Guerrero asked him about it, he shook his head and said, *"They hear everything."*

HC addendum.
Source: Rob MacGregor and Trish Janeshutz, *Fate,* 1984.   Type: G?

Location: Kolomenskoye, Near Moscow, Russia.
Date: 1926.
Time: Night.

In a ravine near Moscow which in ancient times was the scene of Pagan worship of 'Belesa,' ruler of underworld, by the Finno-Ugric tribes that once lived in the area, long before the Slavs. This entity was later identified with the patron saints of animals and wealth. The name of the entity derives from the word 'volohaty' meaning hairy one. Encounters with strange hairy entities in the ravine are described in the chronicles of the times of Ivan the Terrible.

In 1926, at an uncertain date, a local policeman was walking near the ravine when he encountered some thick fog. Suddenly out of the fog stepped out a huge creature at least 2.5m in height, completely covered with hair. Terrified, the policeman emptied the entire magazine of his pistol at the creature without any apparent effect. The eerie entity then vanished in plain sight.

HC addendum.
Source: http://paranormal-news.ru/publ/6-10-867   Type: E

* * * * * * *

Location: Mt. Isa, Queensland, Australia.
Date: 1926.
Time: Night.

A small Aboriginal tribal group living in the Mt. Isa back-blocks, told others that they had been visited one night as everyone sat at the edge of a waterhole campfire talking. From what they told the other Aborigines of the region, "a big black object" came down from the sky and apparently a large number of pygmy-height beings emerged and rounded up the twenty or so tribespeople and their children, herding them into the craft.

Then the little beings for some reason unknown took away the children for some time but later returned them. The craft apparently rose into the air and flew away "somewhere beyond the clouds" it was said. The details are hazy, but it appears that the craft returned its captives through the clouds early the next morning to a location a few miles from where they had been abducted. The side of the craft opened and the terrified Aborigines ran out screaming.

HC addendum.
Source: Blue Mountains UFO Research Club newsletter, January, 2012.
Type: G

Location: Zaragoza, Spain.
Date: 1926.
Time: Late night.

17-year old Pascual Vazquez Arraco had left the offices of a local paper "El Heraldo de Aragon" late one night and was on his way to the local government building when a strange man suddenly blocked his path. The stranger told Pascual that he was from 'another planet,' Pascual then held a conversation with the stranger; at times oral and at other times telepathic.

The next night, Pascual came upon the same man, this time near a strange object shaped like a metallic disc which was on the ground. The strange man appeared to have trouble walking and wore dark tight-fitting clothing. He also wore a belt whose belt buckle was a sort of screen which the man manipulated in order to record the conversation and to display a large screen that appeared in mid-air which displayed events that would occur in the future, the Spanish Civil War, the Second World War and many aspects related to Pascual's life. In the morning, the man entered the disc which departed at incredible speed, disappearing over the horizon. From that day on, Pascual reported seeing other discs and receiving telepathic messages.

HC addendum.
Source:http://www.looculto.260mb.com/ovnisenespana/ovnisenespana.htm also Miguel Pedrero 'Contacto: Comunicacion con seres de otros mundos,' (Editorial EDAF, Madrid, 2005).   Type: G

* * * * * * *

Location: Near Freemantle, Gloucestershire, England.
Date: February, 1926.
Time: Various.

"Excitement has been caused in Gloucestershire, England, by the discovery of a Lilliputian living in the Poolway Colliery. Miners exploring old workings caught a mysterious creature 11 inches high with a round head, the size of a teacup. It strikingly resembles a human being. It is covered with soft, brown hair; has two eyes, eyebrows, and eyelashes; small round ears; flat nose. The mouth contains a fine set of pearly white teeth. The neck is short. The arms are tiny, and the hands perfect. The figure is robust. The legs are four and a half inches long; the feet human. When trapped it snarled like a monkey.

It was in such an extremity of fright that it lived only an hour. The miners left the creature lying on the coal bank. When their story was investigated, it had disappeared. It is believed to have been retrieved by relatives of a miniature tribe.

The story was at first regarded as a fantasy of drunken imagination. Suddenly it was confirmed by a family living in Coleford. It seemingly proves the existence of subterranean beings. A Mrs. Williams when serving supper was alarmed by a movement in the coal scuttle. Her daughter screamed, seeing a terrifying little creature, like a tiny, half caste miner. It was well proportioned, with shapely hips and smiling face. It was seated on a lump of coal. The husband in view of the children's hysterical rendition, threw the scuttle with the tiny creature out of the front door."

HC addendum.
Source: *Western Star* and *Roma Advertiser* (Toowoomba, Queensland: 1875-1948), February 13, 1926.　　　　　　　　　　　　Type: E?

* * * * * * *

Location: Kolomenskoye, south of Moscow, Russia.
Date: Summer 1926.
Time: Unknown.

A group of teenagers; the so-caller pioneers (boy-scouts), suddenly stumbled upon a 2.5m tall humanoid entity completely covered by dark dense hair or fur that was doing something in a fruit garden. The brave pioneers decided that the entity was intent in stealing fruit (apples) so they tried to approach and catch the strange creature, but the hairy visitor escaped and disappeared; dissolved into thin air right in front of the stunned teenagers. This type of entity has been seen in this area for hundreds of years and the place is reputed to be some type of portal or gateway into another dimension.

HC addendum.
Source: Vadim A. Chernobrov, *'Encyclopedia of Mysterious Places in Russia,'* First World Guidebook of Anomalous Zones and other Mysterious and wonderful places, Moscow, 2004.　　　Type: E

Location: Matsuyama, Ehime-ken (prefecture), Japan.
Date: Summer 1926.
Time: Night.

A two year old boy named Warabe (involved in other encounters) was in bed in his house when suddenly he was filled with a happy frame of mind and a warm feeling. He thought he heard someone calling, *"Come out my boy!"* Going out of the house (traditional Japanese houses in the country at that time tended to be open in summer because of very sultry weather); he found that there was a tall young man standing by the house.

The stranger was a white man with golden hair and wore a long white robe as the missionaries do sometimes. With a gentle smile he said in standard Japanese, *"Let me hold you boy."* Then he took a stroll with Warabe around the village for a while. After that he walked the boy home and disappeared. While walking, the little boy was very happy because there seemed to be much human warmth in the young man.

Every summer the strange tall man appeared near the boy's home from nowhere and called out to him by using mental telepathy. Warabe took great delight in going out with the man, for the stranger had already become a good friend of his. Warabe did not know his name, so he called him "Uncle." Sometimes "Uncle" gave the boy such rare gifts as a velocipede which was a great novelty then, and a small metallic box on which a curious design was carved. It was a triangle just like a pyramid on the surface of the box, and on each oblique side was a snake climbing out.

HC addendum.
Source: Hachiro Kubota, UFO Contactee, GAP-Japan Newsletter No. 2 February, 1986. Type: E

* * * * * * *

Location: Ujazd, Poland.
Date: September, 1926.
Time: 4-5:00 p.m.

The witness (Zofia) was alone in a meadow grazing three cows when she suddenly turned around and saw three gray discs (about 2 meters in diameter) hovering just above the ground and three strange entities standing in front of them. There was total silence. All three objects had something resembling opened doors. The humanoids were less than 120-130 cm tall, maybe about 80cm, and wore dark-green suits and something like belts or ropes around their waists. She was unable to see any hair or facial features as the humanoids stood about 100 meters away staring at her. Very scared she began running away. She briefly turned around and everything was gone.

HC addendum.
Source: Bronislaw Rzepecki and Marcin Mioduszewski.   Type: C

* * * * * * *

Location: Bradford, West Yorkshire, England.
Date: September 5, 1926 and after.
Time: Various.

"A strange figure in white was reportedly seen on several occasions in the area. The figure made its first recorded appearance at 3:00 a.m. on the above date in Grafton Street and was subsequently seen every night that week in Grafton Street or the nearby Fitzgerald or Earl Streets. Those who saw it, described the figure as completely dressed in a white garment with the head covering slit near the eyes and the majority are unanimous in declaring that it is at least six feet two inches in height and makes practically no noise when running.

After the first few appearances, one of which caused a young woman to faint, the whole neighborhood aided by the police were roused to dramatic action, to once and for all rid the area of this "thing." Despite the activity being kept up for many nights, and more than a few innocent pedestrians being accused of being the figure, the appearances of the figure did not let up, often now appearing on house rooftops and coal bunkers.

A theory went around that the figure was that of a local man who had agreed to appear in the area, dressed in outlandish garb for fourteen nights, for a bet, but no proof could be found of this allegation. Night after night the figure was seen, becoming something of a tourist attraction and after dinner diversion for those with little else to do."

HC addendum.
Source: Andy Roberts, *UFO Brigantia,* July/Aug, 1986.   Type: E

Location: Bierley, near Bradford, West Yorkshire, England.
Date: Mid-September, 1926.
Time: Various.

"The mysterious white-clad figure appeared to have moved to this location where he took to peering through windows, standing in the shadows and knocking on doors, only to vanish when confronted. Bierley had a reputation of being haunted and many thought the figure in white was the ghost returned. The residents of Bierley like their counterparts in Bradford took to the street with sticks, dogs and guns.

After a few nights in Bierley, the entity traveled a few miles up the valley to Bingley, again to lurk in shadows, leaping at passersby and then vanishing into nothing. The police was out in force, but the culprit, if it was a flesh and blood culprit, could not be found.

A Mr. Whitehead saw the entity "flapping its wings" on the canal bank and was of the opinion that "he wore a white cover in front of him and immediately his appearance was seen, wrapped it up, put it in his pocket and scampered off." He may have been right, but no one could scamper fast enough to catch him."

HC addendum.
Source: Andy Roberts, *UFO Brigantia* July/August, 1986.　　Type: E

* * * * * * *

Location: Dewsbury and others, West Yorkshire, England.
Date: October, 1926.
Time: Various.

"The enigmatic entity in white was reportedly seen at several other villages in the area. These reports differ in that the eyes are now mentioned as "glowing" and "staring incessantly" both which are features of entity reports the world over. One account of a sighting describes the figure as being "on springs," and others speak of 'flashes of light' being aimed at them. Searchers of these areas by the police and groups of vigilantes youths all intent in bringing the figure to justice failed and the appearances carried on, finally petering out towards the end of October."

HC addendum.
Source: Andy Roberts, *UFO Brigantia* July/August, 1986.　　Type: E

Location: La Combe De Morbier, Jura, France.
Date: Winter 1926.
Time: Evening.

A woodcutter reported seeing a large brightly lit sphere hovering at treetop level. Several figures, human-like in appearance could be seen inside the object. These apparently ignored the witness.

HC addendum.
Source: Joel Mesnard and Michel Morel Seythoux, *FSR* Vol. 37 #1.
Type: A

* * * * * * *

Location: Yankton, Oregon.
Date: 1927.
Time: Various.

At least 28 people reported sightings of a huge hairy creature of an apparent intelligent nature. One report stated that the creature ran alongside a moving truck and looked inside the cab. Around the same time sheep and chickens were disappearing in the area.

HC addendum.
Source: Oregon Bigfoot.com   Type: E

* * * * * * *

Location: Corbola, Rovigo, Italy.
Date: 1927.
Time: Morning.

One morning while the witness; a young woman, was going to fetch drinking water at the River Po, she saw a shiny and round object come from the sky; it later crashed in the water seven meters away from her. After a couple of minutes, the witness noticed a big bubble in the water and later the object resurfaced and flew away disappearing in the sky.
The girl had the chance to observe the interior of the object and saw a little man who seemed to be seated because he was only visible from the neck and above. The facial features were human looking and he was not wearing a helmet. The object, which emitted a hissing noise, had a diameter of 2-3 meters.

HC addendum.
Source: Paolo Fiorino, *UFO Universe* Oct/Nov, 1991.   Type: A

Location: Anderson, Indiana.
Date: 1927.
Time: Afternoon.

A young boy was hiking on a trail through the bottom of an overgrown gravel pit near a river when he came face to face with a little man only about two foot in height. The little man had dark blonde hair and a round pinkish face, slightly sunburned. The little man was barefoot and was clad in a long light blue gown. The man suddenly turned and walked swiftly away into the ravine quickly disappearing from sight. (Interpreted by the source as a "Puk Wud Jies," an ancient tribe of forest dwelling little people that possibly still live in Indiana.)

HC addendum.
Source: Paul Startzman, *Fate* magazine Vol. 48 #3.   Type: E

* * * * * * *

Location: Brooks Bottom, Mt View, Tennessee.
Date: 1927.
Time: Afternoon.

A mother and her children were down past the barn working in the garden, when she turned back to see what the kids were making over and saw what she described as an "angel." The figure looked like a human; it was full sized, dressed in a flowing type garment. It had wings and long golden tresses that were curly and very shiny. It was beautiful and bright. The "angel" was fluttering in the air about head high. She said that it came so close to them that they could see its fingernails and toe nails. It had no shoes on.
The mother turned and ran toward the house to get the gun but her husband said, *"Stop, you can't shoot it, because it is a heavenly being."* She said they went on about their business and left it alone. They were not afraid of it. It is not known if it flew away or disappeared or exactly how it ended or if it was ever seen again.

HC addendum.
Source: http://www.mysterious-america.net/reality309.html   Type: E
Comments: Date is approximate.

Location: Orange, New South Wales, Australia.
Date: 1927.
Time: Afternoon.

A Mr. Cecil McGann saw a 'saucer' at Fernvale (Murwillumbah area). That same year at Orange a farmer saw a 'saucer' type craft which landed in a field in broad daylight. Out of it emerged three weird beings. The craft had the appearance of a "Mexican sombrero" with a high, pointed dome. As the man watched from some distance away the three beings proceeded to collect soil samples from the ground with some kind of digging implements, then returned to the craft through a side door from which they had emerged.

Shortly afterwards the craft rose with a hissing sound and zoomed westwards high over the surrounding hills. The farmer later described the strange visitors as having heart-shaped faces and long trunk-like noses. He did not see their mouths due to the distance. They were clothed in dark, tight-fitting garments, with high neck collars. The men thought they had hands and fingers similar to ours and were wearing very large boots.

HC addendum.
Source: Rex Gilroy, the Temple of Nim Newsletter, November 2006.
Type: B

* * * * * * *

Location: Salem, New Jersey.
Date: 1927.
Time: Night.

A cab driver suffered a flat tire while headed for Salem. He had just finished changing the tire when the car began to shake violently. The driver looked up to see a gigantic figure covered with hair pounding on the roof of the car. The driver left his jack and flat tire behind and jumped into his cab and sped away. He was under the impression that he had encountered the famed "New Jersey Devil."

HC addendum.
Source: Michael Norman and Beth Scott, *'Haunted America.'* Type: E

* * * * * * *

Location: Fernvale, New South Wales, Australia.
Date: 1927.
Time: Night.

During a period of bizarre phenomena occurring at an isolated farm that included strange dancing aerial lights, mysterious deaths of cows, dead pigs found with mysterious punctured marks (another went missing.) A 10-year old boy was awakened by strange noises for about three nights in a row. One morning several footprints were found leaving behind the front door to the back. Others saw a brightly lit object land in a valley leaving behind an area of scorched grass. Other family members saw large, unfamiliar birds in the neighborhood.

One night the family had gone to a social event at their neighbor's. The oldest son remained behind. A strange man dressed in clothes resembling a white suit arrived at the neighbor's house. Everyone thought he was with one of the other visitors. He said nothing and only stayed for a short time. Back in the house the oldest son was in darkness. He heard a noise in the house and yelled, *"Who is there!"* The boy got out of bed in time to see someone in a white suit disappearing into the darkness. The stranger was never seen or heard from again.

HC addendum.
Source: Bill Chalker, *'The Oz Files.'* Type: D

Location: Ventanas de Quintero, Loncura, Chile.
Date: January 20, 1927.
Time: 3:00 a.m.

The lone witness was traveling through the area and had just passed by the Naval Base at Quintero, he was on a Ford pickup truck and was keeping a route very close to the water. However when high tide came in he was stranded and was forced to waited out and the highest point on the beach. As he rested half sleep on a small sand dune he was suddenly startled by the presence of a strange figure standing in front of him.

Terrified and curious at the same time, the witness stared fascinated at the strange figure. He described the strange figure as a little more than 1 meter in height, his body including his head were covered in an impenetrable metallic opaque metallic mesh, where the face would have been there was a sort of mask with a circular aperture which shone with a pale light, similar to the light emitted by modern day computer monitors.

The witness then heard a very soft voice which said, *"Don't be afraid of me, I won't hurt you. 20 meters from here I have my ship where my friend is waiting for me, we could take you with us, but we don't want to. We have known about the Earth for over 1 million years. We come from a planet which is close to Earth but we live in its interior, and we possess scientific knowledge that humans are not capable of understanding yet. However we are unable to predict the future since it all depends in the workings of many different minds. We visit the Earth at all times, since it is not difficult for us to do so. However we cannot live on the Earth, the rays from the sun alone would kill us."*

The alien continued talking, *"We do not have eyes, or ears, but we have very special knowledge and skills. Our nourishment is all based on "nuclear energy" the same energy that your scientists are now recently researching and is based on the atom. What is called the brain for you, for us is just special cells which are capable to connect to billions of other cells and archived memory which has been formed and collected throughout thousands of millions of years. We lack any emotions or passions.*

We are not really interested in studying anything about humans or knowing too much about your planet for various reasons. If we travel to the Earth we do mostly at night and avoid contact with the sun. We are only five thousand in number and only reproduce through chemical means and using special females of our species. The ship you see behind us uses atomic energy in combination with magnetic attraction to travel between the planets."

Terrified, the witness just stared at the entity unable to move. Once he looked down to the alien's feet and noticed these square and shiny metallic in appearance, the creature's arms were also very short. From its belt area the creature took out a sort of rolled out tape and placed it on the ground in front of the witness and then walked back to its ship, before entering the object he turned around and said, *"Don't try to follow us; we travel at light speed."*

Once the alien had entered the craft a soft glow within the object started getting brighter and brighter, there was no sound. He was able to see that the craft was somehow cylinder shaped and was emitting a bright blue-violet light from each end. In seconds it disappeared from sight. Terrified he ran to his truck and attempted to drive away forgetting that it was high tide. At this point the witness remembered the small tape-like device left on the sand by the creature. But it had been apparently washed away by the high tide.

HC addendum.
Source: Liliana Nunez Orellana, OVNIS Chile.　　　　　Type: A & C

* * * * * * *

Location: Anderson, Indiana.
Date: Summer 1927.
Time: Afternoon.

Two boys hiking through the woods near a gravel pit both suddenly became aware that a little man was following them. The little man appeared to be wearing a long-sleeved white gown. As they left the woods and began to cross a large field of overgrown tall grass they noticed that the little man was still following them. They ran into a nearby farmhouse alerting a family member that owned a pair of field glasses and was able to see the little man resting on top of a large rock.

HC addendum.
Source: Paul Startzman, *Fate* Vol. 48 #3.　　　　　Type: E

* * * * * * *

Location: Ramonj, Voronezh region, Russia.
Date: Summer 1927.
Time: Night.

A young man named Hariton Rushko, a technician at the local sugar mill had gone outside of town with some of his co-workers to a location considered to be "cursed" and to be a lair of "vampires." He had indeed gone there in order to expose all the stories as just tall-tales, as Soviet propaganda required him to lecture at the mill. On that hot summer night he sat near the bonfire watching the night sky and soon fell asleep on the grass.

Suddenly a bright light awakened him. He was able to make out the "eyes" of some unseen entities around him in the darkness. The eyes were not like those of wolves or deer and everything around him became permeated by a distinct odor that kept getting stronger. To avoid vomiting, Hariton ran to another location but the glowing eyes followed him. At this moment the bonfire seemed to flare up or become brighter and he was able to see the silhouettes of several "men," their eyes emitting light.

At first he thought that a prank was being played on him and the men were really using pieces of glowing embers or coals to frighten him. Hariton then walked about 50 steps away from the fire and no one followed him, so feeling very tired and drowsy he fell to the ground and fell asleep. In the morning he awoke in an unfamiliar location, he could not find the bonfire and instead of meadows there were mountains surrounding him.

Soon he found out he was in the Carpathian Mountains of Romania as the people around him spoke in an unknown language, the locals thought he was deranged. He succeeded in walking to the Soviet frontier and later was hospitalized in a mental hospital after he was unable to explain how he had somehow appeared in Romania.

HC addendum.
Source: Olga Stolyarchuk, 'Mir Uvlecheniy' (World of Hobbits) Kiev, Ukraine #9, August 21, 2003.   Type: G?

* * * * * * *

Location: Omsk, Russia.
Date: Fall 1927.
Time: Late night.

A laborer living near the city was awakened by loud braying noises coming from the barn where some horses were kept. He went over to investigate thinking of possible thieves. As he opened the barn door, the two panicked horses ran out, knocking him down. The witness then obtained a flashlight and accompanied by several of the neighbors that had gathered at the barn, went inside.

The barn appeared to be covered with thousands of fine silvery hair-like filaments that proved to be very strong and hard to cut. As they made their way through to the center of the barn they noticed a very large hole on the roof. Then they noticed a strange creature lying next to a pile of hay nearby. The creature was described as a round white pumpkin sized mass that pulsated rhythmically.

The mass had what appeared to be traces of human like facial features. It suddenly rolled to a nearby wall emitting several tentacles like protrusions form the top of its head. At this point several of the men armed with sticks and axes attacked the creature, apparently killing it, and reducing its body to a whitish blue pulp.

HC addendum.
Source: Peter Kolosimo, *'Sombra en Las Estrellas.'*   Type: E
Comments: Translation by Albert S. Rosales.

* * * * * * *

Location: Stoke, Sherbrooke, Quebec, Canada.
Date: September, 1927.
Time: Early morning.

The witness, Arsene Laventure had decided to trek up Mount Stoke and as a precaution he had taken his hunting rifle with him. Near the summit of the mountain Laventure suddenly encountered four man-sized figures wearing all black clothing. The beings approached him and spoke to him in a language he could not understand, it wasn't English or German, which were spoken frequently at the time. At first Laventure thought the strangers were looking for a local gold mine which it is said had existed on the mountain in the distant past.

Suddenly Laventure apparently blacked out and later woke up at the edge of the forest without his hunting rifle. He walked for hours at random without knowing where he was. He was finally found by friends which he apparently does not recognize and was taken home in a completely confused state. Not until the morning did his memory return and he told his family what had happened to him. Never again would he return to the mountain. Around the same time many locals in the area had reported seeing strange lights high up on the mountain.

HC addendum.
Source: Donald Cyr, Quebec, Canada.   Type: G?

Location: Near Bottlebush Down, Dorset, England.
Date: Winter 1927.
Time: Evening.

Pre-historian C. C. Clay was driving on the B3081 road when he became aware of a horseman riding on the downs in the same direction as himself. Clay was fascinated, and slowed his car down. At one point the horseman was galloping parallel to Clay's car at a distance of only 50 yards away. Clay noticed that its legs were bare and that he wore a long, loose cloak. The horse had a long mane and tail, but apparently was not fitted with a bridle or stirrups.

The horseman turned his face towards Clay periodically though the witness could not make out any features and waved an implement or weapon threateningly above his head. After about 100 yards, the horse and rider abruptly disappeared. Clay stopped his car and went over to the spot where the apparition had vanished and found the trace of a round barrow that he had never before noticed.

HC addendum.
Source: Paul Deveraux, *'Haunted Land.'* Type: X

* * * * * * *

Location: Vancouver Island, British Columbia, Canada.
Date: 1928.
Time: Unknown.

A Nootka Indian and trapper; Muchalot Harry, was plying his trade around the Conuma River and had been sleeping, when he felt someone picking him up, bedding and all, and carried for about three miles by a large Sasquatch-like creature. When set down, he found himself surrounded by about 20 of the creatures, both male and female, which he at first thought planned to eat him, as their campsite was littered with large bones.

The creatures poked and prodded Harry, seemingly puzzled by his clothing. After a while, they appeared to grow tired of the human curiosity, and many left the camp. Seeing his chance, Harry made a run for it; running right past his own camp to his canoe on the river. He never went trapping in the woods again.

HC addendum.
Source: *'Timeline of a Mysterious Universe.'* Type: G?

Location: Lake Vedlozero, Karelia, Russia, USSR.
Date: 1928.
Time: Unknown.

An amphibious human-like being was reported in this lake. The creature was repeatedly seen in the lake by local residents. A group of researchers from the Petrozavodsk University arrived to investigate the case on location. Unfortunately the findings were classified and the members of the research party eventually perished in the Gulag.

HC addendum.
Source: Rafic Garifdjanov, Baku.   Type: E
Comments: Unfortunately there no additional information on this intriguing case.

* * * * * * *

Location: Shuknovolk, Karelia, Russia.
Date: 1928.
Time: Unknown.

Local peasants including one man, F. P. Fedotov reported seeing something like a large cylinder with red flame streaming from its rear end collapsed into a lake. Some say that is still lying on the bottom of the lake and hampers fishermen to fish there. After the fall of the object, local residents started noticing a strange 1-1.2meter long creature. The creature's body appeared slim and its hands were touching the ground. Each hand had four fingers. The creature was incredibly fearful, it would always hide in the water whenever approached by humans.

HC addendum.
Source:http://english.pravda.ru/sceince/19/94/378/12757_underwaterCiv.html

* * * * * * *

Location: Between Buxerolles and Poitiers, France.
Date: 1928.
Time: Afternoon.

One afternoon while checking his cows in a pasture the witness saw a kind of "boiler lid" fall to the ground about three or four meters from him. There was no noise. At once there was a great flash of red and green light and the "boiler lid" suddenly became an enormous "machine," as large as a truck of a gray "scintillating" color. Then two small "nude fellows" walked through the wall of the object and dragged the witness inside the "machine." The witness passed out and woke up to find himself covered in a kind of gelatin, which made him loose "contact" with the environment. He could not recall how long his abduction or flight took place; he has no recollection on that aspect.

Moments later the gel seemed to melt away and he heard a voice who spoke to him in French. *"Do not be afraid, we mean you no harm. Pass through the wall, touch it with your hand and you will see that it will go through. Go ahead."* The witness then walked through the wall and found himself standing in a large room.

Across from him stood a group of short nude humanoids, smiling at him; the wall behind them was shiny. He described the humanoids as about a meter in height, light gray in color, hairless, large round staring eyes, a round face and two hole-like indentations where the nose would have been. The skin appeared to be translucent. They had no ears, but in their place there were two small bump-lie protrusions. Their feet and hands were similar to humans and they appeared to be sexless with again only a small "bump" where the sexual organ would have been.

Apparently after a short flight the witness found himself in a place (planet?) where he was escorted into some buildings. Curiously he neither felt tired, hunger or thirst. Soon he found himself in a white round room, with a flat floor. He was breathing normally and felt neither heat nor cold, and moved easily like on Earth.

The witness had numerous questions to pose to the aliens. In perfect French one of the humanoids explained several facts to the witness including that the walls of the room were made of pure "energy." By putting one's hand through the wall, one could either pass through or pull the "wall" towards oneself, one also, if he wished, could see through the walls. In this case it would become transparent like a scintillating mirror (one could recall the innumerable reports of UFOs with "mirror-like" surfaces).

He was told that later several French speaking humanoids would come to visit and "instruct" him on several manners. He later found out that these extraterrestrials, did not breathe, eat, sleep or reproduce, (!) they were always very busy working. At one point the witness went through a kind of cleansing procedure in which he was given a place in a wall of energy and instantaneously a kind of vacuum cleaner disencumbered the witness of all, impurities, including some unwanted hair.

A certain time after his arrival, an extraterrestrial suddenly appeared within a circle of light on the wall of energy; similar in appearance to the other aliens, except that he carried a sort of luminous box under his chin where the neck, which was hardly visible, was supposed to be. The humanoid remained upright without moving, staring at the witness. Eventually the witness was face to face with humanoid, which began speaking to him in French, with his mouth hardly moving. The humanoid said, *"I came to speak to you, because you have many questions to pose. We will come to see you often. We will inform you all that you will need to know and all of what you want to know. All of our knowledge is stored here. Even for me to speak to you I must carry this small box, which delivers the necessary air (?) for me to breathe. When you exhaust your personal questions, your instruction will begin at your own rate or rhythm. But it will be very fast, your motivation will be curiosity."*

After numerous questions posed by the witness almost all at once, he asked the aliens what would become of his parents, since they were apparently ill. He was told not to worry too much of what occurs on Earth, including your family, since the life on Earth was very short. *"Your future after life on Earth would be much better."* The witness learned much about a number of different subjects, including information about the nature of "God," and man's place in the cosmos. He was eventually returned to same location where he had been initially abducted from.

HC addendum.
Source: GREPI Switzerland, *'New Testimonies.'* Type: G

* * * * * * *

Location: Chesterton, Lincolnshire, England.
Date: 1928.
Time: Night.

Several witnesses watched a glowing hooded "monk-like" figure emerge from a nearby swamp. A similar glowing figure was seen hovering by a nearby iron bridge. No other information.

HC addendum.
Source: Paul Devereux, *'Earth Lights Revelation.'* Type: E

* * * * * * *

Location: Ferdrupt, Vosgues, France.
Date: March 3, 1928.
Time: Evening.

Several youngsters reported encountering in a field; a luminous and beautiful female figure they interpreted to be the Holy Virgin Mary. She wore a simple robe and beams of light seemed to emanate from her hands.

HC addendum.
Source: CNEGU Catalog case #5, Denys Breysse Project Becassine.
Type: E

* * * * * * *

Location: Near Yakima, Washington.
Date: Late April, 1928.
Time: 4:00 p.m.

    Harry Dillon was driving along an unpaved country road when, as he reached the top of a slight rise, he saw an object slowly coming into the view. The object was described as resembling a metallic hexagon with a dome on top, olive drab in color. The witness could see rivets along a vertical section and a two by three foot window set in a metallic frame.
    In the window he could see the upper torso of a man dressed in a dark blue uniform. The man had a dark complexion and was totally human-like. He looked intently in the direction of the witness's car, and then the object rotated, flew across the road, and shot away at terrific speed.

HC addendum.
Source: Jacques Vallee, *'Confrontations, A scientist's Search for Alien Contact.'*
Type: A

* * * * * * *

Location: (Undisclosed location) Colorado Rockies.
Date: Summer 1928.
Time: Night.

    Paul M. Vest was staying at a local resort and one night was walking on a forest trail when he strayed into a deeper part of the forest. When he grew tired, he looked for the trail only to discover that he was lost. He kept searching for the trail but seemed to be getting into deeper woods. Finally he came upon a small clearing and some yards ahead he saw a tumbledown mountain cabin. As he approached it an overwhelming sense of foreboding like a cold, clammy hand stopped him dead on his tracks.
    At that moment the moon went behind a cloud and in the darkness he stood gripped with a fear of impending evil and violence. Cold perspiration broke out on his forehead. He started forward again but once more an invisible hand seemed to stop him. Then about 10ft ahead of him a soft glow appeared. Astonished, he saw the light formed the outline of a tall robed figure, the details of which were not visible. The

figure pointed off into the forest to the witness right. All fear left him and a warm feeling of peace possessed him.

Almost as though a voice were speaking, words echoed in his inner ear, *"Have no fear for you are not alone!"* Then the figure vanished. The following morning the alarm was spread that a violently insane murderer had escaped the previous day and was believed to be somewhere in the woods. He was captured late that day in the tumbledown cabin where he had been hiding the night before when Vest was in the woods.

HC addendum.
Source: *'Mystic Experiences,'* compiled and edited by Jennifer Spees.
Comments: Who was that robed figure? Vest was a well-known esoteric writer, who for publications like *Fate*. Type: E?

* * * * * * *

Location: Lake Geneva, Wisconsin.
Date: October 15, 1928.
Time: Unknown.

Velma Thayer, who owns a farm near Lake Geneva, remembers well a flying saucer landing there and remaining for 10 days. The occupants were "blond little fellows 4'6" to 5'3" in height. She was able to establish communication with one, named 'Ramu,' from Saturn, who told her the saucer was a scout ship form a mother ship 16-60 miles long far out in space, and that their intentions were completely peaceful. A U.S. guard was placed upon the saucer.

During the 10 days it was there, C. F. Kettering of Kettering Labs and Phil Wrigley, the chewing gum scion, were among those who inspected it. When the guard fell asleep, the saucer flew away. "She is in contact with the little men at odd times."

HC addendum.
Source: Jack Rame of the *Cincinnati Enquirer*. Type: B

Location: Bolton, Lancashire, England.
Date: Early November, 1928.
Time: Evening.

Figure 2. The three entities spotted by the witness.

Henry Thomson, playing with a gang of friends, was running through a dark alley when he saw in the backyard of a house three strange figures peering into a lighted living room. The central figure was tallest; it turned and looked at the witness. He mumbled at the other two and they all turned. A wide black eyepiece divided down the center by a ribbed silver piece covered the face of the tall entity.

All three appeared to be wearing inflatable rubber suits with dark boots. On their heads were transparent dome-like helmets. Tubes came from these and joined tanks that were on their backs. They had pale heads shaped like light bulbs, slit-like eyes, scarcely any nose, and no visible mouth. One made a strange noise, and all three began to move toward the boy. He ran away from the area in terror.

HC addendum.
Source: Norman Oliver, *Quest UFO* magazine Vol. 11 #4.   Type: E

Location: Roblin, Manitoba, Canada.
Date: 1929.
Time: 3:00 a.m.

A farmer was confronted in his fields by several "aluminum" little men. No other information.

HC addendum.
Source: www.canadianuforreport.com/survey/data/MBdata2015.pdf
Type: E?

* * * * * * *

Location: Crolly, County Donegal, Ireland.
Date: 1929.
Time: Daytime.

A six-year old boy and two ten-year old friends were playing at a location called "Fairy Rock" when suddenly four three and a half foot tall bearded men appeared. They wore red hats, green jackets, and brown pants. The children stared at the little men for a few minutes then decided to leave.

HC addendum.
Source: Scott S. Smith, *Fate*, March, 1993. Type: E

* * * * * * *

Location: Hertford, England.
Date: 1929.
Time: Morning.

A sister, 5, and brother, 8, were playing in the garden one morning, at that date the road was a lane, with just two pairs of houses, one of which was theirs, and behind the houses there was an orchard. As they played, they heard the sound of an engine; years later the sister would likened it to a quiet version of a trainer plane. Her brother and her looked up and saw, coming over the garden fence from the orchard, this small aeroplane (of biplane type) which swooped down and landed briefly, almost striking a dustbin.

It remained there for possibly just a few seconds and then took off and was gone, but in that short the girl had a perfect view of the tiny biplane but also of a perfectly proportioned tiny pilot wearing a leather flying helmet, who waved to them as he took off. Neither she nor her brother spoke of the strange sight until years later. She estimated the wing-span of the tiny aircraft at no more than 12-15 inches, with the tiny pilot in perfect proportion thereto.

HC addendum.
Source: Janet and Colin Bord, *'Modern Mysteries of Britain,'* also *FSR* Vol. 16 #4.　　　　　　　　　　　　　　　　　　　　　　Type: A

* * * * * * *

Location: Llanystumdwy, North Wales, England.
Date: 1929.
Time: Afternoon.

A boy was collecting firewood and smoking a cigarette in an orchard near the village, when he saw a little man coming out of some bushes. He was about 3ft tall, green from the waist down, and wearing a red cap. Nothing was said and the boy does not remember the little man leaving. He was quite sure that he did not imagine the incident.

HC addendum.
Source: *'Fairies, Real Encounters with the Little People.'*　　Type: E

* * * * * * *

Location: Ranton, Staffordshire, England.
Date: 1929.
Time: Afternoon.

A woman recalled that, as a girl, she witnessed the starting sight of a group of "tiny little pixies," all adorned in dark green clothing, and all prancing wildly around the larger and mighty oak tree that stood at the foot of her parent's back garden. But what had begun as an overwhelmingly friendly encounter, with smiling little creatures that playfully tipped their hats in the direction of the entranced young girl, became far more sinister when the atmosphere changed dramatically and the little folk mutated into malevolent, sinister figures.

The old woman explained that they slowly began to move towards her in a stalking fashion, complete with menacing frowns on their suddenly-wizened faces. Needless to say, the petrified witness fled for the safety of her home, never again to see the strange, unearthly parade.

HC addendum.
Source: http://mysteriousuniverse.org/2013/04/ranton-a-magnet-for-the-macabre/　　Type: E

Location: Paraguaco, Minas Gerais, Brazil.
Date: 1929.
Time: Night.

A large shiny white metallic craft with several window-like apertures was seen on the ground. Two giant humanoid figures about 2.50 meters in height stood next to the object. These wore silvery outfits and brown boots and gloves. No other information.

HC addendum.
Source: Antonio Faleiro, Brazil. Type: C

* * * * * * *

Location: Near Spring Valley, New York.
Date: Summer 1929.
Time: Afternoon.

Nine-year old Ellen Sutter (pseudonym) was playing outside her Spring Valley Home, thirty miles north of Manhattan, when she saw a glint of light in the sky. Looking up, she saw a large metallic object "shaped like a dirigible, with, many, many portholes, and you know, this peculiar light." Sutter could barely believe what happened next. "It was like I was rooted to the spot.

All of a sudden these peculiar things; came out of it, and seemed to be floating. This is why I never told anyone, because as I said, it sounds like a dream. These people; I call them people, I don't know what they were; looked like a diving suit with a head shape at the top and a much distorted, short-looking body. It was weird."

There were about three or four short figures, each floating above and in front of Sutter at about thirty feet in the air. Al the animal sounds stopped and time seemed to stand still. She's not sure how long the encounter lasted. At some point, the figures floated back into the craft through an opening that appeared. When she returned home, her mother scolded her for having been away for so long.

Following the experience, Sutter developed a phobia of being alone. She also suddenly became afraid of falling ill and having to visit the doctor, while at the same time she wondered if she might have caught a disease from the strange visitors. She also began having nightmares of being chased by the figures. In the dreams, the figures were no longer floating and had approached her on the ground

HC addendum.
Source: Budd Hopkins. Type: G

Location: Roccagloriosa, Salerno, Italy.
Date: Summer 1929.
Time: 2:00 p.m.

A girl was working in a field when she looked up and saw a stationary ball of white light in the sky. This then descended vertically, stopping just a few centimeters above the ground, while descending the ball greatly dimmed creating a sort of "opening" in the center of the sphere. After 5 or 10 seconds, a female figure emerged from the opening wearing sumptuous black garments, "like those from the 19th century."
Inside of the ball; 2 or 3 small beings moved slowly and peered outward. The female figure walked toward the witness, without her feet touching the ground. Thereafter, she turned left and was lost in some trees. The girl was frightened and made the sign of the cross. She then ran to call her father. When he arrived at the landing site, he smelled the fragrance of roses.

HC addendum.
Source: Maurizio Verga, 'When Saucers Came to Earth.'   Type: B
Comments: Indeed a bizarre case combining elements of alien encounters and Marian apparitions.

* * * * * * *

Location: Fermeneuve, Quebec, Canada.
Date: About June 15, 1929.
Time: Unknown.

Louis Brosseau, riding home to Fermeneuve, saw on a hillside a sort of black "cloud" with a yellowish light coming from within. Approaching on foot to within 150ft, he saw it to be a dark object on the ground; he could indistinctly see, in the darkness, 4 or 5 small "yellowish" colored men running around in a 20-foot radius.
The dark object rose and passed over him at about 50 mph, "purring like a milk separator." With a rush of air; coming from it he heard two voices as if in argument. The object was about 50ft in diameter, with windows "lit like the moon," and with black protuberances 3ft apart all around the circumference.

HC addendum.
Source: Henri Bourdeleau.   Type: C

Location: Morgan's Ridge, near Morgantown, West Virginia.
Date: July, 1929.
Time: Night.

A Croatian immigrant named Frank Kozul was walking home alone from his shift at a coal mine. He decided to take a shortcut through the woods on Morgan's Ridge. It was a decision he would regret. Kozul suddenly found himself confronted by a savage "thing." It was about two feet high at the shoulder and was built like a large dog with oversized jaws and a bushy tail. It was completely covered in white shaggy hair. The creature stared at him for a few moments and then sprang, snapping its huge jaws and snarling.

Kozul swung at it with his empty lunch pail, but the pail went right through the creature as though it were made of thin air. Kozul ran. The creature paced him, slamming against him. It had foul breath. But if Kozul tried to hit it or push it away, he connected with nothing solid. Kozul stumbled and fell near a graveyard, and the white thing vanished. When he got up, Kozul was surprised to see that he did not have a scratch, bite mark, or any kind of wound on him; yet he had definitely felt contact with the beast.

HC addendum.
Source: Rosemary Ellen Guiley, *'Monsters of West Virginia.'* Type: X

* * * * * * *

Location: Near Burns, Oregon.
Date: July 5, 1929.
Time: 2:00 p.m.

The witnesses were traveling east of town, climbing up through a cut in the rim rocks when an object, very slowly flew over the top of the car, about 50ft above the rim rock. The object stopped and through a transparent window the witnesses could see two completely human-like figures that appeared to be pointing down at them using their arms and hands. One of the witnesses stepped out of the car but his mother demanded that he get back in. He stood on the running board observing the craft, which was two shades of brown. The craft, which had windows in the middle section, hovered for about 40 seconds emitting a soft hum. One of the figures then moved to another window and the craft suddenly accelerated and was gone in a blink of an eye.

HC addendum.
Source: NUFORC. Type: A

* * * * * * *

Location: Pestovskiy area, Novgorod Region, Russia.
Date: August 1929.
Time: Daytime.

17-year old Anna Petrovna Poletayeva was walking on a road on her way to visit her parents. The road passed next to Gusevskoye Lake and as she glanced to the side, she noticed a flying craft hovering above the lake. The object was round, small, without wings. Its lower part was yellow-reddish in color, resembling copper. The upper part was a glassy cupola. The glass from the cupola was joined to the lower part by large "copper" bolts.

The UFO hovered about 15 meters above the water. Anna could see two small sized "people" inside the glassy cupola; one male the other female. They were dressed in gray tight-fitting suits. Both were smiling, looking at the witness. Their faces were very much like ordinary humans. Feeling initial fear she panicked and ran from the area stumbled and injured her elbow. She looked back and the object was still hovering in the same place.

HC addendum.
Source: Aleksey K. Priyma, Anton Anfalov. Type: A

Location: Krini Village, Chalkidiki, Greece.
Date: August 1929.
Time: About midnight.

Theocharis Moustakas was carrying flour in his cart, returning home after the grinding of wheat at Krini mill. Suddenly he saw an object like a "parachute" (semi spherical) land on a nearby field and observed three "little people" speaking a very curious language between themselves. They were dressed in white clothing with white hoods and their skin was also white. Near them was a fence and the small men repeatedly jumped over it with ease. The witness was terrified and went to the village running. Some of the villagers told him that he had seen "devils," while others laughed at him.

HC addendum.
Source: C. Trantafyllou, and Homer Carajas.   Type: C

* * * * * * *

Location: Lackawack, New York.
Date: Winter 1929.
Time: Night.

In an area south of the Roundout Reservoir, "Bud Landis" was walking home one night after visiting a friend who lived a mile away. A full moon was just rising over the hills, and a slight chill filled the evening air. As the moon became fully exposed, its illumination bathed the surrounding countryside in soft light. As Bud strolled along, he noticed a strange stillness in the air. An eerie silence filled the night. As he walked briskly down the dirt road, the surrounding woods seemed to close in from all directions. Glancing to his left, Bud saw a weird light coming from among the trees. It seemed to pulsate and was near the ground.

Thinking the moon might be reflecting off something shiny, Bud continued on. Ultimately curiosity got the best of him. He stepped off the road and moved in among the trees. After stumbling through the thick underbrush for some ten yards, Bud came upon a sight that froze him in his tracks. Before him was a dome-shaped, yellow-green, translucent light. It measured about four feet across and some eighteen inches high. Bud thought perhaps the phenomenon might have been caused by some unknown fungus growing within the radius of the circle. He examined the earth beneath but found nothing unusual.

Suddenly the glow intensified, and Bud dived for cover behind the brush. From his place of concealment he saw two small men a foot high, slowly materialize within the light. They seemed to sense his presence and looked directly at him. Bud jumped backwards, stumbling over his own feet and fell. A second later, both little men leaped back within the glow and they and they light suddenly vanished. But was quite shaken by the weird experience and sat for a while to regain his thoughts before leaving. A week later he returned to the site, and discovered the grass was slowly dying where the glow had been seen.

HC addendum.
Source: Ron Quinn, *'Little People.'* Type: B?

* * * * * * *

Location: Krasnyi Shar, Omsk region, Russia.
Date: 1920-1930 (year unknown).
Time: Unknown.

Several witnesses saw in the sky "something like a window" and the image of "a woman in white inside." They interpreted the figure as "God itself." (!)

HC addendum.
Source: Mikhail Gershtein ufo_miger@mail.ru quoting letter from relative of deceased witness. Type: A?

About the author

Albert S. Rosales, was born in Cuba on January 3, 1958. After living for some time in Spain, in 1967, his family moved to New York City before ultimately settling down in Miami where Albert became a US citizen and attended school. Albert had many strange incidents as a child and developed an interest in UFOs and unusual events from the time he was in high school.

He joined the United States Navy after high school and traveled the world. Later on, after being honorably discharged from the Navy, Albert went into the jewelry business with his father. After his father passed on, Albert joined a local law enforcement agency in Miami and has now been there for over 30 years. Albert is married, with five grown children, one girl and four boys.

For over 40 years, Albert has been studying UFOs, and since 1993, has been regularly updating his Humanoid Encounter catalogue.
You can forward your own humanoid encounters to Albert at:

garuda79@comcast.net

Printed in Poland
by Amazon Fulfillment
Poland Sp. z o.o., Wrocław